Never Saw Me Coming

How I Outsmarted the FBI and the Entire Banking System—and POCKETED $40 MILLION

Tanya Smith

Little, Brown and Company

New York • Boston • London

Little, Brown and Company
Hachette Book Group
1290 Avenue of the Americas, New York, NY 10104
littlebrown.com

First Edition: August 2024

Little, Brown and Company is a division of Hachette Book Group, Inc. The Little, Brown name and logo are trademarks of Hachette Book Group, Inc.

The publisher is not responsible for websites (or their content) that are not owned by the publisher.

The Hachette Speakers Bureau provides a wide range of authors for speaking events. To find out more, go to hachettespeakersbureau.com or email Hachettespeakers@hbgusa.com.

Little, Brown and Company books may be purchased in bulk for business, educational, or promotional use. For information, please contact your local bookseller or the Hachette Book Group Special Markets Department at special.markets@hbgusa.com.

ISBN 9780316569163

LCCN 2024934386

Printing 1, 2024

LSC-C

Printed in the United States of America

In memory of my dad, Ira Smith Jr., and my mom, Bennie Ann Smith.

To my daughter, Makala, who encouraged me to tell my story.

People will forget what you said, people will forget what you did, but people will never forget how you made them feel.

—Maya Angelou

CONTENTS

CONTENTS

I WALKED RIGHT OUT

January 5, 1988
Federal Reformatory for Women, Alderson
Summers County, West Virginia

I stood at attention outside my room. Two male guards—one tall and slender, the other medium-sized and mean faced—walked through the cottage where I was housed with fifty other women. I eyed the guards as they passed each room and dorm and started walking toward me, their eyes expectant, confirming what they needed to know: that I was present for the 4:00 p.m. inmate count.

As I waited, my heartbeat quickening and my palms moist with anxious sweat, I looked out the window. It was a gloomy winter afternoon. Puffy clouds blocked the sun from the sprawling campus. When the guards passed me and moved to the next cottage, I knew it was only a matter of time before they finished the count and sent the status report up the chain of command. After the guards confirmed they were not short inmates in the hours since the last count, it was back to business as usual.

Buzzzzzz.

The horn sounded, notifying everyone the head count was successful, and now it was time to head to the dining hall for dinner. But, for me, that meant it was game on. I exhaled deeply to slow my breathing and dried my hands at my sides. I needed to be in control, smooth and confident.

"She won't even bring my boy to see me. What kind of shit is that? You volunteer to keep him and then you don't even bring him here for six months?"

"Where's his daddy? Can't he bring the boy?"

"That fool's locked up too. Part of the reason I'm here."

"Mama, that's all of us."

The other inmates in my cottage chitchatted as they gathered to rush the dining hall to feast on what passed for food before it had been picked over. The food at Alderson wasn't too bad, but it wasn't Mr. Chow either.

I nodded, pretending I was interested in somebody's child but hardly listened. When they started heading toward the dining hall, I stood back and looked to see if any eyes were on me. No one was paying attention, so I peeled off from the group and cut over to the administration building to the left of my cottage.

I slid into a cracked metal door and froze against a wall. It was an aging brick building with murky sand-colored tiles covering the floors and walls. I listened and watched to make sure no one was around. By then, all hands were on deck in the dining hall as guards policed the inmates to put down inevitable mealtime skirmishes. I expected the building to be empty, but I was unsure. I waited a few more seconds in case there was a straggler running behind. There could be no mistakes. Not today.

When all was clear, I dashed into the bathroom, locked the door, and rushed to the last stall.

I looked beside the toilet, and a bulky black bag was on the floor. *Yes, it's here!* With a sigh of relief, I opened it and started pulling things out: a conservative blue blazer, a knee-length black skirt, a crisp white blouse, pumps, a briefcase, tortoise-shell glasses, and coral lipstick. I slid out of my inmate uniform and stashed it in the bag.

Everything fit perfectly. But when I slid my feet into the shoes, I quickly realized they were too small. When I had entered Alderson, I was a size ten, but now I could have used an eleven. Still, I crammed my big feet into those tight, pointed-toe pumps. They had to do.

Adrenaline flooded my veins. I rushed to the mirror, raked my hair into a bun, put on the lipstick, slid the glasses onto my nose, and picked up the briefcase. I stepped back and peered at my reflection. I was two years shy of thirty, but I still looked like I was in my early twenties. I had my mother's smooth brown skin and my father's purposeful chestnut eyes. In those clothes, with the bright lipstick on, it looked like I was already coming back to life—changing, melting away invisible layers of sorrow and confinement.

When I opened the bathroom door, it was showtime. I had a part to play. I was to imitate a distinguished lawyer who'd visited her client and was now leaving Alderson. I straightened my back, poked my chest out, and held my head high like my mom, Bennie, taught me. I strode out of the bathroom and navigated the halls of the administration building as if I'd done it countless times before. My heels clicked against the floor tiles with each step. Instead of playing small and trying to be invisible, I decided an air of confidence, privilege, and freedom would get me past anyone in my path. They were accustomed to seeing me as a bummy, docile, controlled prisoner, not a refined, successful young woman wearing nerdy spectacles and carrying a leather briefcase. I told myself to *slow down*. Calm every cell in my body. There was no rush.

As I exited the administration building, I passed a few inmates who hardly looked in my direction. If they had, if one peered close enough and realized it was me, they'd rat me out for sure. I hadn't told any of the inmates about my plan, because in prison information is currency. I didn't want to put anyone in a position to be forced to share intel that might hurt me, because it could help them.

One woman I didn't know walked near me as she headed toward the dining hall. She stopped in my path and scanned me from head to toe. My heart quivered. My jaws tightened with anxiety, but I kept walking.

When her hazel eyes reached my feet, she licked her dry-ass lips and slid her eyes back up to my breasts, her mouth curling into a devious, suggestive grin. "Damn, momma, you shonuff lookin' fine in that skirt. Wanna be my lawyer?" she flirted before exposing her wriggling pink tongue and worming it up and down to show what she'd do to me.

I gave no response. My mind was working overtime to stay focused as that initial adrenaline rush dissipated into a flood of self-conscious thoughts.

I kept moving, one foot in front of the other, my hand gripping the briefcase as I walked along the pathway from the administration building to the parking lot. With each step I wondered if any inmates had noticed me or if some random guard was trying to be the day's hero. The pathway seemed to get longer, the length of a football field. I stayed smack in the middle, keeping my eyes fixed on my goal—the gate at the end of the pathway. The closer I got, the more those stupid pumps hurt. My damn feet started cramping and puffing up around the edges of the leather, like muffins rising in a pan. Chilling sweat rolled down my back. I reminded myself, *Keep walking like a queen. You can make it.*

When I reached the gate, I turned to the guard standing in the doorway and waved. He squinted as if he was seeing someone he knew. I was the lawyer who always walked by, right? I smiled and waved again. A heavy lump formed in my throat as I waited for a response. *Come on!* Every second counted. At any moment, someone could realize I was missing, and the alarm would sound. My plan would be a bust. *Tick . . . tock . . .*

After the longest pause in history, he nodded, returned my wave, and opened the gate. *Thank God!*

At the sound of the metal bars rolling up, my heart started pounding like a drum on a plantation, letting all the slaves know freedom was on the horizon. I wasn't nervous though. I wasn't afraid. I was prepared, acutely aware. My mouth started salivating. My fingers started tingling. I couldn't feel my feet anymore, but everything in me wanted to run across the freaking threshold into the world. I had to keep cool. *You got this. You got this.*

I kept walking until I saw my friend Wesley's old burgundy Cadillac Brougham parked a few feet ahead. When Wesley saw me in the rearview mirror, he exited the car and opened the back door for me while gesturing like he was my chauffeur. His jet-black Jheri curl was holding up a furry Kangol 504. He was tall and skinny, wearing creased blue jeans and a nice rayon shirt that made him look like he was in a nightclub—he was always dressed up nicely. I hugged him quickly, slid into the back seat, and kicked off those pumps with relief.

"Damn, sister, that's all I get for driving all the way from Minneapolis to pick you up?" Wesley joked, getting back behind the wheel.

His sister, Jackie, was beside me. Rob, a shorter guy I didn't know, was sitting in the front. They all looked happy to see me. Wesley and Jackie went to school with my older brother, Mason, and lived in the neighborhood. They'd watched me grow up. They liked the flyest clothes and cars and always needed money. That's why I was sure they'd say yes when I called offering cash if they'd drive down to Alderson to pick me up when I was released. For their own good, I didn't tell them I was escaping.

"My girl, you're out!" Jackie cheered, pulling me into a sisterly embrace. "It's so good to see you." She smelled like Carolina Herrera. Her hair was cut into an asymmetrical bob. Like Wesley, she had cinnamon-colored skin and a beautiful smile.

I returned Jackie's greeting but then I quickly turned to Wesley.

"Go! Let's get out of here!" I told him.

"Why? You in some rush?" he asked, starting the Caddie.

"Wouldn't you be if you just got released from prison?" Jackie asked, laughing.

"Right? Let's get her the fuck out of here before they change their mind about letting her out." Wesley took off down the long prison road that led back to society.

Rob turned on the radio and asked if I wanted to hear anything in particular.

"No. I'm fine," I answered.

He scrolled the channels, searching for the local R&B station. Whitney Houston's "So Emotional" started playing. Jackie sang along—*Every time I think of you-oo-oo*—and elbowed me like I should join in. I had no time for singing, not yet anyway. I kept my eyes peeled and focused on the road. There weren't any other cars around us, just unending pavement ahead and tall trees springing up from the brush along the shoulder.

When we reached the highway, I said, "OK, we can slow down, Wesley. You're driving too fast."

Annoyed, he pointed out that he could drive his Brougham, "the smoothest driving car in the land," as fast as he pleased. Everyone chuckled.

"Whatever. Just slow down and be cool," I said, sounding calm but stern.

Just then a siren *whooped*. There was a police car coming up behind us with the quickness of a lion closing in on a gazelle. A voice shouted over the loudspeaker: "Pull over. Now!"

"What's he pulling me over for?" Wesley asked, annoyed.

"Were you going too fast? Over the speed limit?" Jackie asked.

Wesley pulled onto the shoulder and stopped the car.

"Just keep your composure. Everyone. Keep. Your. Composure. Smile, be polite, and say 'sir.' OK?" I looked around the car, and everyone, nervous and wide-eyed, nodded. "We'll get through. Everything will work out," I said, trying to sound calm and confident while peeking over my shoulder at the pudgy police officer approaching the Cadillac. I wasn't quite sure anything would work out. At that moment, with my freedom and sanity on the line, everything I'd been through, what I'd seen and done, survived and struggled through, flashed through my mind. I'd found myself in a ditch so deep it would take a miracle to climb out and set things straight. Escaping Alderson was supposed to be my chance to make things right, to prove I'd been wronged. With that police officer steps from the car, everything was in question. I looked at Wesley's glove compartment. I hoped he didn't have anything illegal in there.

"Roll this window down, boy," the officer barked at Wesley. "And turn off the ignition."

1

THE GIRL WITH THE BIG BRAIN

When I was thirteen years old, I fell madly in love with Michael Jackson and decided he was going to be my husband and the father of my children. Why not? I was young, Black, gifted, and fabulous—and so was he. To make it happen, we needed to cross paths, which was a major obstacle because I lived on the Northside of Minneapolis, and Michael was two thousand miles away in California and knew nothing about me. I just needed time to figure things out.

"Do you think Michael and I would make a cute couple?" I asked my mother one day as we listened to the Jackson 5 on the car radio on the way home from Cubs, Mom's favorite grocery store. My mother, who everyone called "Bennie," was a Dallas, Texas, beauty with buttery, light-brown skin and a flat, tear-shaped nose. She was whip-smart and the most loving person I've ever known. While she could've done anything with her intelligence and education, she prided herself on taking care of her children and keeping our home beautiful and neat.

"Of course. You working on getting a signed poster from him too?" she answered, bringing up my last heartthrob, swimmer Mark Spitz. After getting a peek at his "trademark" mustache as he competed at the 1972 Olympics in Munich and won seven gold medals, I figured out how to get his home telephone number from directory assistance and called him to confess my love. Unfortunately, while he was happy to get my call, Mark revealed that he was moving on from swimming and, worse, getting married. He agreed to send me an autographed poster even though we could never be. I was happy to get it and hung it up in my bedroom. But after I saw Michael Jackson do the robot while he sang "Dancing Machine" with his brothers on *Soul Train*, I tore Mark's poster down and replaced it with a brand new pinup of the Jackson 5 taken from the latest edition of *Right On!* magazine.

"No, I don't want an autographed poster of Michael Jackson," I said with a slight attitude. It was December and cold outside, and I could see my breath materialize into a cloud as I exhaled. Shivering, I added, "I want him to, like, be my boyfriend."

My mother smiled and nodded along to show support, but at thirteen, I could tell when she thought I was in over my head and was just being nice.

"That would be great," she said. "But I'm sure you'll have to fight a million other girls just to get to him. How are you going to do that?"

I peered at her. She had no idea about the skills I'd developed while cracking directory assistance to get to Mark Spitz. After requesting numerous transfers throughout the telephone company's employee directory, I pretended to be from billing and requested a list of all the telephone numbers dialed by Mark's coach from another employee. When that trick worked, I used the same system to get numbers for every celebrity my girlfriends and I could think of as we hung out in my bedroom after school. We'd called everyone from Todd Bridges to Leif Garrett. Getting to Michael would require a little more work, but I was confident in my ability to get what I wanted.

"I'll find a way to get to Michael," I replied to my mother. "We'll be together."

The declaration set me in motion. When we got home, I took Black Power, our family dog, a loyal Doberman pinscher, up to my bedroom to figure out a way to get in contact with my future boyfriend. Imagining myself arm in arm with Michael in the centerfold of the next *Right On!*, I did my usual research. From articles in teen magazines, I learned that he lived in Encino, California, with his parents, Katherine and Joe Jackson. But from what I'd read, his dad, Joe, the group's manager, sounded too strict to approach.

"I need another way in," I explained to Black Power. Considering how I'd gotten to Mark using his swim coach, I decided to look for other people connected to Michael. I discovered that Samuel Jackson, Michael's grandfather, lived in Phoenix, Arizona. He had a listed phone number.

I waited until my identical twin sister, Taryn, came home to dial it. The youngest of the children, we were close, automatic playmates. Mom often dressed us alike, and we loved playing the classic twin trick of trading places at school and making our teachers guess who was who. No one could tell us apart. However, as we grew, we developed different personalities. While I was a precocious people person, Taryn was more skeptical and could be a loner. Still, like our other four siblings—sisters Barbara (Babs), the eldest, and Iris and brothers Ryan and Mason—we both excelled at school and were always at the top of our class. If I was going to meet Michael Jackson, Taryn, my right hand, was coming with me.

When we called Michael's grandfather, he seemed glad to talk. I think he was kind of lonely.

"I want to meet Michael," I told him. "Or even just get him on the phone. My sister and I"—I nodded at Taryn standing nearby and egging me on—"just love the Jacksons and would give anything to talk to them. Won't you help us?"

"Oh, darling, you sound like such a sweet girl. I sure wish I could. But I don't think Joe would allow me to do that," he said, his voice soft and a little shaky, aging him to his midsixties.

I wondered if he might be a little scared of Joe, though he never said anything explicit. It didn't stop him from freely gossiping about "the boys." After our first phone call got us nowhere, Taryn and I called him another time, and he told us, "Michael's on tour now." On a different call, he said, "The boys are recording a new album." Most maddening were the times when he'd say, "I just spent Thanksgiving with the boys," or, "Well, you just missed Michael. He was here."

Did you tell him about me? I wanted to scream. But I knew not to push him. I didn't want to upset my future grandfather-in-law. And if I did, he might tell Joe about our calls, and Joe would for sure change his father's telephone number.

I didn't want to lose contact. Though I wasn't getting what I wanted, the constant flow of facts from our nearly weekly phone calls made me feel close to Michael, like a family friend. I could scatter tidbits of information to impress my friends as we ate bologna sandwiches on the bleachers at school—"Michael will be in Chicago next week"—but I mostly basked in the illusion of intimacy.

Samuel, too, was enjoying our connection. Sometimes I'd call and he'd have nothing to report. "Tanya, I haven't talked to the boys for a day or two. I don't know what they're up to."

"OK, I'll try back tomorrow in case there's news," I'd say, watching a spring shower water our back lawn through my bedroom window.

"I look forward to that," he'd tell me. "You make my day."

He was a true sweetheart. But, much as I liked him, those calls were just a distraction from my real goal of meeting Michael. I soon reverted to my old tactics of calling the phone company and asking the operator for a random department and then having that department transfer me to billing or facilities to make my call look like it was coming from within the company.

Using that method, I got the address of the Jackson family compound—4641 Hayvenhurst Avenue—along with every phone number connected to the place.

With Taryn anxiously waiting beside me, I made a test call. I was sure I had the right number when a young woman with a soft voice answered the phone.

"Hi, LaToya. What's up, girl?" I said, guessing who it might be and trying to sound nonchalant. Taryn nodded along. I was on the right track. We were almost in.

"Hey, who is this?" the woman said, sounding annoyed. I hung up immediately.

"We did it!" Taryn and I were high-fiving and laughing. "We found the Jacksons!"

Now we had to get Michael on the phone. To do it, I kept chatting with Samuel to keep track of when "the boys" were in California.

When Samuel finally tipped me off, I tried calling all the numbers for the house, one by one. When someone picked up, I'd ask for Michael, claiming to be a friend. After failing a few times, I started trying different voices and realized I could keep people on the phone longer when I used my "white voice." I'd go up an octave to sound chipper and privileged. "Gosh, I'm grateful for this sunny day we're enjoying in Encino. Hey, is Michael there? I can't wait to see my guy." The person answering would pass me on to a higher-up, who would then take the time to figure out exactly who I was and what I needed. If I was white, I had to be someone important. "What's your name?" they'd ask before pulling in another person, who'd eventually turn me down saying, "Michael doesn't know any Marys. Sorry." They'd actually apologize like they were sad to let me down.

After all that, Michael never came to the phone. I was bummed but still persistent. Something had to work.

I figured he'd have to answer sometime and kept pushing, which is how I got cussed out by Joe Jackson.

"Where the fuck did you get this number?" he screamed.

"Michael gave it to me," I said sweetly.

"Don't you ever call here again."

But I did, and he kept raging. "I'm going to put you in jail."

"Just let me talk to Michael one time," I pleaded. "Then I'll never call you back."

Slam. He hung up.

As I predicted, Joe changed the phone numbers, which, of course, didn't faze me at all. I'd just make a few calls to the phone company and get the new ones from facilities. I felt sure I was close to catching Michael on the phone, even if I was driving his father crazy.

One day Joe picked up and said, "Tell me who the fuck you are!"

"I'm Michael's friend. He told me to call."

"That's a lie! Michael doesn't know this number. No one in our family knows it. This is a pay phone we had put on the grounds for construction workers," he said and then he got very angry. "Who is giving you these numbers? I'm calling the police!"

I clicked right off.

*　　*　　*

Cuddling with Black Power on my bed, I admitted to myself that my scheme wasn't working this time. I became depressed and started moping until I came up with a plan B. I wasn't trying to get Michael on the telephone. That was small time. I needed the real thing, an in-person meeting that could lead to a real-life kiss.

Hoping to drum up support one summer morning, I drifted into the kitchen, where my parents were enjoying steaming cups of Maxwell House. It was where they commonly met to plan their day, which wasn't easy with multiple children who were always busy and into something. Babs, who was ten years older than me and Taryn, was still in high school and captain of the dance team, the Polarettes; on the yearbook staff and student council; and in Junior Achievement, Y-Teens, and a slew of clubs. My other big sister, Iris, a tall beauty with light skin and long, straight hair, was crowned Queen of North High. My brothers were sports stars: Ryan, the fastest in the state, was an acclaimed quarterback and running back, while Mason excelled at basketball and football. Taryn and I played volleyball, softball, basketball, badminton, and ran track in a park league. Needless to say, shuffling us around town to make all of our appointments was no joke. Those morning cups of Maxwell House in the kitchen were needed and earned. It was also the perfect time and place to get their attention.

I tried my mother first.

"Remember when you agreed that Michael and I would make a cute couple?" I probed.

"Michael?" she asked.

"Jackson. Michael Jackson."

"Sure, honey. Why are you bringing that up?"

"I think I'm ready to meet him," I said.

Having already endured the angst of four teenagers, my parents were sympathetic but distanced. "Well, maybe you will one day," my mother said, glancing at my dad for backup. Eternal sweethearts, they'd met while studying at Texas College, a historically Black, Christian, Methodist, Episcopal school in Tyler, Texas, in 1950. First-generation college students whose parents were one generation out of slavery, they fell madly in love and married young.

"Would it be OK with you if I met Michael Jackson?" I asked my dad. If my mother was the family's loving cheerleader, Dad was the ever-dedicated coach. Standing five foot eleven inches, Ira (Smitty) Smith Jr. was a former college basketball player who worked as a warehouse foreman at Ed Phillips and Sons, a family-owned high-spirits distilling company. He was an intelligent, socially conscious extrovert who never met a stranger and tried to help anyone in need.

"Of course you can meet Michael Jackson. Why not?" He agreed.

"I think I will go meet him," I said, hoping my soft declaration would sound like the only plausible conclusion to our exchange. All they had to do was cosign.

"OK, sure . . ." came their joint, distracted answer. It was exactly what I was looking for. Though they didn't know I was serious, they weren't the kind of people to go back on their word.

Dashing upstairs, I found Taryn in the bathroom applying way too much Maybelline eyeshadow.

"Get ready. We're going to California to see Michael Jackson," I announced like a game show host.

"What? Do Mom and Dad know?" Taryn turned to me with gobs of sea-blue eyeshadow over her eyelids.

"Yes, I told them I was going."

We invited our friend Shirley to accompany us to Los Angeles since she loved Marlon Jackson. When I called her, she said she doubted that her mom would let her go, but she couldn't miss an opportunity to meet Marlon and was game.

Pretending to be my mother, I called Dayton's department store, which had a travel department, and ordered three airline tickets to Los Angeles. I told them my daughter would come pick up the tickets and had full permission to use my credit card. "Sounds good. I'll see you in a bit, Mrs. Smith," the travel agent said.

I rode the bus downtown to Dayton's and went up to the fourth floor. I walked around for a bit to relax. I wasn't nervous. I just wanted to make sure I knew what I would say to the travel agent and that I didn't seem rushed or unconfident about the purchase.

"I'm here to pick up three tickets to Los Angeles," I said to the travel agent while handing over my mother's card. I made sure to make direct eye contact and smile, casually, not too big because then it would seem like I was hiding something.

The woman was petite with big gray hair and looked like she'd been working at Dayton's for twenty-five years.

"Her name is Mrs. Smith," I said, trying to distract the agent and keep her on task.

"Oh, yes," she finally responded, taking the credit card from me. "Your mother called not long ago. So good she has you to help her out."

"I try my best," I said.

After a few pecks at her keyboard, she handed over the tickets. As she slid the envelope into my hand, a high settled over my body. Any misgivings I felt about using my mother's card (I fully intended to pay her back) or flying all the way to Los Angeles to see someone who didn't even know I was alive dissipated to nothing.

On that adrenaline high, I rushed home, threw my cutest outfits into my travel bag, and called a cab. On the way to the airport, Taryn and I stopped at Shirley's house to pick her up. She was nervous about going. Her two younger sisters were there. They told her their mother would be upset if she went to Los Angeles and advised her to stay home. Worried we might miss our flight, I kept my response simple and to the point: "I'm going to Los Angeles to meet Michael Jackson. You can stay home and miss all the fun. It's up to you." Taryn and I started walking toward the door to get back into the cab. Seconds later, Shirley was heading out behind us.

Once we made it to the airport, Taryn, Shirley, and I rushed to the terminal to board our Northwest Airlines flight to Los Angeles. None of us had ever been on an airplane before, but we knew to get dressed up for the occasion. Taryn wore stylish denim bell-bottoms with a matching vest, and Shirley chose a striped, ankle-length maxi dress. I rocked a red miniskirt and a loose-fitting peasant blouse. I wanted to look mature for Michael.

"You guys ever hear about a plane crashing?" Shirley asked nervously as the plane started taking off. "I hope that doesn't happen to us."

"No. It's 1974. Planes are totally safe. They've even started using some computer technology in the cockpits. No need to worry," I said, trying to calm her with information I'd read in a magazine. It was only half true. Most planes didn't have computer technology. The article was just projecting how advanced avionics and digital flight-control systems could be used in the near future.

As the plane pushed through the clouds and started rocking due to turbulence, I wished it was the future and a computer was piloting the vessel. I wasn't nervous at all, but the jerking movements made me feel like I was on a roller coaster, and I was sure my hairstyle was ruined. Plus, the air pressure had my ears popping, and it felt like my brain might explode.

Taryn anxiously clutched my left hand; Shirley clutched my right.

"Don't worry, guys. Everything will be just fine. In a few hours, we'll be poolside with the Jacksons," I said to them, but really, the vision was for me. I closed my eyes and imagined I'd made it to Encino, floated past Joe, and locked eyes with Michael, who was happy to see me and burst into song: "Got to be there . . . beeeee there in the morning. . . ."

I was proud of the trip I'd orchestrated and confident everything would go off without a hitch. Before we left, I called Flo Jenkins, the editor of *Right On!*, to say I could get her an interview with Michael Jackson—all she had to do was meet us at the airport. "Oh my God, I'll be there," she promised. She must have assumed that I was a publicist who was dangling a rare opportunity.

Hearing that Flo would meet us at LAX was reassuring to Shirley and Taryn. Being a grown-up, she'd get us around the city and find us a place to stay—or so I told them. I gave myself an extra pat on the back for calling her. I deserved congratulations for pulling together such an excellent plan.

When I woke from my nap, the plane was circling, beginning its descent.

"We're almost there," I announced. "Soon, we'll meet our future boyfriends."

The three of us were giggling and dancing in our seats, unable to contain our excitement. As the plane touched down, we fell silent as if marshaling strength for the next incredible leg of our adventure. "Welcome to Los Angeles," the pilot announced.

We exited the plane single file with the other passengers and then clasped hands as we entered the jet bridge and began skipping like we were traversing the yellow-brick road leading to Oz. But then Taryn slowed her pace. I turned to see her eyes peering at something ahead.

"Why are *they* here?" She stopped walking altogether.

I looked at the end of our yellow-brick road and saw two police officers.

Nowhere to go but forward in the sea of people exiting the plane, we had to keep walking. When we reached the officers, they immediately pulled us to the side.

"Are you Tanya and Taryn Smith and Shirley Summers?" one of them asked.

I don't remember saying anything. In fact, I'm sure I didn't. Nevertheless, we were escorted down a long, winding hallway to a small holding room, where a cop explained that Shirley's sisters had squealed and told her mom that she was headed to California. Horrified, her mother called my mother, who was equally shocked. Hearing this, I glared at Shirley. If looks could kill, she would have been dead on the floor. I felt betrayed. Why had she told anyone about our plan? I learned a valuable lesson—be careful who you let in on the action. Some people just weren't built for it.

"Sir, I told my parents I was coming out here," I insisted to the cop who was interviewing us. "Let us go, and we can forget about all of this."

"I don't think so," he said, amused.

"You have the wrong people; you really must let us go." I pushed. "What's your badge number?" I asked, trying something I'd seen in a movie. "Can I speak to your captain?"

He didn't bother to answer. As he picked up the phone to call our parents, I wanted to argue, to prove him wrong. I knew in my heart that I'd vastly exaggerated a few careless words, but I couldn't bear to surrender my dream.

"What in God's name were you thinking flying to California without even telling us?" Dad barked through the phone.

He wasn't one to raise his voice. Taryn was startled, but I kept cool.

"I did tell you. Remember? In the kitchen. You were having coffee," I reminded him.

"Don't play mind games with us, young lady," Dad said. "You scared your mother and me half to death."

"I'm not playing mind games. You said I could meet Michael Jackson."

"That's not what we meant and you know it, Tanya Marie Smith." Mom jumped in. "Taryn, what do you have to say for yourself?"

"I'm sorry," Taryn uttered. "It sounded like a good idea."

"Whose idea was it?" Mom asked her.

"Both of us. We came up with it together." Taryn looked at me. We were in this together. My sister wouldn't rat me out.

Before hanging up, Dad told Taryn and me to wait until one of his two sisters who lived in Compton could come and pick us up.

"You wanted to be in California? Well, here's your chance," he said like being there would provide some kind of life lesson Taryn and I weren't ready for. I wasn't falling for that, though. Dad hadn't taken us to meet our family on the West Coast—aunts Ada and Frances, uncle Louie, or cousins Cheryl, Lucy, and NaNa. But if staying with them meant I'd get to linger in California a little longer until I figured out how to get to Michael, I was up for it.

Shirley, who was sobbing, had to fly right back. She didn't even glimpse Los Angeles outside the airport. Her mother had already bought the return ticket. As she headed to the gate, I thought, hopefully, she'd keep her mouth closed in the future.

Taryn and I waited to be escorted to Compton, which I was sure would be the cinematic slice of Los Angeles we'd seen on television—palm trees, sandy beaches, and celebrities galore. We were ready.

When we met Aunt Frances, she looked like my dad in a dress with a short, semicurly Afro. I wanted to laugh. Driving us back to her house in her Chevrolet Impala, Aunt Frances's first words were, "What's wrong with you twins? You scared Junior," her nickname for my dad, "half to death running all the way to California like you ain't got no home training. I won't be having none of that silly business at my house. You can believe that." Looks like Aunt Frances wasn't to be toyed with. Taryn and I traded stares and looked out the windows.

I noticed the surroundings were changing outside the car. The whole neighborhood was covered in spray-painted graffiti. We also passed boarded-up shops and homes, trash-filled alleys, and random drunks begging for change on street corners. It was nothing like our upper-middle-class, mostly Jewish neighborhood.

"It looks dangerous around here," Taryn whispered in my ear. I nodded in agreement.

Aunt Frances's house was scrubbed to a shine—but it was tiny, with iron bars on the doors and windows.

"Now y'all girls listen here," she started when we got settled in. "Don't go outside alone. This ain't Minneapolis. And don't ever go out at night. And whatever you do, don't wear the colors red or blue. We got these stupid gangs here that will kill you if they even suspect you might be repping the wrong set."

"But I have a red skirt that I was going to wear to see Michael Jackson in Encino," I said, pointing to my red skirt, which was all wrinkled. "Can I wear my skirt in Encino?"

"Girl, you ain't going to see no Michael Jackson in Encino. The only Jackson you're going to see is Darryl Jackson up the street. He can sing and dance, though. He might even sing 'Got to Be There' if you give him a dollar. Dope makes people do crazy things," Aunt Frances said, laughing and sounding happy to break my heart. "You in Compton now. Minneapolis is a whole world away from here."

I came up with a plan to rope my cousins Cheryl, Lucy, and NaNa into my pilgrimage to Michael, promising gifts, even cash, if they could get me to Encino.

"The Valley? We don't go to the Valley. Ain't nothing there but white people," Cheryl, the oldest, said bluntly.

"They'll lock you up for anything," Lucy added. "They don't want Black people up there."

NaNa nodded along.

"But the Jacksons live there," Taryn pointed out, backing me up.

"They rich Black people," Cheryl said. "White people up there accept rich Black people. But poor Black people? They don't like us."

I knew they weren't lying. I'd witnessed some of what they were talking about—the division between the haves and have-nots. It got me thinking about money and how it impacted people's lives for better or worse. My father worked two jobs to keep us in a middle-, upper-class neighborhood. He was a warehouse foreman by day and a bouncer at night, securing elite white socialites at private parties and clubs. He'd rub elbows with corporate lawyers, judges, financiers, and politicians.

From what I saw in Compton, it was clear money was a powerful thing that determined so much about a person's life: where they lived and how they lived and what they could do about it. It seemed California was a place of extreme wealth and opportunity, but something was stopping it from flowing to the Black community in Compton.

As the days moved forward, I was having a good time bonding with my relatives. My cousins were incredible singers, and as we were mostly locked up in the house, we had elaborate talent shows where they sang Jackson 5 hits like professional performers. They had moves and could groove. Taryn and I had to keep up.

It was cathartic connecting with my family, people who looked like Taryn and me and had the same blood pumping through their veins. And in time, even Aunt Frances came around and admitted that she enjoyed our company.

"Junior sure made some beautiful baby girls," she said, serving Taryn and me pork chops she had fried for us on our last night.

I didn't give up on meeting Michael Jackson. Of course, I didn't admit that to my mom and dad after Taryn and I arrived home in disgrace. My parents' main attitude was relief, tinged with disappointment. While I was truly sorry for hurting them, my determination to meet Michael continued.

It took me a full year to finagle a return to California. I did it by convincing my parents that I wanted to form a singing group with Cheryl, Lucy, and NaNa. My parents were reluctant, but soon Aunt Frances also requested that Taryn and I return to Cali, saying, "Send them twins back out. I miss them."

Taryn decided she didn't want to go. I wasn't surprised. As we approached our sweet sixteen, we were beginning to drift apart. While we'd been inseparable for most of our lives, there was always a little friction and division between us because of our differences. The reality was that we were totally different people who were stuck in identical bodies. Because of our differences, our friends and some family members would comment that I was the "nice" twin, the sweet one, and she was "rebellious." Some people would say I was smarter. I disagreed. Sometimes, I could see the labeling was affecting her. Though she preferred being different from me and finding her own way, she didn't understand why that meant people seemed to think I was somehow "better" than her.

This was most apparent in the summer of 1975. Through summer sports, we made a friend who lived in a middle-class community on the south side of Minneapolis. She introduced us to her brother, Nico. Taryn fell madly in love with him. He was handsome, Mexican and Black, and he had a muscular physique. What Taryn liked most about him was the seemingly endless stash of pot he shared with her. I wasn't against smoking weed; it just wasn't something I wanted to do. I liked having my whole mind at work at all times, and floating on a cloud wasn't a goal of mine.

"Taryn, why don't you put that joint out and come home with me," I proposed the night I found her high. I knew her answer would be no. Nico was rolling another joint at the kitchen table, and soon, he'd have another cloud ready for Taryn.

"You're not my mom. You can't tell me what to do," she said when I managed to drag her out of the house. She was stumbling, unsteady on her dragging feet.

"You're going to get hurt messing around with these people. They don't want what's best for you," I said.

"And you do?" She laughed. "No, Tanya. You only want what's best for yourself. That's how you operate. The leader of the pack. Right? Tanya is perfect, and Taryn is so messed up that her perfect twin has to come and save her. No, thank you."

I had always been the leader. I knew it made her feel small, an outlier. I didn't blame her for going off on her own, trying to find her own way—if only it were someplace else. Someplace safe. But there was no sense trying to explain all that to Taryn in her state. I actually had to wait until she was even higher to make her leave without an argument.

It was the first real rift in our relationship, and there was nothing I could do about it. I had to focus on myself, my dream. California.

I had to scare up a traveling companion for my trip. I didn't want to go to California to meet Michael Jackson alone.

It occurred to me to ask Angela—a girl my age who'd hang around Taryn and Nico—if she wanted to meet the Jacksons.

"No way do you know Michael Jackson," she said.

"I don't know him, but I have his address."

Angela was skeptical, but she was game to come along. The two of us flew to California, and after a couple of days of playing with my cousins, we set off on our quest.

It would take three hours to get from Compton to Encino. We had to wait a while at the transfer points, but we easily made our connections. Angela whined the whole way, but I reminded her that we had the address. "We're going to march right up and knock on the front door!"

I'd played that scene in my mind many times: someone—not Joe Jackson!—answering the knock, like a maid or even a butler wearing a formal tailcoat and white gloves. We'd introduce ourselves, explaining that we'd traveled from Minneapolis. We'd be shown into a sunny living room with Italian white furniture. Michael himself would come greet us, saying, "Minneapolis! You came all that way? How good of you! I'm so glad you're here." He'd then compliment my psychedelic jumpsuit—I'd upgraded from the miniskirt—and send his driver down to Compton to get my things for me to stay with him.

The trip took two-and-a-half hours on three different buses that seemed to get progressively hotter and less packed with people the farther we traveled into the Valley. With each ride, I felt my hair withering in the heat as my bangs moistened and began lifting from my forehead. I hoped Michael liked natural hair because, by the time we got there, I was sure I'd look like Don Cornelius.

Finally, sweat wetting my armpits, I was tugging the cord, signaling to the bus driver to stop at the corner of Hayvenhurst Avenue and Ventura Boulevard.

"Where the hell are we?" Angela snapped. "How far are we from Michael's?"

"We're going to have to walk a couple blocks," I said. I was exhausted, too, but I hid it so Angela didn't completely abort the mission.

"I'm thirsty," she complained as we braved the overpowering Valley heat, which took our breath away and warmed our insides like we were ducks baking in an oven. It had to be almost a hundred degrees out there in July. Compton was twenty degrees cooler. It made no sense.

For relief, we headed into a Gelson's grocery near the intersection. When we opened the door and crossed the threshold, I felt that we'd been transported to an immaculate alternative universe. The food was displayed beautifully, much more artistically than in any Minnesota supermarket I'd ever seen—and definitely better than Compton. The green apples shined like someone had buffed them that morning. The radishes were the brightest red I'd ever seen. Even Angela was impressed, and I'd never seen her eat a fruit or a vegetable. Clearly, we were in the right elite neighborhood. "This place is neat," she said, forgetting her many complaints.

Then, fortified with drinks and snacks, we headed down Hayvenhurst, which was a long road with massive gated compounds on either side. There were no sidewalks, and we walked in the street, occasionally stepping onto the grass to dodge a passing car. And what cars they were: we saw a Rolls-Royce and a Porsche. And then some guy with wavy blond hair sped by in a red Ferrari. He slowed when he saw us and quickly glanced in our direction, just enough to let us know he'd seen us. Two Black girls, the only people on foot in an exclusive neighborhood, peering through gates and up long, curved driveways to see the magnificent mansions that lay on the grounds. We must have been quite a sight.

"These are gorgeous places," Angela said.

I was too excited to dawdle much. "We're almost there! Come on!"

Our destination, 4641 Hayvenhurst, looked impenetrable. I don't know why I'd dreamed we could just knock on the front door. It was ringed by privets at least twelve feet tall, with a formidable black entry gate. Through a small gap between the hedges and the gate, we could just glimpse the driveway but not the house, which was off to one side. On the driveway, we could see two German shepherds on patrol. How I wished Black Power was by my side. He could chat with his canine brothers to get us inside.

"We ain't gonna never get in there," Angela grumbled. "The place is locked down."

"Just wait," I said. "See that camera above the gate. If I hit the buzzer, they can see we're here."

I pushed the buzzer, and nothing happened.

"Don't you tell me we came out here for nothing," Angela said.

She was really starting to get on my nerves, but I blocked her out and pushed the buzzer again. This time, a woman answered.

"Yes, who is it?"

"Hello?!" I said, sounding surprised. When she didn't say anything, I went on, "My name is Tanya Smith. I came to see Michael Jackson all the way from Minneapolis." I tried to make it sound exotic like Minneapolis was Mauritius.

"Hold on, please."

"See," I told Angela. But behind her back, I was clenching my teeth with anxiety, mouthing, "You've got to let us in."

Suddenly, a new voice came over the intercom. "Hello?" It was a woman. "You say you came from Minneapolis?"

"Yes, we did. Please, we'd like to see Michael."

"Precious, he's not here. None of them are. The boys are on tour." When the woman said "precious," I knew she was watching us on camera and saw that we were young girls. She sounded like one of my aunts.

"All of them are gone?"

"I'm afraid so."

"Well, can't you just let us in for a minute?" I couldn't stand the disappointment, and I wasn't about to ride all the way back to Compton listening to Angela saying, "I told you so."

"I can't do that. I'm so sorry. I'd let you come in if they were here," the woman said.

I then realized who was on the line. "Are you Katherine, Michael's mother?"

"Yes, I am. And again, I'm sorry that you missed them. Be careful. Goodbye."

When she clicked off, my mind was still racing, trying to find an angle—words I could say, anything I might do—to salvage the situation. I'd spent two years researching, scheming, and conniving to meet Michael, only to have it come to . . . what? A big nothing burger! Deep down I felt that this quest was over and that I'd never muster the strength or the will to try again.

I sat on the curb, hyperventilating, almost too overwrought to cry. My cute jumpsuit was getting dusty in the dry San Fernando Valley dirt, but I didn't care. I was done.

Angela, meanwhile, was cussing like crazy, stomping back and forth in front of the gate. *Is the camera off?* I wondered—and hoped it was. I didn't want Mrs. Jackson to see this mess.

Just then, a black limousine nosed into the driveway. I jumped to my feet, thinking, *Thank God! It's them! At last!* My heart started beating fast; my thoughts started racing. My dream, it was happening. I would return to Minneapolis as part of the Jackson clan. Michael was about to see me, and we'd begin our life together. I started smoothing out my jumpsuit and shaking the dirt off my knees.

But when the window lowered, I saw that the passenger was LaToya. She gave us a friendly smile and a wave. The gate slowly opened to admit her, and I had a moment's impulse to rush it, to just barge onto the grounds and make a run for the house. But I didn't. Instead, crestfallen, I told Angela, "We better head back."

The sun was setting in the Valley, and at least it wasn't piping hot as we trudged back to the bus stop. Angela didn't say a word. I think she knew I was hurt and didn't want to make things worse. I was grateful for that.

*　　*　　*

A few days later, I was back home with Mom and Dad, and I was still in a deep funk I couldn't shake. I told them the whole story, looking for comfort or simply to reconnect. My secret celebrity stalking had me feeling isolated from my family, especially since I'd gone to Encino without Taryn.

"You did well," my dad said, and I could tell he meant it. "You chased your dream. It didn't work out, but maybe there's a valuable lesson in all this."

"Like what?" I looked at him like he'd gone mad. How could spending a couple of years of my life and failing at meeting my true love be a valuable lesson?

"I think what Dad is trying to say is that maybe you could stand to start using some of that brain power of yours on something more substantial, more meaningful than chasing a celebrity. You're a smart girl. You have so much more to offer," Mom said.

"You can do or be anything you want. Why don't you concentrate on your schooling? Focus all that intellect and energy on something worthwhile," Dad added.

I rolled my eyes, though I knew they were sincere—and maybe right. I never told them about my telephone company plotting, but they were seeing some of my obsessive tendencies and how they were interrupting my life.

"I guess you both are right," I said, agreeing to move on from Michael.

Later, my parents got me and some friends tickets to see the Jacksons (the group's new name) when they came to town. The tickets included VIP passes that let us go backstage and meet "the boys." I dressed up in my best-fitting jeans and pulled my bangs down to curl on my forehead under a big-brimmed hat that framed my face. I knew I looked cute.

The concert itself was a blur of teenage girls screaming and the Jacksons proving why they were the most talented teen boy group in the world. They were high-energy, with slick moves and honey-laced vocals. I tried to pay attention, but really, all I could think about was seeing Michael.

When the show ended and my friends and I headed backstage, I expected to be welcomed into an elegant lounge decorated with big furry couches and lava lamps. Mega celebrities like Diana Ross and Gladys Knight would pull plump shrimp off platters and sip glasses of champagne that were being passed around like cups of water. And then, at the perfect moment, the Jacksons would perform an impromptu number to entertain their adoring fans up close and personal. Last, Michael would pluck me from the bunch, serenade me, and ask me to complete the rest of the tour with him. Sorry to say the experience was nothing like that.

Backstage was noisy and bustling with chaotic energy. There were groupies and producers, agents, and handlers. It was hard to even get to the Jacksons. And when I finally did, it was Marlon, not Michael, who locked in on me.

"Wow, Marlon keeps staring at you," one of my friends said. It was true. I'd already noticed his gaze. Still, I held out for Michael, the boy who'd taken up residence on my bedroom wall.

One problem: Michael never so much as shot a glance my way—or anywhere else for that matter. His eyes never left the floor. Dynamic as he was on stage, he was withdrawn in person. I could have reached out and touched him—I was that close—but his vibe was unmistakable: "Please, leave me alone." He seemed out of place, overwhelmed by all the attention. I decided to let him be and move on.

2

FROM THE GREEDY TO THE NEEDY

My family went from recognition on the Northside to luminary status in the city's Black community. My father had the idea to open a theater and secured a loan from Wheelock Whitney Jr. He was a founder of Northwest Equity Partners, whose investments launched International Dairy Queen, Life Time Fitness, and Rosetta Stone, and was the future president and part owner of the Minnesota Vikings. My father first leased and then purchased the Capri Theater from his good friend Ben Berger, a businessman who owned a chain of nineteen movie theaters and was the co-owner of the Minneapolis Lakers (later the Los Angeles Lakers). It was a glorious old art deco movie house with more than five hundred seats, a grand lobby with a concession stand illuminated by a glittering chandelier, and a stage.

My father had long dreamed of establishing a cultural center for Black and lower-income people. The Capri became that and more. In addition to being our family-run business where we all helped out—taking tickets, working the concession stand, and picking up trash—Dad let community groups like Eden House, a halfway house for addicts, use the space to hold meetings and seminars free of charge. Additionally, he showed free films to a group of underprivileged kids from Chicago who played in a Minneapolis basketball tournament. He opened the door to a group of local elderly people as well. He also employed people who needed work, including John, the Capri's caretaker. He was an old white guy my dad had rescued from the streets. Dad let John live rent free in a backstage room and paid him to clean the theater each night. That was how giving and committed to community uplift my dad was.

In addition to giving us up-close and personal views of the lives of Minneapolis's elite, Dad's connections also exposed us to those who were less fortunate. Smitty, as my dad was known, was a community organizer who was always on the phone trying to help someone. "He just needs work," I'd hear him say, drumming up a job, or, "The funeral expenses are too much for them."

One day, he invited a homeless white man to dinner. Peering into the kitchen, where they stood with my mother cooking, Taryn and I were scared by the stranger's filthy clothes and raggedy beard. "He looks weird," I whispered to Taryn. "I'm not sitting near him. I bet he smells."

Daddy caught us spying and took us aside. "He's a regular man down on his luck and in need of help," he said, quashing our complaints. "Anyone could find themselves in the same position. I've been there," he added, reminding us that though he had a good job, solid credit, and money saved up, he and Mom—like other Black borrowers—couldn't get approved for a home loan, so one of his wealthy white friends got the loan in his name and promised to give my dad the deed when the house was paid off. "Looking out for each other is our job as human beings. This man is lonely and hungry, so he will share our meal."

Hearing this, my siblings and I rose to the occasion. We nervously took our seats at the dining room table and joined hands with the homeless man to pray over the meal my mother had prepared. After the prayer, the man thanked my dad for everything he'd done and joked that he would try not to eat all the food on the table but that it would be hard because it was clear my mother was the best cook. We laughed and nodded in agreement. By the end of the meal, we were laughing and joking with him like he was a part of our family.

In time, the Capri Theater became the city's chief distribution outlet for martial arts classics and Black films, with directors like Gordon Parks and Sidney Poitier and stars like Richard Pryor, James Earl Jones, Bill Cosby, Cicely Tyson, and Louis Gossett Jr.—but he also showed top-billed movies after they were no longer at the major theaters, which made leasing them more affordable. The Capri was also a concert venue, showcasing up-and-coming local artists and providing a space for them to hone their craft. Like the community groups, Dad didn't charge these artists to use the space, because he wanted it to be accessible to all.

One of those artists was my friend Tyka Nelson's big brother, Prince. The Nelsons lived six blocks away from us. Taryn and I would often pack up our Barbie dolls and head to Tyka's to play. Born in 1960, like us, Tyka had a beautiful singing voice. Her parents were both jazz musicians. Her father, John, played the piano and used the stage name Prince Rogers; her mother, Mattie, was a singer. There was always music playing in their house, especially in the basement, where her big brother played the drums or the keyboard.

"You girls go on downstairs to play," Tyka's mother would say when we got too loud.

We'd pack our dolls and trek down the stairs. Tyka's brother, whom we called "the Ogre," would start banging on the drums to get rid of us. Annoyed, the three of us would stand there, rolling our eyes and grumbling. He'd laugh and keep on banging.

"Mom," Tyka would complain, "Prince won't let us. . ."

"Prince, come up out of that basement," their mother would yell. "You're always down there. Give the girls a chance."

After a few more shouts from his mother, Prince would get all huffy and stomp up the steps. He wasn't a big talker, but his icy sneer let us know he was pissed off.

We enjoyed tormenting Prince. Even when we didn't want to play Barbies, we'd push Tyka's mom to run him out of the basement.

"You twins—why are you here again?" he'd demand. "Go home."

One day, he was waiting when we got down to the basement. "You two," he said, "this is for you."

He'd written a song to taunt us called "Lippy Lippy Lou," about a nasty girl with big lips. I was too mad to take in the words, but I still remember the song's funky beat. All his banging on the drums and keyboard was paying off.

When Prince practiced at the Capri, John was always calling in the wee hours to complain to Dad.

"It's two in the morning," he'd growl, sounding tired over the phone. We'd hear Prince clacking instruments in the background. "That boy is still up here playing."

Sometimes, my dad would go to the theater to remind Prince that it was a school night. But usually he'd tell John, "Well, just let him be," and hang up.

One afternoon, I entered the theater to help Dad set up for an event and found Prince composing music. I opened the door and saw the stage full of instruments—two guitars (bass and electric), drums, a keyboard, hand cymbals, everything. Seemingly in a trance, Prince would play one and then jump to another and play that, like a one-person orchestra—but loud. By then, he was seventeen and quickly growing into manhood. He had an uneven beard and mustache sprouting on his face and a thick, billowing Afro that looked like a halo.

"Prince, what are you doing?" I asked, pointing to the instruments scattered all over the stage. "That looks crazy."

He was lost in his vision and barely heard me. All he could do was shout, "Shut the door! Shut the door!"

And I did.

Eventually, I went back in because the music and his singing seemed to get louder. When I opened the door and peered inside, I found Prince on the stage holding his guitar. His eyes were shut real tight, and his head faced the ceiling as he plucked the strings on the guitar like he was touching a woman in her private parts. I didn't dare move or say a word. I just listened to the erotic tunes emanating from the instrument as he plucked and plucked and plucked. Soon, his notes became more sensuous. He swayed to the beat and appeared to be climaxing, having an orgasm or some heightened trip. When he finished, he stopped playing, exhaled, opened his eyes, and looked at me.

Seeing my wide eyes and mouth agape, he smirked and said, "You liked that, didn't you?" I returned his smirk and left him alone to get back to it. Years later, when I listened to his guitar solo on "Why You Wanna Treat Me So Bad," it was very similar to the music I heard that noisy day at the Capri.

Dad's financial help from Wheelock Whitney Jr. opened my eyes. I'd seen him interact with super-wealthy moguls early on in my life. As a child, I was dazzled by their wondrous shows of glamour and seemingly carefree living.

Taking note of Dad's ability to connect with people and comport himself among sophisticated clientele, every year, during the Christmas holidays, Phillips and Sons would have him deliver liquor to the homes of some of the wealthiest families in the country.

"Ho, ho, ho!" Dad would enter dressed as Santa Claus. The children would gather around him, thrilled for the spectacle of an in-home visit with Santa. One of those homes was that of Minnesota Supreme Court Judge George M. Scott. His son,

Daniel, sat at my father's knee in awe. For years, he thought Santa was a Black man.

My father also befriended George Pillsbury, heir to the food company fortune; Bob Naegele Jr., an investment banker who owned billboards, Rollerblades Inc., and the Minnesota Wild; and James Binger, the CEO of Honeywell, who would later own the city's landmark Butler Square development.

He was invited into their homes and private lives, not as an employee but as a trusted friend. Sometimes he'd take Taryn and me along when he visited their magnificent homes, probably to show us off because we were bubbly and smart, and twins are cute by definition. But I also think my father was trying to show us how other people—wealthy people—lived.

"Today, you girls are going to meet Mr. George Pillsbury. He's a good man, very rich and powerful. He inherited his family's food-service business," he explained, peeking back at us from behind the steering wheel as we drove to the lush Pillsbury estate.

"You mean the Pillsbury Doughboy?" Taryn asked, sitting beside me. We wore adorable matching tartan print dresses my mother had picked out for the visit.

"He's not the Doughboy." Daddy chuckled. "But, yes, they are that brand. They make millions selling flour, biscuits, dinner rolls, sweet rolls, cookies—a bunch of stuff you girls eat. That's why I want you to meet him. You could learn a lot from a businessman like him."

Taryn huffed and sank back into her seat. She hated these visits.

"Cool," I said, intrigued. I loved being exposed to an opulence most people see only in movies—vast lawns and gardens, swimming pools, hot tubs, tennis courts, and furnished terraces that were as big as pavilions overlooking Lake Minnetonka. We once attended the wedding of one of the Pillsbury kids on an island on the lake. As we were transported by a private ferry, I was beside myself. Looking out over the water, I pretended I was alone on my own private island.

The homes themselves were colossal and architecturally grand. Inside were marble foyers rising several stories to dramatic medallioned ceilings or leaded-glass skylights. Floors, staircases, and archways leading to living spaces were marble or gleaming wood. Golden light streamed in through walls of windows. Every sumptuously upholstered chair or love seat, every thick, soft carpet, every gossamer or heavy silken drapery exuded luxury.

Most interesting of all was how the people, the families, lived their daily lives surrounded by such grandeur. It was like they didn't even notice. The women talked about mundane things like the weather and country club gossip as servants tended to their every whim in dining rooms large enough to host banquets.

"Did you hear Lyle broke his leg in a ski accident last week?" a wife dripping in real diamonds and sparkling emeralds would share at the dinner table with a hint of amusement beneath her pretend concern. "Aspen is a total death trap. I only go to keep tabs on the old crowd." Meanwhile, I was keeping tabs on her mansion, which I would never leave for any reason. The walk to the pool house alone required a snack. Why go anywhere?

How much money did it take to be rich like the Pillsbury family? How much did it take to live in relative comfort, as we did, but close to the edge and with no slack for extras? I wondered about my Northside neighbors—were the Kerns, who owned an interior design firm, as rich as the Bogarts, who sold furs?

There was no easy way to get this information. I couldn't ask anyone directly. Rich people never talked about money, and poor people didn't have any money to talk about. Walking Black Power downtown one day, I saw a wealthy-looking white man enter the bank in a rush. Peeking into the lobby as the door closed behind him, I realized that the bank was the only place where all the numbers I sought could be found. Rich people kept every dime they had in the bank in some capacity, and smart poor people did the same.

"Let's get home, Black Power," I said, patting his head. "We have work to do."

Infiltrating the phone company and connecting with Mark Spitz and the Jacksons taught me important lessons. Number 1: Never talk business with the first person you reach but ask to be transferred to look like an in-house caller. Number 2: Say you're trying to solve a problem because people love to help. Number 3: Let people assume you're white. People are less suspicious of someone like themselves. Number 4: Be nice, not demanding. It calmed me to start calls with pleasantries like, "How's your day going?" Number 5: Stick with it. The person might be hard to find, but someone, somewhere, in the company holds the key to what you need. In the 1970s, most business was transacted through person-to-person contact. Understanding how to finesse those relationships was extremely important.

Time and again, the worth of these five lessons—which I called my "power tools"—was validated. And I knew I'd need them to succeed on my new mission with the banks to find out how much money people had.

Minneapolis was a small city served by a handful of banks. If I hit the three major ones, chances were good that I could check out the accounts of everyone I knew. I started with the Kerns. I was transferred to the extension after calling a local bank and asking the operator for information on safe-deposit boxes. When the representative answered my call, I said, "Oh no, I must have the wrong extension. I'm trying to get my balance. Can you help me?"

She answered, "You want personal accounts," and transferred me over.

"Personal accounts," someone said.

"Hi, this is Gloria Kern. I'm trying to figure out how much cash I have in my primary account. Can you help me?" I asked.

"What's your account number?"

"I'm afraid I don't have it with me. Could you look it up another way, by my address, say?"

"Sure."

After sharing the Kern's address, I was given their bank balances, and the representative asked if I needed anything further.

"The Kerns have fifty-thousand dollars in the bank!" I later told Taryn. (This is roughly two-hundred-and-fifty-thousand dollars today.)

"Woooo! That's a lot of money!"

Taryn was the only one I told about what I was doing. She'd always been good at keeping secrets.

While my power tools usually got me the intel I wanted, often, the bank employees were challenging, either refusing to release information without account numbers or asking for other means of identification. This led me to develop a new strategy: instead of posing as a customer, I'd claim to be a fellow employee who needed help.

"Tom, I'm so glad I got to you. Please help me fix this issue for our customer. How much do they have in their account?" I'd ask.

"Can I get an account number?"

"I don't have it here, but they are trying to get approval for a loan. You know how tense these situations can get," I'd complain.

"I sure do. I'll help you out this time. How do you spell the last name?"

"Brooks. B-R-O-O-K-S. Thanks a bunch." I'd smile at Black Power as Tom delivered the account balance.

That ruse almost always worked. Using it, I diligently worked my way down the Northside, picking random addresses in high-end Golden Valley and then heading south to where the poor lived. Our house was a block from Golden Valley, in the middle. I got some big surprises checking people's accounts. For one thing, I could never have predicted which of my immediate neighbors would be well-to-do or broke. For another, while most of the white people were at least treading water, none of the Black people had any money at all—none of them.

I checked out one Black millionaire and a few well-known professionals and was relieved to see that they, at least, were prosperous. But they were the rare exceptions.

"Dad, why are so many Black people poor?" I bluntly asked over dinner one night.

He sat back and closed his eyes to think. He was always careful with his words. "We could sit here all night talking about this, Tanya," he started. "I'll keep it short, though. The truth is that in this country, it takes power and access to make any real money. Those are both things that were historically kept away from Black people after slavery due to systemic racism. Between that, a lack of generational wealth, and poor financial practices, it's tough for Black people to escape and stay out of poverty."

Hearing all this and having had a peek inside so many accounts, I viscerally understood my father's commitment to community service. He'd been trying to level the playing field for poor people. What I'd seen as mere generosity or kindness, praiseworthy virtues, was a one-man fight to help people survive. It made me even more proud of him and solidified in my mind that Dad was a better man than most of the rich men he had befriended. Everything he had, he earned using his brain and body, and still, he was trying to help others. Smitty was a superhero.

I felt I had to do something too. I wanted to join the fight.

I found my path when I overheard a classmate complain that, at home, their lights had been cut off. I had no idea that even happened to people, that utility companies were cruel enough to plunge whole families—with children! Even babies!—into darkness over an unpaid bill. With some elementary sleuthing, I got the family's address and called the electric company. I did the little dance of asking for a random department and getting switched to billing to seem like an in-house caller. Once I learned my classmate's family owed $342, I called back to try a new ploy.

"Hi, this is Jackie Johnson. Is your computer down?" I asked a fellow employee.

"No, mine's fine."

"Maybe you can help me. This guy with interrupted service, Roland Burke on North Upton Street, just paid his bill of $342. But I can't get into the system to restore it."

"I can input that payment for you. Is that B-U-R-K-E?"

Just like that, the problem was solved. What a revelation! All it took to ease human hardship was a poof of digital magic. I felt like my childhood hero, Samantha on *Bewitched*. But even more, I felt satisfaction. I'd used my power tools for something worthwhile, as my father had urged.

Inspired, I wanted to rescue people on a bigger scale. It struck me that utility companies had lists of cut-off customers and that I could get them by working my usual routine. I'd go down the list and select a mix of strangers and families I'd heard of through school or sports and set about restoring their gas, lights, phone—whatever they needed. When Taryn was home, she'd be my sidekick, picking customers' names off the list—"Let's do the Clyburns on Chestnut. Do we know them?"—and whooping joyfully when the scheme worked. It felt good working with Taryn. We were a good team, and I enjoyed having her around.

My restorations didn't always stick, though. The utility company would sometimes catch what was presumably its error and cut off the service again.

Word got around. Partly because Taryn and I would whisper a bit, unable to stifle such a big secret. Kids would tell their parents: "Tanya can fix it."

My most poignant encounter was with a classmate's grandmother. I didn't know the family well but heard the kids lived with her. One day after school, she was waiting—a small woman in a shabby winter coat, but tidy, with matching gloves and hat.

"Are you Tanya?" she whispered, pulling me away from the other kids. "I have a problem."

I could see she had been crying. I led her to a bench and offered her a napkin to wipe her tears before they froze to her cheeks in the bitter Minneapolis cold.

"How can I help you?" I asked.

"I can't believe I'm doing this, asking a teenager for help. This is rock bottom," she said. She covered her face with her hands to shield new tears. "I'm so ashamed."

Not knowing what to say, I placed my hand on her knee and squeezed to let her know I was there, and I wasn't going anywhere.

After a few minutes, she opened up to me. She was behind on her mortgage payments, and that month, she was about to come up short again.

"I could lose my house. Then where will we go? I'm all my grandkids have. They'd have to go into foster care." She started crying harder.

"That won't happen. I promise it won't," I said, embracing her. "I'll do everything I can to help you."

At that point, I hadn't messed with mortgages but figured I could wipe out her arrears, given my success spying on bank accounts.

She thanked me but could barely look me in the eye. What's more, my promise didn't ultimately cheer her up. Her burden shifted a little, but she still seemed overburdened.

Between the ages of fifteen and sixteen, I managed to void people's utility bills, at least temporarily, around three hundred times. I also handled a few overdue mortgages. I'd come home from school, change clothes, eat a snack, and then Black Power and I would head upstairs and start phoning before the close of business. Office workers tended to be weary and a little more careless at that hour, which helped.

I realized that what people needed more than relief from bills was money. Not paying bills was just a symptom; the disease was cash deficiency. There wasn't enough cash for groceries, gas, clothing—everything cost too much. The only difference between my dad's mogul friends and the average person—even my family—was dollar signs. When I was calling the banks, I learned where I could find lots of dollars.

As a faux coworker, I could ask direct questions about bank functions—which departments handled what, who had decision-making power, and more. Through this process, I discovered that banks don't just hold customer deposits; they also have their own pools of funds, called reserves, which are unconnected to accounts. These reserves could be enormous.

I'd discovered millions of dollars in those reserve funds at the banks, money that didn't belong to any particular person. If I managed to extract small sums—a few thousand here and there—to distribute to my neighbors, I wondered if the banks would even notice it was missing.

Trying to figure out how to access the reserve money, I discovered that wire transfer departments moved millions of dollars all over the country—even the world—every day. Most of those funds went into established bank accounts, but there was a way that anyone could wire money to someone else: the bank where the sender had put down cash would alert its wire transfer department, which would transfer the money to the destination bank, which in turn would release that sum from reserve funds. The recipient could then come to pick it up. This transfer method was called PUPI: paid upon proper ID.

There were restrictions: any cash transfer over $9,999 would be reported to the IRS. And there were small hurdles to request a transfer, such as knowing the destination bank's name, routing number, and code of the day.

Armed with my power tools, I knew I could get all the information and transfer money. Though I wanted to get ahold of those dollars to help everyone around me, it seemed too risky. I needed more information and more hands to pull it off without getting caught. Basically, I needed more time and a lot more nerve and then I could break the banking system wide open.

3

REGINA

The exciting education I was getting about the banking world left me with a lot to be desired at school. Taryn and I had been coasting at our local public school, Patrick Henry High, and by the tenth grade, we were bored by the dumbed-down classes, which felt like they'd been created to keep kids in their seats as the teachers babysat them for eight hours. We craved something more stimulating: to be in an elite learning environment with top-tier teachers and peers who could keep up with and inspire us. I was also socially curious. Having observed the lifestyles of my father's wealthy friends, I wanted the chance to walk in their children's shoes—to learn what they learned, to share their experiences, to see how it would feel to have endless resources, comfort, and privilege.

Regina High School is an all-girls school founded by the Sisters of Notre Dame. It's one of the most exclusive and prestigious parochial schools in Minneapolis. I decided Taryn and I should transfer there. After filling out the application, we took a qualifying exam, which we both passed. I did best in the English section, and Taryn got a higher score in math. I was sure we'd be accepted, but I knew there was no way our parents could afford to send us.

"Greetings, Mrs. Shivers, I'm so thrilled to recommend my shining stars over here at Patrick Henry High. Taryn and Tanya Smith are scholar athletes. They'd be perfect for Regina's scholarship program. How do I finalize this?" I said, posing as a dedicated teacher once I got the counselor who doled out the school's scholarships on the phone. I'd become quite comfortable speaking in an adult tone, and puberty helped add a deep timbre to my voice.

"We have lots of candidates from Patrick Henry High and other local schools. I'll have to consider their applications first. It's only fair," she said, her tone dismissive. "Maybe next year."

She was about to hang up, but I pushed forward, like it didn't even register that she could be turning me down. If I forgot about it, she'd forget about it.

"Did I mention that they're twins? Adorable twin girls. They'll look cute in their Regina uniforms on the school's brochure next year. Adding another layer of real-world experience for its legacy population will really make it clear that Regina's doing great things to improve integration," I noted. I could practically feel the woman's ears perk up and her mouth begin to salivate.

"What are their names again?"

Hearing this, I smiled at Black Power. We were in.

In the fall of 1976, at sixteen, Taryn and I proudly donned our new uniforms (brown blazers, white blouses, and plaid skirts) and prepared to leave the house to begin our private school education. Our parents made a big breakfast—sausage and bacon, Cream of Wheat, waffles, scrambled eggs, and fresh orange juice—as our big send-off.

"I still don't understand how all this happened, girls." Mom repeated what she'd been saying since we told her we'd been accepted to Regina with full scholarships. She was excited, of course, and knew we had the academic chops to get in and excel, but she and Dad were suspicious since they hadn't been involved in the process.

"We're so proud of you girls," Dad said, kicking off his one-hundredth pep talk. "As I always say, you can do anything you set your mind to. Don't worry about those kids at Regina. They need to be worried about you two."

With Dad's advice as the wind beneath our wings, Taryn and I headed out to our new bus stop on the corner of Vincent and Twelfth Avenue North. It was the first time the Regina bus had ever been routed through the Willard-Hay neighborhood of Minneapolis. Our neighborhood friends were impressed. "How did you get into Regina?" they'd ask, seeing us standing there waiting for the bus in our plaid skirts. There was a degree of respect connected with such a fancy school.

Compared to noisy and bustling Patrick Henry High, arriving at Regina each day was like entering a serene spa that also happened to include lesson plans and nuns in habits. The bathrooms, lockers, hallways, classrooms—everything—were neat, clean, and ready for use, like we were in a five-star hotel. Our teachers never complained about not having enough resources for experiments and lesson plans or that our textbooks were too old. Everything was new, untouched, and top of the line. If we wanted to make a rocket, the supplies would suddenly materialize. And, most noticeable of all, there were no boys. The girls at Regina had good etiquette and table manners and wore expensive shoes, blouses, and backpacks.

Taryn and I quickly made friends. As it had been everywhere we went, the other students loved seeing identical twins, and now we had to dress alike each day. It was kind of a teenage spectacle. The Regina girls practically gathered around to inspect us. Sometimes, in the bathroom or study hall, I'd catch them staring. One girl rubbed my shoulder in the cafeteria. But they kept things pleasant. No one was ever overtly rude; stereotypical Minnesota niceness was the norm among the mostly affluent white-girl population. They'd introduce themselves, ask the usual questions to see if we were of their pedigree, and then, if we passed, move us up the chain to the "possible friend" zone. But in some cases, there was a strange racial undercurrent to the friendship, as if we'd been chosen for bragging rights because we were Black.

Piper Prescott was one of those girls. She sat beside me in religion, a class where we were supposed to study the Bible, but really, everyone was just doodling in their notebooks as one of the nuns droned on about the Ten Commandments. One thing I quickly learned about academics in private school was that most of the kids hardly paid attention in class but excelled because they were well prepared at home by tutors and other educational programs. The classes were challenging, but the students always seemed steps ahead of the teachers. Years later, I learned that some of the kids had actually been gifted lesson plans and exams that had been stolen from the teachers and passed down among the elite.

"Your hair is, like, gorgeous," Piper chirped, reaching over and combing her skinny fingers right through my hair. I yanked my head away, but I don't think she even noticed. Or maybe she pretended not to. White girls, I was learning, had lots of power tools. "You look just like Diana Ross. Do you know who she is?"

Of course, I knew who Diana Ross was. Who didn't? She was a real-life goddess. Unmatched. *Lady Sings the Blues?* Like every other Black person in the world, I got chills when Billy Dee said, "Success is nothing without someone you love to share it with" to her in *Mahogany*. Yes, I knew Ms. Diana Ross.

"Yes," I said.

Piper had a straight, medium-length blonde bob. She looked like Barbra Streisand. She was always pleasant, succeeded in all of her classes, and had wealthy parents. Her dad was a banker, and her stay-at-home mom was a trust fund adult. Everyone wanted to be in her good graces, even the nuns.

After this interaction, Piper and I were kind of inseparable. Taryn had somehow found the weed-smoking crowd and stayed to herself, and I was bonding with Piper and her acolytes, a crew of girls who collected *Seventeen* magazine and only dated boys from the top private schools in the area—like Breck and Benilde-St. Margaret's.

"You hanging with us this weekend, Tanya?" Piper asked randomly one Friday. Up until then, our friendship had only played out on school grounds. We sat together at lunch, gossiped in study hall, and did laps side by side around the track in gym class. We never spoke on the phone or visited each other's homes. She hardly even asked about my life outside of school. I knew she and the acolytes hung out on weekends at country clubs and took tennis lessons, and I assumed I'd be invited when the time was right.

"Cool. I'd love to," I said. "What's going on?"

"Just a little party at my friend Blake's house in Kenwood Isles. His parents are trying to fix their marriage in Bora Bora, so we have the place to ourselves. His nanny will be there, but she stays in her quarters."

"Count me in," I said, intrigued. Kenwood Isles was one of the most affluent neighborhoods in the state.

"Rad," Piper cheered, writing the address on my memo pad.

Walking into Blake's cavernous abode, it occurred to me that I was going to be partying with rich white teenagers. I was the only Black person there. It was wild. They had bottles of every kind of liquor, weed brownies, and joints floating around like cigarettes—just out in the open like they knew they wouldn't get caught, and if they did, nothing would happen to them. Jess, Piper's main acolyte, who maintained her size-zero figure via anorexia, got drunk and stumbled off to the pool house to have sex with two boys. Lilly, Piper's other friend, hopped on Blake's parents' massive oak dining room table and stripped down to her bra and panties before running and jumping into the pool. The next thing I knew, I was staring at a room of nude bodies as half the kids stripped naked and made their way to the pool to skinny-dip. Someone tried to pull me along, but there was no way I was getting naked in front of all those people. I decided to take the weird turn of events as my cue to exit before things got too crazy.

By Monday morning, it appeared that they'd all forgotten what they'd done on Friday night. Piper and the acolytes went on with the day as if the party hadn't happened. Not one peep until I was alone with Piper in religion.

She turned to me, looking worried, and asked, "Did something happen at the party? You left early."

"No. Nothing happened. I just wanted to get home."

"Cool. I was so worried. I thought maybe someone did something to, like, offend you." She lowered her voice to a whisper when she said "offend."

"Not at all. Everyone was super friendly," I said. "But, honestly, I was a little put off by all the alcohol and drugs . . . and the sex and nudity."

Piper chuckled. "I can see how all of that could be alarming, but it's all in good fun. We study hard and party harder. It's the seventies. Free love has taught us that we have to free our bodies and our minds. You'll get used to it," she said. "I'm just happy I didn't ruin things with you. I was actually thinking . . . would you like to come to my house for dinner sometime? My parents would like to meet you."

"Really? Your parents want to meet me? Why?"

"They're a little leery, not as open-minded as us. But I told them they need to get on board and make room for my best friend."

Hearing I was Piper's best friend felt good. Being away from all the kids I'd grown up with in public school, I was beginning to feel lonely at Regina. Piper's invitation to meet her parents was a solid step forward.

Piper's home looked like something in a magazine. It was a seven-bedroom, ten-thousand-square-foot mansion in Kenwood Isles. Every room, including the bathrooms, had an ornate crystal chandelier and marble floor tiles. Following Piper through the mansion, I wondered how many people lived there aside from Piper and her parents. She was an only child. What could they be doing with all those extra rooms?

Her bedroom looked like an adult's apartment. She had her own bathroom, a walk-in closet, and a queen-size bed.

At dinner, Piper's parents watched me like I was an alien who'd invaded their home. They carefully observed everything about me: how I held my utensils, where I placed my napkin, and my mannerisms. Piper's mother, who seemed medicated and a little detached, started asking me questions: "How do you like Regina? Where do you live? What do your parents do?"

When I had answered, she said, "You're articulate. You speak well."

I was immediately offended. What did she expect?

Piper picked up on my energy and tried to defend me. "Mother, that's offensive," she said. "Tanya is very smart. There's no need to highlight that, like, it's strange or unique."

After her mother struck out, Piper's father tried to carry the conversation forward, but he was worse. "Let me know if it's too cold in here for you, Tanya. Let me know if you need flat water. Let me know if that chair isn't comfortable enough for you," he said.

I kept saying I was fine, but his attempts to make me feel comfortable made it clear he assumed I lived under a bridge somewhere.

Finally, Piper, who was growing more frustrated, jumped in, saying, "Tanya, please forgive my father. He's never had a Black friend, not one, and he doesn't know what to say to you."

I nodded along, but I didn't say anything further.

When Piper's father drove me home in his brand-new Mercedes-Benz, I had him drop me at the wrong house—not because ours looked bad but to impress him with a much grander one.

By senior year, Taryn and I had mentally withdrawn from Regina altogether. It wasn't about the school or our classmates; the situation with Piper was in the past, and I'd made a few close friends. The problem was that neither of us could really focus on academics. We'd get dressed, hide till our parents left for work, and then pursue our true interests. For Taryn, that meant Bobby and the drugs that he brought around, which were now heavier than weed. For me, it was using my power tools. By twelfth grade, I was doing five or six account adjustments, a process that I now called "doing transactions," per day, and I needed to do them during business hours, which also happened to be school hours.

When the school called to check on us, I pretended to be my mom: "The twins are sick today . . . yes, both of them . . . a month . . . they'll be back in a month." We were out sick so much our friends started sending "get well soon" cards in the mail. Finally, I ran out of excuses and decided that we'd better withdraw. We wound up getting high school diplomas from a correspondence school in Florida. Our parents were crushed.

"I keep telling you girls that education is the most important thing. How could you let this opportunity at Regina slip through your fingers?" Dad said in a long lecture in the living room when we broke the news. "You both have the potential to be anything you want to be. You can only compete in this world with an education."

"And what about college?" My mother cried. "This won't look good on your applications." After our enrollment at Regina, her plans for our college education had grown more ambitious. Considering our test scores, there was talk of Ivy League enrollment, which my dad wanted, but my mom said we would have more fun at a historically Black college, like Spelman in Atlanta or even Howard in DC.

Sitting on the sofa, Taryn and I watched our parents heatedly pace the floor. We felt bad, terrible, about letting them down, but there was much more going on with us than competing with our classmates at Regina and applying to college. I had ambitions, but none of them included enrolling at an institution.

I was helping many people with my transactions and started keeping files with names and account information—whose mortgage was due and what contacts I had made at the bank who could correct it. I started thinking of the employees I had connected with on the telephone as my actual coworkers. We'd laugh about headline-news gossip and chat about the weather. The intimate moments of communication made me feel adult and seen. Sometimes, I'd forget what I was doing was illegal.

4

MACHINE DREAMS

Calling the banks and getting account information was small time. I needed to figure out how to get ahold of the reserve funds without getting caught. While doing a transaction, it occurred to me that everyone I spoke to—at the phone company, the electric company, and the bank—used a computer. They primarily entered the information I provided over the phone into their systems and then the computer directed the next steps.

I'd always been obsessed with computers. When I was in fourth grade at John Hay Elementary School, my classmates and I arrived at our room to find our teacher had set up a movie projector and hung a screen over the chalkboard. She instructed us to take our seats and quiet down. While most of the kids were excited by this series of events, as it indicated that we were about to watch something on the projector—a rare treat in the late sixties—I was sad because it meant a break from my social activities, which were pretty robust. Quiet time at my desk in the dark wasn't my idea of an eventful day at school.

When the teacher finally got the projector running, an animated film about computers started to play. It was all about how computers would run our lives one day—automatically cooking dinner and turning the lights off and on, aiming and steering our cars to the desired destination, and sparing us from doing dangerous and tedious jobs. As the narrator revealed all these fascinating, almost unbelievable, tasks this thing called a computer could do, my eyes widened, and I was sucked into the possibility of a future where everything a person could need and desire would be manifested through and by a machine. Something in my brain latched onto this idea. I loved figuring things out, breaking concepts down to their bare bones and building them back up to arrive at a conclusion, an end result. With computers, that would all be made easier and faster.

I ran home from school, found my mom and dad sitting in the family room, and announced, "Computers are the future!" with the same gravitas as the narrator in the film.

"OK," they said in unison, unsure of where I was going with this.

"Can we get one?" I asked. I wanted my family to become the Jetsons.

"Not right now," my mom said, letting me down easily. "But you just keep getting those good grades and then maybe one of these days, you can have a computer."

"Really?" I cheered. I started dancing around the family room with Black Power jumping at my feet.

It would be months before I finally got my hands on a real computer. That summer, my sister Babs, home from college in

Los Angeles, had a summer clerical job downtown. She took me along on a Saturday when she had to work.

I roamed the office while Babs typed and filed paperwork. I found a room full of huge, rumbling machines.

"Get away from there," Babs warned. "Don't go near those computers."

I tore myself away but kept trying to sneak peeks at the mysterious blinking towers that seemed to be communicating with each other. I was hovering near the door when one of Bab's bosses came by.

"Oh, you're working today too?" he asked her, impressed. Moving his eyes to me, he added, "And who's this young lady?"

Babs introduced us, and since he could see how enthralled I was with the towers, he asked, "Would you like to see the mainframes and—"

"Yes," I blurted before he could finish his offer.

The computer room was cold. "Is that so they don't overheat and explode?" I asked.

"We keep an eye on them," the boss assured me. "But being so powerful, they generate a lot of energy." He rattled off numbers, explaining that these towers, about as tall as he was, could even control other computers. Up close, I could see that one of the towers had lots of switches and colored lights, while others had spinning reels of tape. They seemed efficient, whirling and humming as they processed data at lightning speed.

"We call these the Big Iron," the boss said.

As he described what the different towers did, most of his words went over my head. But I was mesmerized. The Big Iron had besieged my imagination.

Considering how the utility companies were using computers, it seemed everything I'd learned about their future use was coming to pass. I wanted to be a part of that.

While doing research about banking systems at the library, I learned that I could connect to the bank's mainframe using a computer terminal, a so-called dumb terminal, which relied on a central mainframe for processing. From there, I could access every department in the bank and even link to other financial institutions via the American Banking Association's routing number system, which was essentially how banks identified each other while doing financial transactions, including money transfers.

After learning that, I consulted reference books at the library to get the local banks' routing numbers, addresses, phone numbers, and other identifying information. At the library, reference books were stamped Do Not Remove, but one day, wanting to continue doing research at home, I slipped the two black books into my backpack. When I was walking out, the librarian called my name and came running after me. As seasoned as I was at doing illegal transactions on the telephone, I nearly fainted. I couldn't get caught stealing. "Hey, Tanya," the librarian said, out of breath, when she reached me. "I just wanted to make sure you know we're closed for Labor Day next week. We'll be open the following day, though." I thanked her and rushed out.

Once I got home with the reference books, I decided I had to get a computer to put them to use. If I had my own computer that could interact with their systems, I could bypass risky person-to-person interactions, cut straight to the action, and control it. With a couple of strokes on a keyboard, I could do whatever I wanted.

While skimming the routing numbers, I thought of all the daily transactions the banks had to do—thousands or hundreds of thousands worldwide. And for every transaction, there was a computer involved. With that much work being done, I thought some banks might have used terminals that were just sitting around. I called a coworker I'd met at Farmers and Mechanics, one of the banks downtown, who thought I worked at another branch. I told her my computer had died and I needed a replacement.

"You guys have an extra one down there?" I asked.

"Yeah, sure, we do. Do you need one?" She said I could come pick it up that afternoon.

I panicked, thinking, *She'll see I'm only seventeen!*

I told the woman I was swamped with work and would have an office assistant pick it up. "It might take more than one," she said. "It's pretty heavy."

I immediately called some neighborhood friends I'd been hanging around to ask for help. Randall and Terrell were my age. They hung out in my bedroom, where they'd try on my shoes, clothes, and makeup, along with my mom's wigs.

"Darling, you are a star," Randall would tell Terrell as he pranced around in my mom's black kitten heels. They could work heels better than most women. I'd giggle and encourage them to keep going. They were unlike any boys I'd been around because of how free they were with their bodies and ideas. They loved fashion, music, and art. Terrell wanted to travel the world as a male model, and Randall dreamed of dancing in revues in Paris, like Josephine Baker—he had the legs for it. We called ourselves "best girlfriends."

They were a lot of fun and always up for an adventure. I was sure they'd be excited to help me get a free computer.

"How the hell are we going to do that?" Randall asked when I broached the subject.

Terrell was sitting with me at the vanity, applying the perfect lip.

"We'd all have to look professional," I explained. "I'll wear a nice blouse and slacks, with heels, and you should wear dress pants and ties. Randall can come into the bank with me, and, Terrell, you can drive your old jalopy as the getaway car."

"You trying to get us locked up, Tanya Marie?" Terrell asked.

"No way. You know me better than that," I said. I'd never do anything to harm them. Sometimes, when we hung out downtown or at the mall, other boys who sensed their queerness would tease them and threaten bodily harm. I'd jump to their defense.

After sharing a few more details about the operation, Randall and Terrell agreed to come along to pick up the computer.

On the way to the bank, I coached Randall. "Let me do all the talking. Don't act scared or nervous, no matter what," I said. "Remember—we're employees from another branch."

Randall was too anxious. "This isn't going to work. We shouldn't do this," he said. "We could get in serious trouble!"

"Don't worry," I insisted. "It's going to be fine."

We asked for the security head at the bank as my coworker had instructed.

"I'm Lauren Johnson from the Lakeside branch, and I'm here to pick up the terminal Kimberly has for my boss, Ms. Sanchez," I told him, all friendly and matter-of-fact. I'd brushed my hair into a bun and wore one of my mother's dark pantsuits and pearl earrings to look older, at least twenty-one. The guard seemed to be buying it. He was there to guard the money. No one was thinking about computers.

"Oh yeah," he said, oblivious to Randall shivering beside me.

He led us to the basement to get the terminal, which looked like a small TV. It was an IBM, yellow-beige with a green screen, and it was heavy. We pushed it into the elevator on a little cart, which we steered outside so we could load the terminal into Terrell's car. We thanked the guard and took off. During the car ride home, all of us were giggling nervously. It felt like a scene from a heist movie.

My parents were out when we got to the house. That was lucky because Randall, Terrell, and I had a hell of a time wrestling the terminal up three flights of stairs to the attic, which I'd decided was the safest place to stash it. There was an old desk up there. We set the computer on it and stared at it in amazement. When it hit me what I'd just done—and what I could do with this wondrous machine—I started crying.

After that, I was in the attic all summer, trying to get the computer running. From another coworker at Farmers and Mechanics, I got the name of the outside tech firm that handled troubleshooting for the bank. There, I befriended a technician named Phil, who told me I needed a "coupler," a device to link the terminal to my phone line and, through the phone, to the bank's mainframe. I found a coupler in a computer magazine and ordered it. It took forever to arrive. When it did, I called Phil, who walked me through the steps to install it and get online. This included hiring a network electrician to complete the wiring.

I usually had the house to myself in the daytime. Mom was at work. Dad was often busy with theater or political business. Babs, now in her twenties, was in Amsterdam doing research for a television show she was producing. Iris, also in her twenties, married one of her college professors and lived in Pasadena, California, with their young kids. Mason still lived at home but was always off doing his own thing. Ryan was in the hospital. Then there was Taryn, who had gone from smoking weed to boozing and doing cocaine. But she still hung out with me during the day and was home when I mastered Phil's instructions. Suddenly, the computer came to life. There was a weird screeching sound, and the glowing green letters LOG IN appeared on the screen.

"Taryn!" I screamed.

Taryn came charging up the attic stairs.

"What's going on? What happened?" she asked, running to my side. "Did it work? Did you get in?"

"I think I did. I made it. I'm connected to the system, just like a bank employee."

The two of us stood there watching the neon letters shine, afraid to do anything.

"Do you know what this means?" I asked, weighing the magnitude of the moment in my mind. There I was, just months shy of my eighteenth birthday, and I'd not only scored a computer terminal from a bank, but I'd figured out how to get the thing up and running and online. No one I knew, not in my neighborhood nor among the elite Pillsburys on Lake Minnetonka or Piper's well-to-do family in Kenwood, had done anything like this. I was sure of it. I felt an overwhelming sense of self-actualization. I'd fulfilled some aspect of my full potential. It made me wonder what I could do next. My mind started racing.

My twin, connected to my energy, gripped my shoulder to show support.

"You're *in*," Taryn declared. "You did it, sis."

Of course, I wasn't fully connected until I got a login name and password by claiming my "old ones" weren't working anymore. Phil helped with this. And then my computer studies began in earnest.

Initially, I had no real idea what the terminal could do. I started experimenting by collecting information, just as I had by phone. Only now, instead of checking my neighbors' bank balances, I could look into celebrities' accounts. Using the library reference book, a few strategic phone calls, and my computer, I discovered that Diana Ross was richer than her manager / soon-to-be ex-husband, Robert Ellis Silberstein. I also checked the accounts of Suzanne Somers, Erik Estrada, and Rick Springfield. I'd see a celebrity on TV and then zip upstairs to the computer to check their finances. I also looked at their credit card statements and checks paid—to whom and when. It revealed a great deal about people and their spending habits—$500 for a brunch at the Ritz-Carlton, $6,500 at Bergdorf Goodman. I'd lay in bed at night, imagining what they'd eaten for brunch at the exclusive hotel. Were they poolside with their agent or in a room with a secret lover? And what had they purchased at that prestigious luxury store? A gown for a premiere, perhaps? A watch for a scorned wife? Peering into other people's lives proved to be an irresistibly fascinating game.

Sometimes, the mechanical screech of the coupler was so loud that I swore my parents would hear it in the family room, three floors down, with the TV on.

"Quick," I'd tell Taryn, "Grab that blanket. Throw it over the machine." Then one of us would try to distract Mom and Dad until the line connected and the whining stopped.

Things got more interesting the summer Grace, my sweet Texas grandmother, visited. She spent a few weeks with us every year when she got time off.

"Where are the twins?" was her first question when she entered our house; she always had little gifts for us. When we were young, she'd bring us live turtles, which we'd keep in a deep dish with water. She loved cuddling with her "babies" and reading us stories. Taryn and I adored her too. Having reared my mother alone, Mom seemed rejuvenated and joyful whenever her mother came to visit. She'd stock the refrigerator, and she and my grandmother would cook excellent meals—pot roast, banana pudding, ham, turkey, steaks, and homemade biscuits.

Grandma Grace was a tall, good-looking woman with gleaming, thin, black hair. She radiated strength and cheer. But that year, she seemed different, less energetic. She was worn down. She even seemed shorter and smaller in her clothes.

"What's the matter, Grandma Grace?" I asked as we cuddled in the family room, watching the news as Mom made dinner.

"Nothing. I'm just tired," she told me. She'd been a maid for a white, wealthy Dallas family for years, raising their kids instead of my mother and now looked after those children's kids on top of the cleaning and cooking. "All that work is getting to be too much for an old lady."

"You should quit," I suggested.

"That would be nice, but I can't just up and quit." She chuckled at my youthful naivete. "I have to work. I need the money."

"Maybe you could get a different job that wouldn't be so hard."

"Keeping house is all I know."

She rubbed my knee, and I could feel hard callouses all over her hands, which were arthritic and swollen after decades of scrubbing floors and picking up after people. The work had also taken a toll on her back, which was constantly aching. She'd have Mom rub Bengay on it. I wondered if she'd have to endure such body-breaking work until she just keeled over and died. That couldn't be it. I had to help her.

One day, while sitting in the backyard eating BBQ chicken Dad had brought home, I asked Grandma Grace where she would vacation if she could afford it. Mom told me she loved to travel.

"All over the world," she said. In her eyes, which had a gray tint now, I could see she was imagining globetrotting on a private jet. I imagined I was right along with her. "But you know the first place I'd go?"

"Where?"

"Neiman Marcus." She laughed and described how elegant the store was—the most glamorous in Dallas—with practically a whole floor of fancy makeup and perfume counters. You could spray on some cologne to try it out. "Then, after a whole day of shopping, I'd go to Dunston's and get a big steak charbroiled on the open-fire grill," she added. "My boss took me there once, and I promised myself I'd return."

Later, when I recounted the conversation to my mother, suggesting we find a way to send Grandma Grace on that shopping spree and out to dinner at Dunston's for her birthday, she said, "Well, that would be wonderful. It's a good thing you want to help your grandmother."

Then Mom told me to sit at the kitchen table and held my hand as she said, "There's something else bothering your grandmother. She has glaucoma. According to the doctor, she may eventually go blind. We didn't tell you girls, because we didn't want to upset you. But I think you should know."

I was devastated. I wanted my grandmother to be able to slow down, live comfortably, and have a few indulgences, like that chargrilled steak. She'd certainly earned it. She told me everything would work out, but we both knew she could not know that.

The next day, when the house was quiet, I was in the attic looking at the computer and thinking about Grandma Grace. I had to bring her some peace. What good was a shopping spree at Neiman Marcus, dinner at a fancy restaurant, and a trip around the world if you couldn't see it?

After all my research and practice transactions, it was time to see how the terminal would perform. I reminded myself that the point of taking the risk of getting the computer, going through the trouble of installing it, and figuring out how to use it was to take the next step: making money transfers without being detected.

With some sleuthing, I discovered where Grandma Grace banked in Dallas and got her account number. I then got the bank routing information from the library reference book. Next, I placed my calls, cycling through bank departments to cover my tracks until I reached a likely prospect to get the code of the day.

"Hi, this is Sandy from checking and savings. How's your morning going?" I began. "We didn't get the code for today. Do you guys have it?"

"Yeah, we have it. It's *monster*."

"*Monster*? Is that M-O-N-S-T-E-R?" I confirmed.

"Yes, that's it."

"OK, thank you so much."

I logged onto the computer. When the screen asked what I wanted to do, I clicked wire transfer and added Grandma

Grace's account information. Knowing any transfer over $9,999 would be reported to the IRS, I typed in $5,000.

It was my first computer transfer. I was terrified. What if $5,000 was high enough to trigger some other security check? My face flushed hot with fear as I placed my finger on the button and pushed enter.

Boom. Nothing. The screen went blank. I was frustrated and wanted to scream. After the whole struggle to get the computer, hide it, get the coupler, hook it up, practice—now it didn't even work?

I shut down the machine, too unnerved to try again. I was completely disappointed.

A day or two passed. Then, one morning, as I was coming downstairs, I overheard a snatch of conversation between my parents.

"Well, I didn't send it," my mother said. "Grace doesn't know anyone else in Minneapolis. Let me call her back."

I crept back up the stairs and shook Taryn. "Wake up!" I told her. "She got the money."

"What? You mean it worked?"

"Yes! It worked! It worked!"

The two of us slipped back to the stairs to listen. My mother had talked to Grandma Grace and was telling my dad that she was not touching the money. "She told the bank about it. They insist that the deposit is legitimate."

I was shocked. It never occurred to me that Grandma Grace wouldn't use the money or that she'd alert the bank. Would that trigger an investigation that would lead to me?

I waited a day and approached my mother as she ironed clothes in the family room. "Mom, did I hear you say Grandma Grace got some money?"

"Yes, and it's a big mystery. It just showed up in her account. She's scared to touch it since she doesn't know who sent it."

"Why?" I asked. "If the bank put it in her account, why not keep it? What are they going to do? Send it back?"

"I have no idea," my mother said. "But knowing her, she'll let that money sit there for a hundred years before touching a dime."

I guess that was what people meant by the expression "honest to a fault."

5

NIGHT MOVES

As my dad had hoped, the Capri Theater became a local magnet. Though our weekly movie nights were popular, the concerts Dad organized every few months pushed our little theater into music history. In the 1970s and '80s, Minneapolis was bubbling with an eclectic pool of young musicians dedicated to creating their own sound. Their melodies and rhythms were like a magic spell, an enchanting fusion of funk, soul, and rock that transcended genres.

Audiences eagerly anticipated the musicians' elaborate, well-planned, and meticulously practiced performances. They'd line up down the street and later pack the theater. On those nights, I was often tapped to help out. I didn't mind. Seeing them was inspiring, like witnessing musical evolution up close and personal. Also, I enjoyed running the concession stand, selling our famous popcorn, the best in town—hot, freshly popped, and made with real butter, not the artificial stuff—and chatting with customers.

"It's crazy in there," Dad said one night after we'd sold out of popcorn and everything else in the concessions. "If we keep this up, we will need a bigger theater."

"Is Morris Day here tonight? I came from St. Paul to see him and Champagne. I had to pay my brother to drive me here. I would've walked to see Morris. He's sexy," a woman in a royal-blue dress that was so small it might've been a tube top said, stopping by the concessions stand to profess her love. He played drums for one of our regular bands, Grand Central, affectionately known as Champagne. Morris was the second drummer after Prince's cousin Charles "Chazz" Smith departed. The other group members included Prince, keyboardist Linda Anderson, and her brother, bassist Andre Anderson, who'd later be known as Andre "Cymone," the visionary behind Minneapolis's funky underground music scene. Their performances were a spectacle of energy and charisma. And they weren't alone. Flyte Time, featuring the powerhouse vocals of Cynthia Johnson, keyboard virtuoso Jimmy "Jam" Harris, and groovy bassist Terry Lewis, was also on the local scene.

While I loved working in the theater with my parents, I did start to feel restless. I wanted to get out on my own and have a social life outside the theater. Minneapolis had a growing nightlife scene where some of my friends went to party, listen to music, and find people to hook up with. At seventeen, I didn't know how to navigate that scene, but when I read about Tempo, a new club in South Minneapolis, in the newspaper, I started having ideas. It sounded glamorous and exciting.

I cut the article out and handed it to Taryn one Friday night after our parents had gone to bed. She was also looking for something more to do than spend nights with her boyfriend or at the theater. She'd work a shift here and there, which included a "loan" from the cash register.

"Do you think they'd let us in?" Taryn asked since we were underage.

Though I didn't know either, I said, "Yes. Of course. Look at us!"

We'd grown into shapely brown beauties with full bust-lines, narrow waists, and luscious, pouty lips.

Hoping to get into Tempo, Taryn and I pulled out these beautiful dresses my mom had bought us from Young-Quinlan. The snug-fitting dresses made us look sophisticated and adult. Standing before the mirror on our closet door, we commented on our club looks.

"You look great," Taryn joked, marveling at my pose.

"What's your telephone number, pretty lady? Can I buy you a martini?" I proposed to her.

We laughed and took turns doing each other's makeup. I liked seeing soft colors, pink lips, and blush on my brown skin. Taryn liked neon colors, blue shadows, and pink lips with light gloss. We looked like *Jet Magazine*'s Beauties of the Week when we were done.

After sneaking out, we took the number twenty bus down to Franklin Avenue and Cedar, where Tempo was located. Standing on the sidewalk among the crowd of young people waiting to get inside, I could feel the beat of "Love to Love

You, Baby" by Donna Summer playing in the club and pulsating through me.

Knowing we looked good, Taryn and I skipped the line and walked to the doorman. Seeing us standing together, he looked from Taryn to me and then from me to Taryn and grinned.

"Oh, they're going to love you sexy twins," he said, waving us right in without bothering to ask our age. Being cute, we discovered, was the only ID we needed. We were immediate VIPs.

Inside Tempo, a mirrored disco ball refracted shards of light over the dance floor. It was everything I'd imagined a nightclub to be: dark, smoky, and exciting. Taryn and I walked around to get a peek at the crowd. Most of the people were a little older than us, midtwenties to thirties, but they all looked attractive and like they were having the time of their lives. The women flaunted their cleavage in too-tight halter dresses. The men showed off their hairy chests in button-down shirts with gold chains. It wasn't too late, but some partygoers had already had too much to drink. One woman was slurring while being held up by her two girlfriends.

After going to the bathroom to make sure the bus ride hadn't melted our hair and makeup, we stood near the bar, rocking along to the music.

"Do you know that guy?" Taryn asked. "He keeps staring at you."

"What guy?" I turned to look across the dance floor, where Taryn had discreetly nodded. It's when I saw him—this

NEVER SAW ME COMING

handsome Black man in an expensive-looking, light-brown blazer, T-shirt, and slacks with matching leather shoes. He looked sharp and oozed a mix of confidence and masculinity that made him undeniably sexy. And Taryn was right; he was staring hard and clearly wanted me to notice. When our eyes locked, he smiled. I looked away to break the stare and then looked back to be sure I was receiving what he intended, and sure enough, his eyes were still set on me, and he was walking in my direction.

"Tanya, he's coming over here," Taryn said to prepare me.

"I know. I know," I sputtered. His eyes glued on me, I didn't know what to do with myself. I started fidgeting and looking around the club at random things to appear unbothered. I felt like Billy Dee Williams was approaching me in a romance movie.

"Hello, gorgeous. My name is Puegot," he said, holding his hand out to take mine. At that moment, I could hear Billy Dee saying, "You want my arm to fall off?" as he held his hand out to Diana Ross in *Lady Sings the Blues*. When I finally gave Puegot my hand, instead of shaking it, he kissed it like it was a ripe strawberry. Against my skin, his lips were as soft as pillows. I could feel Taryn staring. "And what's your name?"

"I'm Tanya."

"Well, Tanya, I wanted to come over and say you are the most stunning woman here. You might be the most stunning woman I've ever seen. In fact, I'll just say it right now, right here—you are." Puegot looked me over again, undressing me with his eyes.

82

I felt blood rushing to my cheeks. I never had a man compliment me like that. It made me feel sensual.

"How haven't we met before?" he asked.

Looking at his well-groomed mustache, which made me want to kiss his lips, I wondered the same thing. How hadn't we met before? He was five eleven and about 190 pounds. Not muscular but fit. He looked like he could pick me up and swing me around the room. I was immediately smitten. Of course, I'd had crushes and a few gentlemen callers in the past, but this man had taken my breath away. I could tell he was a little older—probably too old to be hitting on me—but that made him more attractive. I was outpacing most of the boys my age, and Puegot seemed like he could teach me things.

"I know why we haven't met. It's my first time here," I replied.

"Oh, really. A newbie. How old are you?"

"I'm eighteen." I lied. I could see Taryn grinning out of the corner of my eye. I ignored her and hoped he didn't notice. But suddenly, when Diana Ross's "Love Hangover" started playing, she grabbed my arm.

"This is my song. Let's go dance!" She squealed, pulling me away from Puegot.

"Bye," I said to him, stumbling behind Taryn while being dragged to the dance floor.

"Bye, beautiful."

I kept looking back at Puegot while Taryn found a spot for us. He didn't move from where I had left him and kept his eyes on me. When Taryn and I started slowly snaking our bodies back and forth like we were doing a lap dance—the only way to dance to "Love Hangover"—Puegot stared so hard at me everyone else in the club disappeared, and I was dancing for him. Wanting to draw him in, I let go of my inhibitions. I ran my fingers up and down my hips, caressed the back of my neck, and lifted my arms over my head. "'Cause if there's a cure for this, I don't want it, don't want it," I mouthed to him. He licked his lips and crossed his arms. He was about to come to the dance floor, but again, Taryn grabbed my arm.

"Shit, we need to get out of here," she said.

"Why? I'm having a good time."

"The bus. We're about to miss the last bus home."

I looked back toward Puegot to say goodbye, but I couldn't find him. Taryn and I raced out of the club and made it to the bus stop just in time. Had we missed the bus, we would've been stranded, and our parents would've discovered that we had sneaked out.

After that night, Taryn and I became regulars at Tempo. It was our spot. We both enjoyed dancing, music, crowds, and all the attention. We quickly went from being just twins to being the "Twins."

While I was enjoying all the partying, my mind became fixated on the next time I'd see Puegot. I picked out dresses and styled my hair and makeup, hoping to run into him. When I did, he always complimented me. And he didn't just say I was "pretty," like the other guys at the club. He was specific. He would say, "I love your teeth," "I love your hair like that," or "I love your calves. You have Tina Turner legs." Puegot was such a charmer. He was usually with some of his friends. They called themselves the Brothers. They were a group of upscale guys who threw high-end parties and events around the city.

Although Puegot would watch me like a hawk, he never asked me out or for my phone number. I was growing a little annoyed. I didn't know the next level of our connection, but I wanted to see him outside the club. Maybe we could go on a date. I knew I couldn't ask—he was too masculine for that. I had to wait.

Finally, Puegot offered to drive me home one night. I rushed off to Taryn. "Should I do it? Should I say yes?"

"Go ahead," she said.

I felt like royalty when I got into Puegot's brand-new, brown Mercedes-Benz. He opened my door and held my hand as I slid into the leather passenger seat, which stretched out like a bed. It was getting late, but there were still stragglers, drunks, and lovers hanging out in the parking lot. Familiar faces watched us closely. By then, they knew who we were, especially Puegot. Seeing us get into the car together was a significant statement. We were a thing.

"I'm a lucky man," he said, getting behind the wheel. "Look at you. Everyone out here wishes they were in my shoes."

Being close to him on the drive home, I could smell his spicy cologne with hints of vanilla and oak. It drove me wild. I wanted to put my nose against his neck and breathe in his scent, but I tried to focus on getting to know him.

While Barry White sang "It's Ecstasy When You Lay Down Next to Me" low on the eight-track player he'd had installed in the luxury car, Puegot told me about his life. He was a counselor at Harambee, a group home for disadvantaged and delinquent boys. He said he loved his job because he got to help the boys—most of whom had been written off by their families and society—get on the right track. Coming from a family focused on community service, I was even more enchanted by this guy. He liked to help people like I did. It seemed like proof that Puegot and I were written in the stars shining brightly overhead.

"So how'd you get a name like Puegot?" I asked, watching his left hand work the steering wheel. He didn't use two hands like my dad. He was hardly using one. He was smooth; even the car followed his every command.

"Peugeot is a foreign sports coupe. It's my nickname. I gave it to myself," he said.

"You gave yourself a nickname?"

"Baby, Puegot does whatever he wants," he replied. "My life, my rules."

We laughed and laughed.

He said, "I spell it differently, though—P-U-E-G-O-T."

"P-U-E-G-O-T," I repeated, and I never forgot it. "Nice."

When we reached my street, I had him stop the car a few doors from my house to avoid my parents hearing the motor idling.

When he stopped the car, he said, "A Willard-Hay girl? Classy. Your parents must be doing all right."

I laughed and said, "We've been here for a while. Since I was four." I explained that we'd been one of the first Black families on our street when we moved in, but everyone was welcoming. One neighbor who lived a few doors down in a beautiful yellow house asked us for favors on the Sabbath, like turning on their lights, which they weren't allowed to do. Soon, we did it for most Jewish families in the neighborhood. "To show their appreciation, some neighbors will give us wonderful pastries—rugelach, babka, apple cake, and Hanukkah cookies. Taryn and I are in heaven when they do that," I said.

"I like that. You get to experience a different culture," Puegot said. "That's why you're so sophisticated."

I blushed and said, "Thank you."

"Hey, there's a new club downtown on Fifth Street. It's called the Fox Trap. You should stop by sometime."

"I'll check it out," I answered, hoping that was some proposition for a date. "Thanks for the ride."

"No problem, beautiful."

When I turned to open the door to exit the Benz, Puegot didn't touch me or try to kiss me, though I wouldn't have turned him down if he had. He didn't even ask for my phone number.

The move piqued my interest, and I got out of the car thinking, *He's the one. Puegot is my ideal man.*

The next day, I looked up Harambee in the phone book and found the address. Sitting at my desk before I started my transactions, I took out the pink-tea rose-colored stationary my mother gifted me for special occasions and wrote Puegot the sweetest crush letter about how charming he was and said we would look great as a couple.

When I was done, I signed it, "Your Woman," and sprayed it with Charlie perfume by Revlon. I sent those anonymous crush letters to Puegot at Harambee quite frequently.

One night, Taryn and I got up the nerve to go to the Fox Trap. I wanted to see Puegot again, and she wanted to try a new spot. We hoped they'd let us in just like Tempo. Of course, it worked. Kyle Ray, a friend from the neighborhood, was the DJ. He was spinning funky records like "Car Wash" by Rose Royce and "Get Up Offa That Thing" by James Brown. Everyone was on the dance floor, singing along to the music and doing the latest dance moves.

Puegot was there with his boys. He walked up to me and whispered, "Tanya, you came correct. You're a stallion. Every man in here is staring. You gonna let me take you home tonight?"

To this, I smiled. There was no reason to answer. We'd be back in his Mercedes a few hours later, zipping through the city under the glowing moon.

This went on for months. Taryn and I, the "Twins," were fixtures on the Minneapolis nightclub scene. We stopped going to Tempo and became regulars at the Fox Trap, Riverview, Shieck's Cafe, Moby Dick's, and the Gay '90s, where we always went with Randall and Terrell. Often, we'd encounter musicians we knew from the neighborhood or the Capri, like Jimmy Jam, Terry Lewis, and Morris Day, dancing or performing or both. Prince was always out in the clubs too. One night when Taryn and I ran into him at Shieck's, he said, "I don't know how you twins turned out to be so fine!" I punched him playfully, and we hugged like siblings. Our "Lippy Lippy Loo" days were over.

Still, every night, I'd pray we'd run into Puegot, and when we did, he'd watch me nonstop and drive me home. Again and again, he'd let me go without laying a hand on me or asking for my telephone number.

I was becoming sexually frustrated. While I was a virgin, I kept imagining what it would be like the first time Puegot made love to me: how he'd smell, how he'd hold me and call my name. With my older sisters out of the house, I had my own room. Lying in bed at night after Puegot dropped me off, I'd slide my hands beneath the covers and press my fingers between my thighs, imagining he was there with me, investigating and learning every inch of my body.

6

THE COLLEGE TRY

In the fall of 1978, I enrolled as a freshman at the University of Minnesota. I handled the application process myself. Having upset my parents with my diploma shortcut, I wanted to prove that I embraced their higher education dreams. Since my diploma came from an accredited school, I only had to take an entrance exam to be admitted. I scored high enough to be awarded total financial aid from the school.

My proud parents were happy to treat me to a groovy one-bedroom pad at Cedars 94 in the Cedar-Riverside neighborhood, within walking distance to campus. My mom helped me pick it out, along with a bright-blue Pontiac Sunbird—my first car—and all the other things I needed for the apartment. Together, we hung curtains, cleaned the refrigerator, and stocked the cabinets.

While I was still doing dozens of weekly transactions on the telephone, I'd shut down the computer after the incident with Grandma Grace, fearing that leaving the line open would somehow lead the authorities to me. I left it in the attic at my parents' house.

Though I was thrilled to be on my own, beginning this chapter of my life didn't feel right without Taryn, who wasn't living up to her full potential. She'd become a steady drug user. I kept telling myself she had a right to choose her own path, but the drugs were making her more distant, secretive, and risky. Her boyfriend Nico introduced her to his weed dealer, Mrs. Babcock, who lived across the street from him.

Mrs. Babcock was an overweight lady who sometimes dressed like a man. All kinds of people—older men, hippies, street people, scary people—streamed in and out of her house, day and night, to score. There was always loud music playing, some people smoking, and others lounging around buzzed. The Babcock kids, young ones as well as teenagers, hung out in the chaos. No rules, no need to go to bed or school, and you could stay out all night. I hated that atmosphere, but Taryn loved it. Soon she was going to see Mrs. Babcock without Nico and spending most of her time there. Mrs. Babcock doted on her almost more than her own kids because Taryn was polite and well-bred. Taryn liked the attention and seemed to gravitate to her and seek her approval by doing things our parents wouldn't ever allow—drinking, smoking, whatever.

"Oh my God, where has this stuff been all my life?" Taryn laughed one night after taking a toke from Nico's joint in Mrs. Babcock's kitchen. She was already high, and her eyes were as red as ladybugs. She started dancing and passed the joint along to one of the Babcock kids, who tried to slide it to me, but I declined. I liked it just fine down on the ground. I also didn't like what weed was doing to my sister. I was getting worried.

Ever since we were kids, I had always wanted to make sure she was all right and felt responsible for her safety. It began when we were seven and Mom took us to the Minneapolis Aquatennial Grande Day Parade, which was held every year in July. During all the merriment, which included magical fairies in Grecian chariots, massive ducks spinning on paper-mache water, and bands from local schools marching in sync down Hennepin Avenue, a commotion started in the crowd. Black people started whispering about a police officer beating a Black teen girl accused of stealing a wig. We didn't know, but it was the beginning of what would later be called the "Minneapolis Riot," just one of over 150 riots that swept across the United States during the "long, hot summer of 1967."

With skirmishes breaking out around us, Mom had said, "Let's get out of here," and grabbed my hand. On instinct, I felt to grab Taryn's hand—Mom always told us to stay together—but she wasn't there.

"Where's your sister? Where is she?" Mommy asked Iris, Babs, and me, but she was already looking through the crowd, pulling me along to find Taryn.

"Taryn! Taryn!" I yelled, but it felt like the atmosphere was swallowing my words and no one could hear my small voice. Panic surged through me like an electric shock. My heart was pounding. Was Taryn the Black girl the people were talking about? Were the cops beating my sister? Was she going to die? Was I next? "Taryn!" Hot tears gathered in my eyes, blurring my vision.

Minutes that felt like hours passed until we found her—crying, just as lost in the wave of turmoil as I felt. Mommy hugged us tight, her eyes heavy with dread. Somehow, I felt responsible because I'd taken my eyes off Taryn for a few minutes. At that moment, I promised I'd never lose sight of my twin sister again. I'd keep her safe and out of harm's way.

Seeing Taryn constantly getting high at the Babcock house and heading in the wrong direction, I felt the same conviction. She was every bit as smart as me, and together, we could outshine all our classmates at U of M. I convinced her to try college to get her away from the people who meant her no good. She enrolled but only attended a few classes and quit. It just wasn't her path, and I had to accept it.

I had plenty to do to keep my mind off my sister. Nestled in my new digs, my mind went back to my unfinished business with Puegot. I figured out that he'd been such a gentleman because he suspected I was underage. I was still living with my parents, and I was leaving the clubs in time to sneak back in before they woke up. But now, things were changing. I'd turned eighteen. I had my own place and my own telephone. The little girl Puegot met at Tempo was all grown up, and I was ready to show him.

I invited him to my apartment one Saturday night. Remembering how much he loved my legs and curves, I put on a tight, orange, terry-cloth short set that rode up my butt cheeks every time I took a step. It was cute with a college-girl-next-door vibe but still sexy enough to let him know what I was up to.

Puegot walked into my apartment, looking fine as ever. He had a fresh haircut, and I could smell his cologne. I gave him a short tour and led him to the couch, where he took a seat while I turned on my record player and lowered the needle on Marvin Gaye's *I Want You* album.

"You hungry? I have some leftover Chinese food in the fridge," I said, standing before him. After walking around, those orange shorts were high on my thighs and looked like panties. I didn't bother to pull them down. I took a power pose with my hands on my hips to give him a good look at my body.

He looked at me like I was crazy for bringing up Chinese food and said in a firm voice, "Get yo fine ass over here."

Without a word, I went and stood between his legs.

"Now, take your clothes off," he ordered.

"Why?" I asked.

"Because I said so" was his answer. "Do it." There was sexy confidence in the way he said it. He was in control.

With the window shades still up and the moonlight peeking in through the balcony, I slid my clothes off while Puegot stared at my body. At first, I was nervous, but seeing he liked what he saw and was turned on, I started feeling more like myself. By the time I got to my underwear, I had a slight smirk on my face. I wondered what he wanted me to do next.

"Now turn around," he said sternly. "I want to see your ass."

I turned, and he palmed my ass with a tight grip, examining it like a sweet peach. The warmth of his skin against mine made my temperature rise, and I began melting, becoming soft inside.

Puegot picked me up and took me to the bedroom. He laid me down on the bed, splayed my legs wide open, and looked at me with deliberation and contemplation.

As Marvin crooned, "Breathe in and get a bit higher. You'll never know what hit you" on the record player in my living room, Puegot began stripping off his clothes. The lamp on my nightstand was on, and I could see everything. My eyes slid over his beefy pecks and toned biceps. He pulled off his pants and slowly lowered his underwear. When they hit the floor, he stood to give me a good look.

"This is yours," he said. "And I've been waiting so long to give it to you."

Puegot entered me, and every man I ever knew before him—any crush, any conversation, Michael Jackson and Mark Spitz included—was dead to me. I was immediately in love with that man. I wanted to give him every part of me. I wasn't the type of girl to surrender anything to anyone, not my mind and certainly not my body, but Puegot pulled that out of me. He eased my busy brain and got me to focus on him. He made love to me with passion and intention. I felt like a full woman. Deliciously feminine. He found every single one of my buttons. "Let it out. Puegot's here. I got everything you need," he whispered in my ear, but I could hardly hear him. My every sense was clouded with euphoria, and I didn't realize I was moaning his name.

Just before dawn, I was awakened by Puegot moving around in the dark. He was looking for his clothes. I could hear the needle skipping at the end of the record in the living room.

"You leaving? I was going to make breakfast," I said, wrapping a sheet around myself.

"I have to get to the group home," he said. "Duty calls."

"They're fortunate to have a man like you," I said. "You're such a charmer."

Hearing this, he stopped and looked at me. He said, "Oh, so you're the one who's been sending those letters to me."

"You got it. I'm your woman."

With his clothes on, he hopped into bed and started kissing me again. "You're damn right you are," he said. "All mine."

When I walked Puegot to the door, I asked when I'd hear from him. He started kissing my neck and stuck his tongue into my ear, trying to turn me on again.

"I'm serious." I stopped him.

"You'll hear from me," he said. "Don't worry. I ain't going nowhere."

I perked up. Everything in my new adult life was coming together.

I was whipped. Puegot was constantly on my mind. I wanted him to be my everything, my future husband. After a few days of not hearing from him, I was anxious. I decided to pop up at the Fox Trap to show him what he was missing. Wearing a short lavender dress that cinched my waist and my sexiest pair of black heels, I walked around the club a few times looking for Puegot, but he was nowhere to be found. I was about to leave when I ran into Walter, one of the members of the Brothers.

"Hey, mama, you looking for Puegot?" Walter asked, eyeing my dress.

"Maybe," I said.

"He ain't here, but I'll make sure he knows I saw you. He's a fool to miss seeing you in that dress. No disrespect but you the full package."

I walked out and drove home. By the time I got in the door, my phone was ringing. It was Puegot inviting me to Harambee. He told me to wear the lavender dress with my pumps and no panties.

Sure enough, ten seconds later, I was back in my Pontiac, heading across town.

Harambee was a two-story house that was turned into a group home. When I got there, it was well past midnight; all the lights were out, and the place was quiet. Puegot told me not to ring the doorbell; he would leave the front door open for me. I should enter quietly, take a right, and go into the office. That's what I did. I waited for about fifteen minutes and then he walked in and locked the door behind him.

"So you checking up on a brother now?" he asked.

"I didn't have a choice. I wanted to see you."

"That's fine. I apologize for not calling. A lot has been going on around here, my girl," he said, holding out his hands to indicate that he'd been busy working at Harambee.

"I'm the man in charge, so I have to focus," he added. "But right now, I'm focusing on you. Walter called and told me you had all them fools at the Fox Trap salivating over you."

"At least someone is."

Puegot laughed and told me to stand and spin around. "My boy wasn't lying. You looking correct."

He got up close to me and started examining my body. I could feel his heavy breathing on my neck.

"You trying to drive me crazy?" he whispered softly in my ear. He pulled me to the desk, turned me around, and lifted my dress. "Oh shit." He sighed before entering and stroking me. I started hollering his name and didn't care who heard me.

After, he lowered my dress and kissed me gently.

"You're so special," he said. "I wish I could do this all night, but I have to get back to work."

"Work? But all of the boys are asleep," I said, feeling disappointed. I didn't want to leave, not after what we just shared.

"They *are* asleep, but they could wake up, and if they come to my office, I can't have a beautiful woman in here, now can I?" he explained, and though I didn't want to part ways, I knew he was right.

I agreed to go, but that one night turned into months of Puegot and I having sex in his office at Harambee.

Most nights, at least four times a week, he'd come to my apartment. Sometimes, he'd bring food—BBQ, pizza, or fried chicken—and we'd play our favorite records by Teddy Pendergrass, the Dramatics, Marvin Gaye, the Whispers, and the O'Jays. We'd talk about everything on the news, laugh, dance, joke around, and massage each other with cocoa butter and then he'd fuck me passionately on my desk or against a wall or on my kitchen counter.

On Sundays, Puegot worked the three-to-eleven evening shift at the group home. Sometimes, I would stop by before the boys went to bed. There were eight to ten boys housed there at a time. They all seemed comfortable at Harambee.

As Puegot and I chatted in his office, the boys would come by with problems: "Hey, Mr. P., Curtis and James are fighting."

Puegot would summon Curtis and James and say, "Sit down. Let's work this out like men."

Listening from the sideline, his solutions dazzled me. Puegot was wise and good at his job. These were tough kids whom the state had mandated to a group home instead of prison. That he'd earned their trust and respect sent my pride and affection skyrocketing.

After witnessing one of Puegot's mediations with the boys, I waited in his office until lights out and locked the door behind him when he returned.

"What's going on in here?" he asked.

I didn't say a word. I pushed him onto the desk and fucked him hard with my clothes on.

"You're getting good at this, Tanya." He moaned as I rocked in his lap.

I was getting good, and I was enjoying every moment of it, but the late-night romps were starting to get to me. No matter where we were or what we were doing, just before dawn Puegot would always change his demeanor and say, "OK, time to go. I have business to take care of." I'd complain but then he'd start talking about his plans, his ideas for his future, and how much money he needed to make his dreams a reality. Puegot wanted to be a real estate mogul. He planned to purchase luxury properties and rent them out to make a profit. To do that, he needed capital; to get capital, he needed to work. He'd say, "I'm trying to make big moves, and I need your support, not your criticism."

I tried hard to be understanding and supportive, but I started feeling crazy. Was this love? Were we a couple if we didn't ever spend daylight hours together? Go to the movies?

Breakfast? If I were special, why couldn't we be like my parents? Get married, buy a house, and raise children?

One night after having sex, Puegot got up to leave, and we got into a heated conversation.

"You know I need money. Why do you keep trying to hold me back?" he said.

"I'm not trying to hold you back," I replied. "Actually, I was thinking maybe I could help."

"Help me do what?" Puegot asked.

"Get money. I know where there's lots of money, and I can get it."

Puegot sighed like I was wasting his time. Though I'd shut down the computer in my parents' attic, I was getting better at doing telephone transactions and growing more confident. While posing as an employee to pay someone's car note using Western Union, I discovered that, just like banks, Western Union wired money. To call in a wire, all you needed was the code of the day, the Western Union location where the money was to be dispersed, and personal information about the customer doing the pickup—name, address, and telephone number.

After some digging, an employee gave me the in-house number to call to have funds released through any Western Union counter in the country.

"What kind of ID do they need to have to pick up the cash? I'm so sorry. I forgot," I said.

She said, "Government issued ID, or if they don't have ID, a test question. All they have to do is show ID or answer the question correctly."

"You can get money?" Puegot pushed during our exchange. "You're nineteen, and you don't have a job. How can you get money?"

"Don't worry about it," I said. I wasn't ready to tell Puegot about the information I had, especially since I wasn't sure if it would work. But if trying meant I'd get closer him, I was willing to give it a shot. "Just know that I can get lots of money for us."

"OK. OK." Puegot nodded. "If you say you can get any amount of money, why don't you prove it to me."

"How?"

"I've always wanted a Corum watch. Could you get me one?" he asked. I could hear the doubt in his voice. I was annoyed. I don't like to be underestimated.

"Give me a few days," I said. "You'll have your watch."

Getting the code of the day for the Western Union transaction was effortless. The hard part was finding a reliable person to get the cash. Taryn volunteered, but I knew she just wanted to get money to buy drugs. I asked Randall if he could do it. While he was also game, Randall could be tricky. He moved by his own clock and danced to his own drum. As I wouldn't be with him when he picked up the money, I feared he'd take it all and run off to Cabo with some guy he'd met at the club for a few weeks.

"Call me as soon as you get the cash," I told him before he left my apartment to go to Western Union. I'd already called in the transaction for $3,000 to be picked up by Alexander

NEVER SAW ME COMING

Johnson with no ID. All he had to do was answer the question I provided.

"Calm down, Ms. Lady. I got this," Randall said. "You just make sure you give me my cut, and we are good."

When Randall walked out, I played everything that could go wrong in my mind. The Western Union agent I'd spoken to might have suspected something was wrong, and the police could be waiting at the store to arrest Randall. In another scenario, he could say the wrong name and seem nervous, and the desk agent might suspect something was wrong and call the police. They'd arrest Randall and force him to give up my name and then they'd kick in my front door and take me to prison for the rest of my life.

After an hour of running through these alternative realities, I suspected Randall had gotten the money and was on his way to Cabo. I was angry with myself for trusting him. How could I be so dumb? I swore I'd never speak to Randall again for the rest of my life.

Knock! Knock! Knock!

There was loud pounding on my apartment door. I just knew it was the police coming to put cuffs on me. When I opened the door, Randall was standing there, smiling from ear to ear.

"Open up, fish. It's the po-lice," he said, laughing when he saw my face.

I pulled him inside.

"Did you do it? Did you get the money?"

"Of course I did," he said. He pulled out the thick wad of bills and handed it to me. "So what Western Union are we hitting next?"

Randall and I started squealing and doing a happy dance in my living room.

That day, we did three Western Union transactions. I limited the releases to $3,000, so we made $9,000. I kept $6,500 to get Puegot's watch and gave the rest to Randall.

After counting his take, Randall started walking to the door to leave.

"What are you going to do with your money?" I asked.

"I'm grown. Mind your business," he said and walked out.

When I showed up at Harambee with the Corum watch, Puegot was shocked.

"Ain't no way," he said, examining the watch to be sure it wasn't a fake. It was made of eighteen-carat gold and had a black strap. "I can't believe it. This is real. A real Corum watch." His eyes widened with the wonder of a kid who had unboxed the best birthday gift ever. I could practically see the diamonds on the watch dancing in his pupils. Seeing the man I loved happy filled my heart with joy.

"Put it on, " I said. "I want to see it on your wrist."

Puegot slid the watch on and started modeling it like he was on the pages of GQ.

"That's it!" I cheered for my man. "That watch was made for you."

That night, we made passionate love. The best ever. And Puegot kept the watch on.

When we were finished, Puegot asked how I got the money to buy it. I told him about the Western Union operation, and he started talking about our future and what he could do if I got more money and gave it to him.

"I'd put it all in real estate. I can put things together for our future and help you with your plan to help others," he offered. "That would be great for us. We'd be a good team."

Hearing Puegot use words like *we*, *us*, and *our*, I started feeling a sense of security that made everything he said sound possible.

From that moment on, I gave every cent from my Western Union transactions with Randall to Puegot to invest in the future he was building for us. Puegot eventually moved into a place near Phelps Park. Sometimes, when he had friends over, he would invite me just to show me off. They'd look at me like little boys admiring a pinup model. One of Puegot's friends shared that Puegot used to tell them I had the best body he'd ever seen and my sex was the best he ever had. The lip slip annoyed and embarrassed me, but I loved that Puegot liked showing me off. In front of everyone, he'd shower me with compliments. I felt like the only girl in the world: "I love your wrists"; "I love your skin"; "I love your ears." When the crew left, he'd sing Teddy Pendergrass's "Close the Door" to me before we made love.

As time went on, my faith in Puegot's plans for our future grew stronger. While he was still working at the group home, which I applauded, he sought investment properties and shopped for a dream house "for us." He took me to see some places, empty lots, and amazing properties but kept dithering, saying, "Oh, that one won't work," or, "We need more space."

I'd agree and work with Randall to get more money for Puegot to purchase whatever property he wanted. After a few months of hitting Western Unions, I decided their $5,000 cash limit was too low. I needed more cash to truly invest in our dream. While the computer was still unplugged in my parents' attic, I knew powering it up and taking another swing at the banks was my next step.

7

GETTING FOCUSED

I wish I could say I was shocked when my dismal first-semester grades came in from U of M. But I was so busy doing transactions, pulling in Western Union funds with Randall and Terrell, and spending time with Puegot that I had little time left for my studies. As I sat in class or took exams, all I could think about was how I would unveil my master plan with Puegot and raise the money to make it all happen. After his initial speculations, he'd produced a solid list of potential investment properties, and the goal was to purchase a few units and rent them out. We could even use some to shelter the unhoused and create more group homes like Harambee, which Puegot would operate. Once all the properties were purchased, I could stop doing transactions and focus on my career.

I considered two when I had enrolled at the University of Minnesota. I would either be a broadcast journalist or a lawyer. Mom often said I'd be "good on TV" and compared me to Ethel Payne, the first Black woman commentator on CBS News. "You're just as sharp and intelligent as her," she said. Dad highlighted my intelligence and desire to help others. "Law is a solid field. You would be a wonderful defense attorney," he said. I agreed with both options, but after sitting in a few classes, I was bored. After my first year, I decided to transfer to the University of Southern California. It had the best journalism program in the country and a top law school. I liked challenges, and since USC was known for its rigorous studies and high-achieving students, I decided I had to be there. Though I felt some apprehension about leaving my hometown, family, and Puegot to move to Los Angeles, securing my future was top of mind. And I loved the idea of Puegot coming to visit me at USC. We'd spend our days on the beach and party all night in Hollywood. And if my career kicked off in LA and we loved it there, we could move our operation.

Knowing my grades from U of M would look horrible on my transfer application to USC, I decided to focus on my ACT score, hoping it would show the admissions committee I was capable of more. I got the ACT study guide at the library to prepare for the exam and worked through the modules daily at my apartment.

Taking the English, reading, and science sections was a breeze, but I was guessing through most of the math portion.

Feeling unsure about my test results, I sought refuge at my parents' house, where I still spent a lot of time visiting them.

While out for a walk, I heard someone yell, "Hey, twin—Taryn, Tanya—whichever one you are. Come over here."

I turned to see Prince chatting up his forever crush, Renee Fuller, a dark-brown beauty who was the prettiest girl on the Northside, on her front stoop.

When I reached them, Prince, now twenty-one, pointed to beautiful Renee, sitting on the steps like Queen Nzingha on a throne, and said, "Tell her that I'm going to be a big star." Standing before Renee with one foot on the step where she sat, Prince was spitting his strongest game to convince her to get with him.

Not wanting to get involved, I hesitated.

He prodded. "Tell her Warner Brothers is coming to the Capri to see me play."

It was true. By 1979, he'd made quite a name for himself on the underground music scene and was getting attention from record labels. Warner Brothers wanted Prince to do his first concert at Madison Square Garden, but he declined. He was adamant that his first show would be at the Capri Theater in his hometown.

"They signed me right, Taryn? Tanya? Tell her!"

Renee asked me directly. "All this about Warner Brothers—is he for real?"

"Yes, they're coming," I told her.

"Oh, no way!" She perked up and batted her eyes at Prince. He was in.

I worked at the concession stand with my mom on January 5, 1979, the night Prince gave his first-ever benefit concert as a solo artist at the Capri. He performed for two nights with his band, which included André Cymone. That night, they played future platinum-selling hits like "I Wanna Be Your Lover" and "Why You Wanna Treat Me So Bad?" Those Warner Brothers reps were there and over the moon.

*   *   *

Certain my rejection letter from USC was in the mail, when the spring semester started at U of M, I decided to focus on my studies, hoping to pull my grades up and reapply to USC the following school year. While attending class, I met Jesse Marks, a tremendous all-around athlete. Jesse needed help with his homework. Happy to make a new friend, I agreed to help him, and we became very close. Through him, I got to know the other campus sports stars, including Marion Barber Jr., Brooks Winters, and basketball wizard Kevin McHale.

They considered me "one of the guys," and I quickly became a part of the pack. I got a reputation for being daring enough to accomplish anything. When our basketball team, the Minnesota Gophers, was set to play the Michigan State Spartans, which included media darling Magic Johnson, someone said, "Bet you can't meet Magic Johnson."

I laughed at the challenge. "Sure I can meet Magic. No problem. I can get to anyone."

Posing as a reporter from the *Minneapolis Star Tribune*, I called the Michigan State press office for information. Through them, I learned that Magic was staying at the Marriott in suburban Bloomington. I called the hotel and asked them to connect me to Earvin Johnson's room. When I got Magic on the phone, I requested an interview. We agreed to meet in the hotel lobby at 6:00 p.m. I said I'd call his room from one of the phones in the lobby when I got there.

Everything went as planned. At 6:00 p.m. sharp, Magic floated toward me in the hotel lobby. He was so tall he looked like two people standing on top of each other. He was also devilishly handsome and had an enticing smile.

"Hello, Earvin. I'm Tanya from the *Minneapolis Star Tribune*," I said, holding my hand to shake his.

"No, a hug!" he said, opening his arms.

"That's fine."

He pulled me into a long embrace that made me feel like we'd known each other forever.

"Would you like to do the interview here or grab a bite?" I asked.

"Food sounds good. How about ribs?"

I took him to Rudolph's, the best barbecue joint in Minneapolis. When we entered the restaurant, everyone was looking at Magic and trying to talk to him. I suggested we take the food to my apartment. He agreed, and we got the ribs to-go.

We chatted like old friends as we ate the smoked meat in my living room. Magic had such a warm personality, and he was funny.

After a while, he said, "So, do you have some questions?"

Suddenly, I remembered why we were together. I was supposed to be a reporter. Trying to sound like a seasoned professional, I said, "Let's just talk. That's how I get to know most of my subjects."

"Sounds good to me."

I grabbed my camera to document the visit with some shots of Magic sitting on my couch.

"You're not a reporter, are you?" he said, watching me fumble with the camera.

"No," I confessed.

"How come you went through all this trouble? You could've just asked me to hang out. I don't bite. And you're cool."

"It was a dare," I told him. "You have some big fans in Minneapolis. They bet I couldn't meet you, so I had to do it."

He wasn't mad. He just laughed and shook his head.

Back at the Marriott, Magic left me with another big hug and a story that helped my do-the-impossible image. When I told Jesse and the other athletes about my afternoon with Magic Johnson and handed over the picture taken at my place as proof, they were impressed and cheered for me like I'd scored a touchdown. Hearing them chant my name, I realized they thought this was my peak, the wildest thing I could imagine and accomplish.

Feeling I was ready to move on to the banks, one afternoon when my parents were at work, Randall and Terrell helped me move the computer from the attic to my apartment. Having taken copious notes when setting it up the first time, it was easy to get it running.

I logged in and started doing my usual bank research, looking into account data and transactions. That's when I realized I could see how transfer funds moved between accounts in real time using the terminal. I had access to notes and alerts added to accounts by bank employees and could alter them remotely. While I was still nervous about using the computer to transfer funds, I was confident I could successfully manage the bank's Paid Upon Proper ID cash transfers because I'd been practicing by doing the Western Union transactions with Randall and Terrell. Armed with the day's code, I could call in a transfer and then use the computer to watch the money move through the system.

"It's foolproof. I'll be able to see everything going on from right here. There won't be any surprises," I told Taryn when I summoned her to my apartment to tell her about my plan. I needed to let her in on the operation because I planned to transfer a large sum, and I knew she could handle it. While I was sure she'd probably blow her cut on drugs, she was the only person I knew I could trust with that level of transaction. I promised myself I'd only use her one time. Too much money in a drug addict's hands was dangerous, and I didn't want her too involved. As long as I was making money, or even if I wasn't, I would always take care of her.

"You'll transfer the money into the dummy account in my name and then I'll go into the bank and pick it up?" she asked. "What if they catch me? I don't want to get arrested." Taryn was brave, wild even, but not crazy.

"I told you—it's foolproof. If there's an issue, I'll see it on my computer. I'll pull you out. I promise you won't get caught," I confirmed. "And we will split the money."

Considering this, Taryn said, "I could do a lot with that money. I'll do it."

With Taryn signed on, I got the routing number for a bank in St. Paul from my reference book. I then called the bank and cycled through departments to cover my tracks until I reached someone who gave me the code for the day. Armed with that information and the routing number, I made more calls to set up a wire transfer of $5,000 to be paid to Ms. Taryn Smith.

When I hung up, Taryn and I stared at each other in terror and excitement about what was next.

"You can't act nervous," I advised her. "Just go into the bank, smile, and be polite. People like that. And don't forget to call me from a nearby pay phone before you go in and then—"

"After I get the money, call to let you know I'm headed back here. I got it, sis. Don't worry about me. You just do your part from here and make sure I'm safe."

Before Taryn walked out, I gave her a big hug. The moment felt like a turning point for me, like something big was about to happen. I didn't know what, but I was grateful Taryn, my first best friend, was by my side.

When Taryn left, my mind conjured dozens of dark scenarios just like when Randall did his first Western Union pickup: burly cops accosting Taryn at the bank; Taryn at the police station, either crying or blurting my name; my dad getting called; or worse, Taryn leaving the bank with the money but getting her bag snatched. If any of those things occurred, it would all be my fault. How would I explain that to our parents?

Sitting alone in my apartment, I tried to ignore these thoughts, but I grew more nervous as time ticked by. The bank in St. Paul was about twenty-five minutes away. Taryn was supposed to call as soon as she got there. A little more than an hour passed.

I went to the computer to see if there were any flags on Taryn's dummy account or updates indicating a problem with

NEVER SAW ME COMING

the transfer. If I saw something when she called, I'd tell her not to go into the bank at all. Luckily, there was nothing noted. I just needed her to call.

Finally, after ninety minutes, the phone rang. The receiver was already in my hand.

"You there?" I asked.

"Yes. I'm about to walk in. Did you check the account?" Taryn sounded a little nervous.

"I did. Everything is fine. You are good to go," I said. "Remember to just go in and act natural. There's nothing to this."

"I'm OK," she assured me. "I'm feeling calm. It's going to work."

After we got off the line, I went to my computer. I could see when the banking agent viewed Taryn's transfer and when the funds were dispersed. I sighed in relief. It worked. It was done. Now I just had to wait for Taryn to call when she left the bank to let me know she was done and on her way back.

Once again, time crept by, and there was no word. Ten minutes, twenty minutes, thirty minutes. Nothing.

I paced the living room. I lifted the receiver to check the dial tone. The phone was working but silent. Where was Taryn? Had something happened to my sister? It was the Aquatennial all over again.

After an hour passed, my anxiety was through the roof. Though I had to wait for the call, I couldn't stand being in the apartment. I needed air. Maybe a walk to calm my nerves.

I was about to leave, but when I opened the door, Taryn was standing there.

"What happened?" I said, pulling her into the apartment.

"What do you think happened, square?" Taryn laughed. "I got it."

"You did? Jesus, I was so terrified. I thought something happened to you. Why didn't you call?"

"I was too scared to stop at the pay phone again. I felt like everyone was watching me," Taryn said, taking off her jacket. "I just wanted to get back here and hightailed it out of there. I even took a different route home in case someone followed me."

"Clever. Very clever."

Taryn pulled a thick envelope from her purse and placed it on my desk.

"I didn't open it. I wanted to wait for you," Taryn said, standing beside me as we hovered over the envelope.

I tore it open and pulled out the cash, a stack of fresh one-hundred-dollar bills.

"Holy shit!" I said. "We did it! We broke the fucking bank!"

"Wide fucking open," Taryn said, grabbing the stack and taking a long whiff. "Now that smells like five thousand dollars."

"My turn." I took it back and fingered through the bills, spreading them in my hand and fanning myself. "Looks like it too."

"My turn." Taryn snatched the cash and held the notes tight together while flipping through them. I watched, amazed, as Benjamin Franklin seemed to wink at me.

"My turn." I got the cash and cradled it like a newborn baby.

Taryn laughed, started pulling bills from my baby stack, and threw them in the air.

At first, I thought she'd gone too far but then I joined in, throwing the bills to the ceiling and watching them rain down over us. Soon we were giggling in a shower of cold, hard cash. My carpet looked like the floor of a strip club at the end of the night. Money was everywhere.

When we finished our fun, Taryn and I restacked the money. I gave her half and saved my cut for Puegot.

"What are you going to do with your money? Go shopping or something?" Taryn asked.

"No. Puegot's putting everything away for our project."

"Suit yourself." Taryn frowned. "I'll have a good time for you." She jumped on the phone to call her boyfriend, who lived twenty minutes away.

A half-hour later, he pulled up outside. From my window, I watched them pull off. I knew he either stopped to get Taryn's drugs on the way to my apartment or they were going somewhere to get the drugs then.

After that first bank transaction with Taryn, I felt like the woman let out of the bottle in *I Dream of Jeannie.* I'd discovered a potential source of unlimited funds, which made me feel powerful. It was like everything in my life that came before suddenly made sense. All my passions and obsessions had led me to this moment, and the payoff was about to be significant. Like Prince playing music or Magic playing basketball, this was my destiny, my purpose.

Over the next few months, I worked on perfecting my craft. My apartment was like my office. I would wake up in the morning, read the newspaper, and sit in front of the computer with my telephone and reference books to map out the day's efforts. In addition to Taryn, I recruited Randall and Terrell for bank pickups. Soon we were doing many transactions, and they found more people to help.

As my staff grew, my to-do list became quite extensive. I found a guy who made fake IDs that were good enough for Paid Upon Proper ID pickups. For those IDs, I would make up unique names that wouldn't match anyone in the system and provide fake addresses. I also found fresh banks to hit in increasingly farther-flung cities and scheduled and booked flights for the runners I sent there. Whenever anyone went in for a pickup, I'd make sure they were prepared. Depending on where and what was being picked up, the runner's scenario would be different. It was as if I were a director telling the actors what role to play. Each person had a different personality, and the roles were different. When they were dispatched, I'd watch everything go down on my computer. Sometimes there were flags. The banks would request more identification or be suspicious of the new account. I'd try to erase the notes or respond, but I'd call the transfer off altogether if that didn't work.

Doing this daily, I'd pull in $20,000 to $40,000, roughly $85,000 to $170,000 today. Sometimes, I would get busy and Randall and Terrell would encourage me to take a break. They would beg me to take the day off and come out to the spa with them for relaxation. They offered to book private jets to Paris or Milan for shopping sprees and fine dining. I turned them down and took my cut to Puegot.

"You came correct this time," he said when I handed over the day's take. "You're my miracle girl. You can make anything happen."

"When will we buy that apartment complex you showed me?" I asked. "We should have enough money to pay with cash by now, right?"

"The deal fell through. That white guy wasn't serious about selling it," Puegot complained. When he saw I felt let down, he said, "Don't worry. I'm doing everything in my power to set us up right. I'm your man. You trust me, right?"

"I do. I'm just anxious. I want everything to be perfect."

"It will be. You will see."

Puegot pulled me to him and started kissing my neck and then my ears. Soon, I found myself in his bed. I forgot everything I brought up and remembered why Puegot was the love of my life.

In the spring of 1979, my mother called to say a letter had come in the mail from USC. I asked if it was thin, and she said, "Yes, it is." I was heartbroken that I'd received a thin rejection letter, not a thick admissions packet. When I went to retrieve the mail, I was shocked to learn I'd been accepted. They shared that they were excited to admit a candidate who nearly earned a perfect score on the ACT. The top score was thirty-two; I scored thirty.

"I got in," I said to my mother, who was sitting nearby reading *Essence* magazine. It was the special Mother's Day edition with Iman and her beautiful baby girl on the cover.

"USC? You got into USC!" Mom cheered. She put the magazine down and came over to hug me. "I knew you'd get in. When you put your mind to something, there's no way of stopping you, Tanya Marie."

Hearing my mother's kind words, I grew sad. I was going to miss her if I moved to Los Angeles.

"I'll be right here waiting for you to get back. This is your home. You can go anywhere you want, but we will always be here. Remember that," Mom said, her motherly intuition tapping into my emotions.

While Mom and Dad were excited about me moving to Los Angeles, Randall and Terrell weren't. They were worried about money. With me gone, no one would be there to set up transactions. I couldn't trust them to take over. They were recruiting runners I didn't know. They'd take too long to phone in, complain about basic procedures, and try doing things their way. On more than one occasion, one of their runners just disappeared with the money. It was too much. I was happy to step away from the action for a little while, before the house of cards they were building came tumbling down. Though Randall and Terrell protested, I shut down my operation. I packed the computer and buried it beneath a stack of boxes in my parents' attic.

Puegot also wasn't thrilled about my departure. Like Randall and Terrell, he was worried about money. When I told him about the move, we started having disagreements about how I expected him to keep investing if I wasn't giving him money from the transactions. I wasn't concerned. We'd saved a lot. If we were to put the cash into a high-yield savings account, it could earn us enough returns to purchase half of Minnesota in ten years.

"Just promise me you'll save all the money we've stashed away," I begged him on our last night together before I was to leave for Los Angeles.

"OK. I got it," he said. "You keep repeating it."

"I keep repeating it because it's important to me."

"Well, *you're* important to me. I'm going to miss you," he admitted before kissing me like we'd be apart for ten years. "Come back soon. I'll be waiting."

8

FLYING COLORS

W e're going to miss you," Dad said as he and Mom unloaded my bags at the airport. "If you need anything, and I mean anything, call us."

"Promise you'll come home to visit real soon," Mom pleaded with tears in her eyes.

"I promise. I'm coming back." I committed to them. "And don't worry about me, Dad. I'm capable of taking care of myself. You taught me how."

"I know. I know. Just stay focused and remember who you are." Dad kissed me on the forehead, and we gathered for a group hug.

Moments later, I was sitting on the airplane, heading to take on my new life.

I planned to do the full college experience at USC, starting by living in the dorm. When I got there, I was stunned by the cramped room. It was just wide enough for two single beds and a narrow aisle in between. But my shock was nothing compared to my white roommate's alarm when she realized I was her bunkmate. Hyperventilating, eyes narrowed with panic, she could barely croak out a hello. Clearly, she never expected to share that tiny space with a Black person.

Seeing her reaction and the tiny space, I told her, "You can relax. I'm not staying. The room is all yours." I walked out without bothering to unpack a thing.

From the pay phone down the hall, I called Mark, a Minneapolis friend I'd met through Randall and Terrell who had settled in North Hollywood. "Come on over," he said. "We have room."

I grabbed my luggage and took a cab to Mark's apartment, a decent-sized flat with two bedrooms and a large living room, where I slept on the couch. He and his roommate, Shelly, a petite Jewish lady with black semicurly hair, were welcoming. We instantly hit it off.

"I can't wait to see you on the news," Shelly said when I told her what I planned to study at USC. "You know this is the city of dreams. You can be anything you want if you work hard at it."

One of Shelly's friends, Chang, owned a car dealership and gave me a car to drive to school every day. It was a midsize blue sedan, nothing fancy, but I was grateful for it.

I carpooled to school from North Hollywood with a new friend, Nora, who worked in USC's admissions office. Through her, I got a job in admissions as a receptionist. I loved handling student questions, but the occasional cranky parent could be a trip.

I remember one in particular—Sally Struthers, a costar on the popular 1970s sitcom *All in the Family*.

"Something must've gone wrong. You need to fix it." She shouted in my face when she came to the office to complain about a family member being rejected. She was beautiful on television but absolutely exquisite in real life. I don't think I'd ever seen hair that blonde. I wanted to help her, but deciding who was accepted and rejected was far beyond my pay grade.

While working in admissions proved entertaining, I most enjoyed doing outreach as a peer counselor in South Central. Two or three days a week, I'd visit high schools in South LA to talk to students about the importance of going to college and what USC had to offer.

Of course, part of the appeal of Los Angeles was the glamour. Everywhere I went, there were stars. Through Nora, I met Harold Sylvester, whom I recognized from movies like *Sounder: Part 2* and TV shows like *Barnaby Jones*. Shelly was friendly with the singer Al Jarreau, who often showed up at our apartment. Sometimes we'd gather in the living room, lounging with drinks and takeout. After a few sips, someone would ask Al to sing, and he'd break out in song. His smooth, melodic voice would bounce around the apartment like an exclusive concert hall.

My real introduction to LA's celebrity scene came through Shelly's friend Alejandro. I had always been an R&B fan, but Alejandro loved jazz. He introduced me to fusion, funk, and soul jazz. It quickly became my favorite music. Alejandro took me to clubs like the Baked Potato in Studio City and the Flying

Jib in Encino, where famous musicians headlined and dropped by to jam. You never knew who might sit in—from Stanley Clarke to the guys from Spyro Gyra. I met Herbie Hancock, Earl Klugh, Roy Ayers, George Duke, Carlos Santana, Donald Byrd, Chick Corea, Ramsey Lewis, and Grover Washington Jr.

Alejandro was best friends with Phil Upchurch Jr., son of the lauded guitarist who'd played with everyone from Howlin' Wolf and Muddy Waters to Bob Dylan and Michael Jackson. At the time, he performed and recorded with jazz and pop artist George Benson, who'd won a Grammy for best record in 1976. One of the hottest artists in the country, Benson also recorded the original version of "The Greatest Love of All" for Muhammad Ali's 1977 biopic. I loved hearing him sing. Whether he was crooning a romantic ballad or grooving to a jazz tune, Benson's velvety voice had a timeless quality that was instantly recognizable.

Alejandro, Phil Jr., and I hung out all over Southern California. Eventually, there were eight of us in our group. All jazz enthusiasts, we'd jam, club hop, and dance until the wee hours of the morning before getting breakfast. We were so cool.

Now and then, George would be at some of the sound checks, concerts, or jam sessions. He enjoyed my company and liked that I always had an opinion about whatever the guys were debating. "Tanya, you come sit near me," George would say whenever he came around.

Ola Ray, who appeared in George's "Give Me the Night" video, often accompanied him. Ola was a striking brown beauty with a petite, shapely frame that kept men's eyes on her whenever she was around. When George introduced us, Phil Jr. pointed out that she had been *Playboy*'s "Playmate of the Month" for June. "You two should hang out. Ola's a sweet girl, Tanya," George said.

Wanting to make new girlfriends in Los Angeles, I took his advice and connected with her. She lived in an apartment in Beverly Hills and said she wanted to be an actress. She was dating a few guys who were making promises to her. I told her being arm candy for any guy wasn't enough. "Your brains will always get you further than your looks," I said. While it was clear we weren't going to be close, I gave her my parents' number in case she ever wanted to connect again.

A few years later, looking for me, she called my parents in Minneapolis.

"Tell Tanya I'm going to be in Michael Jackson's new music video. It's for a song called 'Thriller,'" she told my mom. I'm still unsure of why she called—whether to acknowledge my advice or rub her success in my face.

Sketchy men like the ones who were making Ola all those promises were all over Hollywood. I came across one while trying to find work in entertainment. One of George's managers, Dennis Turner of Ken Fritz Management, said he had a job for me and invited me to discuss it over dinner. While I didn't know what the job was, I wanted to look good for my interview and wore a cute, strappy, evening dress that was not too revealing for someone dining with her future boss.

When Dennis and I entered the restaurant in Beverly Hills, we spotted Lionel Richie. Riding high on his megahit "Three

Times a Lady," Lionel was handsome with his bouncy Afro, chiseled features, and calming voice—the man sounded like he was singing when he was talking. I could feel everyone trying to be in his orbit, but Lionel was down home and sweet. Dennis kept trying to make it seem like they were best friends, chatting Lionel up. I could tell he wanted to impress me. He invited Lionel and his guest to join us for dinner, but Lionel declined.

After dinner, Dennis and I hopped into his car to head back to Hollywood. I asked when he wanted to discuss the job, but he kept changing the subject. Halfway home, he pulled over, claiming he wanted to show me an extraordinary view of the skyline, but instead, he started groping me and shoving his tongue down my throat.

"What are you doing?" I asked, pushing him away.

"Come on, baby. We had a good time. Work with me," he said.

"I'm not sleeping with you, Dennis!" I shouted. "I thought you had a job for me. Just take me back to my car."

Luckily, Dennis got it together and did as I requested.

A few weeks later, Alejandro, Phil Jr., and I went to a practice session with Phil Sr., Ronnie Foster, Greg Phillinganes, and David Boruff, a great saxophone player from the Flying Jib whom we'd hooked up with George Benson. Away from the jazz lounges and adoring fans in the practice space, I got a real taste of their unfiltered talent. These musicians were genius craftsmen who elevated each other. Listening to them, I could hear things in the music I hadn't detected before. I could feel the mood swings, the highs and lows. It was like a trip but without the drugs.

Inspired, I'd told everyone about my desire to work in entertainment. Soon, I got an invitation from George Benson to join
him on tour. Of course, I said yes. I was onboard for his giant
arena shows in Dallas, Houston, and Minneapolis; his amphi-
theater gig in Fresno; and his LA appearance at the historic
Greek Theater. My primary duty was assisting the prominent
Jehovah's Witnesses who came backstage after each show. The
Witnesses were old and young and Black and white, and they
all loved George.

George would always share how happy he was to have me
on the team. I knew how much he cherished the Witness's support and appreciated my life-of-the-party qualities.

Through Alejandro, I also met and grew close to Natalie
Trundy, a dainty, fortyish actress who was the widow of
Arthur Jacobs, the famous producer of films like *Dr. Doolittle*
and the *Planet of the Apes* franchise, which Natalie starred in.
Natalie lived in Beverly Hills on Beverly Drive in a sprawling
Spanish-style home with a beautiful pool and one large stone
sculpture of apes commemorating the movies.

She had a nanny/housekeeper, but when I was around, I ran
all of her errands and spent a lot of time with the kids. I drove
her custom Gucci Seville more than she did. The interior and
top were monogrammed with the inverted "GG" on beige with
the red-and-green woven signature stripe.

Natalie's kids adored me. I used to take them to the park
and play with them all the time. Natalie loved to entertain, and
I was honored to be her guest, seated at dinner next to mega-
stars like Robert Wagner, Roddy McDowall, Gregory Peck,
Gene Hackman, and Charles Bronson. At her parties, I met

some of my favorite music artists too. She knew everyone, and having come from wealth, she was great at entertaining all those elites. Sitting in intimate circles around the property, we'd chitchat about how good the steak was at Musso & Frank Grill or gossip about who hooked up with whom at Cannes.

Bonding with people I'd grown up watching on television, I used to ask myself, *How is this possible? I'm a Black college girl from Minneapolis, and Charles Bronson is calling me by name.*

"Tanya, do you like my shirt? Natalie is being cruel about it. Tell her it's cool. We need a young person's opinion," he said once.

I suggested he remove it and show off his muscles.

He laughed.

When I responded like this, just being myself, charming and fun, I knew I belonged. I was my father's daughter in that respect—never intimidated by wealth or fame, equal to and able to talk to anyone.

Hanging out with celebrities didn't make me exceptional. While it was glamorous, it was passive. I was basking in reflected glory. What I was craving was action, the stimulation of being the center of my own operation. It was the sense of mastery, of achieving something that no one else was even thinking about. I enjoyed my classes at USC, but nothing I learned or accomplished was unique. Even the peer counseling I loved didn't involve a rare, inimitable skill. The excitement was problem-solving and planning, assembling the crew, orchestrating the strike, and then waiting with bated breath for the payoff. Sitting behind my computer, I was like the captain of a spaceship, leading a mission into the unknown. Being in

LA, lovely as it was, I felt like I was off mission, and like any true astronaut, I longed to get back to space.

I'd always planned to spend my summer break in Minneapolis. Freeing the computer from its prison of boxes in the attic became an even more powerful incentive to return.

My parents were overjoyed to see me. They practically pulled me into the house when I got home. Mom made my favorite dinner, baked chicken and green beans with potatoes, to welcome me back.

"I cleaned out your old room and put new sheets on the bed," she said as we ate at the dining room table. Taryn and Mason were still living at home, and Ryan was still in the hospital. My parents worked hard to get him help and never missed a weekend visiting him.

"I'm getting my own place," I said.

"Why? You could just stay here with us." Mom recoiled. "Save some money."

"I have leftover college loan money. I can afford it. Plus, I need my own space," I said. It was true. To resume my transactions, I needed a command center where I didn't have to worry about Mom or Dad busting in.

I found an apartment to lease in Edina, one of the city's nicest suburbs. To make my parents proud—and to explain my projected undercover income—I got a job as a receptionist in human resources at Pillsbury. It delighted my dad that I applied and was hired without tapping his friendship with George Pillsbury. After he bragged about my initiative to George, members of the Pillsbury family would sometimes pop down from the executive suite to say hello, which both amazed and intimidated my coworkers.

"So your dad, like, knows *the* George Pillsbury?" Amanda, one of my coworkers, inquired, her mind blown after George visited my desk one afternoon.

"Yes. They've been good friends for years," I said cooly. "I've been to their house."

Amanda's mouth hung open in astonishment. She instantly compared everything about herself to me, trying to make the information make sense, and said, "Wow. I guess we know who's getting the next promotion."

My dad's pride impressed his friend Bob Naegele, who also wanted to hire me. I took an aptitude test at his office and got a perfect score. He offered me a position as a marketing trainee. I was flattered, of course, but declined. I already had a "job"— my transactions—that spun more money than any conceivable corporate gig.

Ready to get back to work on my master plan and missing my romance with Puegot, I reached out to him. When I initially returned home from Los Angeles, he was in Chicago ordering custom clothes, and we had to wait to reconnect. When he got back to Minneapolis, he wanted to see me immediately.

"Yes, yes. You are looking correct, Tanya," he said, inspecting me when I got to his place.

I smiled and posed for him in my tight jeans. I missed his compliments. We hardly spoke over the phone when I was in Los Angeles, and it was good to hear his voice and see his face.

"Get over here. I've missed you so much. You are so fine. Ain't no women in Minneapolis like you," he said, pulling me into his arms and kissing me. "Look at this body," he added, looking at my curves and claiming them as his. "You can't leave me again."

I laughed. "Stop it. I loved LA. And I made so many friends there. You into jazz?"

"No, I'm into you. And I don't want to hear about LA or jazz," he said.

He backed away from me and began sulking. I ignored it. He didn't like hearing about me enjoying my life without him. What I found strange was that he wasn't talking about our money or the real estate investments.

"We got plenty of time to talk about that stuff," he said, changing the subject when I brought it up.

That night, after a passionate lovemaking session, the phone rang, and he said he had to slip out to check on something going on at the group home. He told me not to answer the phone if it rang again.

When he was gone, I looked at the time. It was 2:00 a.m.

A few minutes later, the phone rang. Ignoring his wishes, I picked up.

"Hello?"

"Hello?" It was a woman.

"Hello?" I repeated, unsure of who it could be. What woman would be calling Puegot at this hour?

"Is Puegot there?" She sounded just as confused as me.

"No. Who is this?"

Click. The line went dead.

9

IS THIS LOVE?

Puegot wasn't happy when he got home.

"I told you not to answer the telephone," he said, pulling the phone out of the wall and stashing it. He wasn't the type to raise his voice at me, but his tone was brusque and bounced off the walls in the duplex as he left me sitting in the living room and returned without the phone. "So, you just ignore what I ask you to do now?"

Sitting on his couch with my arms crossed tight over my chest, I didn't offer an excuse. Yes, it was Puegot's home and phone, but he was my man. We were a couple. What was the big deal if I answered his telephone? My focus was on the woman.

"Who was she? And why was she calling so late?" I asked.

"I don't know who it was. It could've been a wrong number. And I shouldn't have to say anything about it. I told you not to answer the phone," he said.

Seeing that Puegot wouldn't tell me who the woman was, I left the duplex without any answers, but I knew something was wrong. In addition to his complaints about the phone, he was busier than usual and accusatory whenever I brought it up: "Here you go again complaining about something," he said when I asked why we were only spending nights together. "Why can't you just enjoy what we have the way it is?"

The next time I stayed over, the same scenario went down: we had sex, fell asleep, and a few hours later, the phone rang. Again, it was the middle of the night. Puegot got up and answered. He hung up, dressed to go out, and said he'd return soon. On his way out, he unplugged the phone and took it with him.

When he was gone, I took the spare phone I placed in my bag in case he pulled the phone from the wall again and plugged it in. It was an old, black rotary phone from my parents' attic. I sat staring at the phone for a little while, daring the woman to call.

After a few long minutes, it rang.

"Hello?"

"Hello? Who's this?" a woman with a completely different voice than the first asked.

"What do you mean, *Who is this*? You're calling my house," I replied, feeling territorial.

"Is Puegot there?" she asked, ignoring me.

"What do you want with Puegot? I'm his wife."

Click.

"Hello? Hello?" Realizing she'd hung up on me, I looked at the phone like she could see me and rolled my eyes, annoyed.

*   *   *

By the time Puegot returned a few hours later, I was hot. I laid into him. *Are you seeing someone else? How many women do you have? Are you my boyfriend? What are we exactly?*

These questions shot from my mouth like bullets. Puegot stood in the kitchen, quietly watching me. He looked like he was trying to read my emotions.

"How could you be planning our future if you have all these women around?" I asked. "I thought we were in this together."

"We are," he said. "Don't even question that. I'm working hard to set us up."

"How? You haven't even shown me any proof that you've purchased property or saved the money. Where is it?"

"Where's what?"

"The money?!" I pushed. "Where's the money I've been giving you, Puegot? It has to be about six-hundred-and-fifty-thousand dollars since I took a million. Let's just use that to buy a building right now." I attempted to sound rational, but really, I was just trying to stop my heart from breaking. I needed proof of something, anything, to confirm his fidelity.

"Now you don't trust me?" Puegot exhaled in disbelief and looked at me like I was the one letting him down. "I always knew you'd do this."

"Excuse me? I never said I don't trust you. I just want to know what's going on. It's very simple."

"I told you what's going on. I'm holding the money to invest it. When the time is right, I'll make a move," he said. "That's it. Either you believe me or you don't."

Realizing I was getting nowhere going back and forth with him, I left and went back to my place. By then, I was confident something was going on. He was being too defensive, too secretive, for that not to be the case. If Puegot was seeing other women, I'd have to figure out a way to get my money from him and then break things off. If he wasn't, everything would be fine, and I'd keep seeing him. But I needed to reassess our plan for the money.

To figure out what path I'd take, I needed information. Since Puegot was keeping me in the dark, I had to get it on my own. I knew where to start—the club.

I put on a tight-fitting mustard dress with a red sash around the waist and went to the Fox Trap. As I was looking around the club, I spotted Jeffrey, an old friend I hadn't seen in a while.

He greeted me and said, "You look beautiful as always."

We hugged and sat at the bar, chatting about our elementary years at John Hay.

"Are you the one dating Puegot or is that your sister?" he asked.

"That's me. Do you know him?"

He chuckled. "Who doesn't know Puegot? The guy with a thousand women?"

"A thousand women." I repeated, urging Jeffrey to share more.

"Come on. I know you're not that naive, Tanya. I'm surprised a woman of your class would be with someone like him. He's a pimp."

"You're kidding." The comment, worse than I suspected, stung. I started to feel sick. My head was spinning. "He has prostitutes?"

"Not exactly. But he's definitely a lady's man," Jeffery said. "I think they are all professional women. I know he was with George Foreman's wife, Adrienne, and she bought him a brown Mercedes-Benz."

The first time Puegot drove me home, it was in his Mercedes. Remembering all the intimate moments I shared with him in that car—all our talks, drives, and hours just planning our future together—I felt like I was going to vomit. I excused myself and told Jeffrey I had to go.

I couldn't breathe and needed to get some air. Hearing about Puegot's other women, I felt like I'd been sucker punched in the gut. I sat in the Pontiac weeping. Why wasn't I enough for Puegot? What was it about me, about us, that made him feel a need to go to other women? He said I was perfect. He said he would spend the rest of his life with me. I wasn't making these things up. It wasn't a figment of my imagination. He'd said those things without provocation. Why say those things and then play me?

Over the next couple of days, I reached out to more mutual acquaintances and learned that Puegot's list of women included a banker and a lawyer. "They're giving him money," one person admitted. Why would he need money from women? He had all my money.

I called him and told him I was coming over. We needed to talk.

Standing in his living room, I suddenly became aware of every upgrade. There was a new leather sofa, a table set shipped directly from Italy, and a Bang & Olufsen record player and speakers. His suit collection, all custom-made in Chicago, had tripled. He had hats of every color. He had shades, blazers, designer shoes, shirts with his initials on the collar, and a diamond in his ear.

"How many women are you seeing?" I asked flat out.

"Who told you that?"

I glared at him.

"I only have one woman and that's you, but I have female friends," Puegot said, and the smug arrogance in his voice was sickening. Did he expect me to accept that?

"Friends, huh? Well how come I haven't met them?"

"You can," he said.

"Who are they? Tell me now."

He started giving up names but added, "They are just friends. Nothing more. I love you. You are the one here with me every night. I work all day, handle my business, and then I call you to come spend the night with me. If I had other women, I wouldn't be able to spend so much time with you." He grabbed and kissed me. "I've been thinking. Maybe it's time to take this to the next level."

"What next level?" I asked.

"I want you to meet my family in Gary. You should come home with me. How do you feel about that?"

Caught in Puegot's gaze, I saw the man I'd fallen in love with on the dance floor at Tempo, the guy who'd driven me home all those times without laying a finger on me. I saw the lover who adored my body and mind and all those nights we'd spent together, all the time we'd shared. He was my great love, and I believed in him. I had to. Meeting his family was something I had always wanted. It was the confirmation of fidelity I was seeking. Hearing him propose that I meet them washed away all of my doubts about what had happened to my money and why he was with those other women.

I wiped my tears and said yes.

When we arrived in Gary, Puegot took me to an apartment. It was very well decorated with matching jacquard furniture and brand-new white appliances. He said it was his brother Bruce's apartment. Bruce was married, and I wondered why he would have a separate apartment.

"Don't worry about it. It's his hideaway. He's letting us stay here," Puegot assured me, rubbing my shoulders.

I decided to let it go. I started doing transactions again and let my mind wander. How much money would I get next?

I took a shower and started preparing to go to his mother's house.

"Don't get dressed. Just relax here. I have some errands to run. I'll be right back," he said.

"I can come along. I'll just throw something on."

"No," he pushed, firmly. "Just wait here for me."

Before I could complain, Puegot was gone.

I took a nap and woke up. He was still gone.

Hungry, I ate the last bit of a turkey sandwich I'd packed for the road trip and watched a rerun of *Charlie's Angels*.

Lying on the sofa in the living room, I took another nap and woke up hours later when the sun had gone down. Puegot was still gone. I got up and looked out the window. It was dark, and the parking lot was empty. Where was he?

I waited there alone for two days. I had no way to get in contact with Puegot or go anywhere because he had taken the car. I felt stupid.

On the third day, Bruce Puegot's brother, showed up and said Puegot told him to take me to their mother's house to meet the family. I hadn't come all the way to Gary to go home without meeting the other members of the family.

"My God. You are the cutest thing I've ever seen," Puegot's mother said when I walked into her house, a boxy ranch in a Black neighborhood. "Come over here and give me a hug. I'm Lorna. You can call me that or Mama."

Her sweet disposition calmed me, and I immediately felt comfortable. At first, I didn't think Puegot looked much like her, but when she smiled, I saw his face looking back at me.

We hugged, and she called Puegot's sister, Eunice, into the living room.

"Come meet Terry's girlfriend," his mother said, calling Puegot by his birth name like everyone else in his family. "She's a beautiful little thing, just like he said." She turned to me and said, "Get comfortable, honey. I'm going to make you some supper to welcome you to Gary."

"Thank you," I said, taking a seat at her kitchen table.

For the next few days, I hung out at Puegot's mother's house, getting to know her and Eunice. We bonded by spending hours laughing and talking about Puegot and his siblings growing up. Lorna took out his childhood pictures. There was Puegot, cute as a button at three years old with his fraternal twin brother, Harry.

When Puegot finally showed up one night after dinner, his mother lit into him right in front of me, scolding, "What do you need all those other women for when you've got Tanya? Out there chasing tail while she's waiting on you."

Eunice parroted these sentiments and added, "She a better woman than me because I would've set your car on fire."

Women? Puegot had women in Gary too? I was heartsick. Is that who he'd been seeing during our visit? I was embarrassed.

Catching it from his mother and sister and my eye lasering him, Puegot became furious; he started pacing and shouting, "Tanya, get packed. We're leaving. We're going back to Minneapolis right now."

As I walked out of the house, Puegot's mother embraced me. "I just love you, darling," she said. "You come back and see me real soon."

"I will," I promised, but I knew that was the last time we'd be seeing each other.

Riding in the Benz on the way back to Minneapolis, Puegot fussed at me, claiming that I'd turned his family against him.

"I didn't bring you here for that. You're supposed to be my partner, my woman. You don't gossip about me with my mother. What kind of shit is that? You didn't even defend me."

"Defend you? You're a grown man. You left me in an apartment for almost three days, and I'm sure you were with one of your Gary women!" I shouted back.

"Oh that's it? That's what you're mad about? You know what? Fuck this."

He pulled over and said, "Get out!"

We were in the middle of nowhere. Outside the car, the night was pitch black and frightening, but I stepped out to the side of the road.

"You can't just leave me out here!" I cried.

Puegot ignored me. He drove off into the night. I watched his car until the red taillights disappeared.

I looked down the road in both directions. I was completely alone.

I was distraught with fear and anger. How was this happening to me?

Moments later, I saw headlights heading toward me. It was Puegot returning to pick me up. I had no choice but to climb back in, thinking, *It's over*. We drove back to Minneapolis in complete silence.

Once we got home, the floodgates opened. I knew it was over, but I needed to gather as much information as possible to truly understand who I was dealing with and be completely done with him for good.

One day, I rented a car to prevent Puegot from spotting me and waited outside the group home until he got off work. I tailed him to a house and watched from the car as a woman met him at the door and kissed him before walking inside. I wrote down the address and went home to look it up. Puegot owned the house. He used the money I'd given him to buy it, but instead of telling me about it, he had some other woman living there.

After making that discovery, I started following Puegot every day, collecting information. He'd purchased a handful of properties and had women living in the homes. They were white, Black, Mexican, Indian, everything. They had kids, some of which were his, and one was pregnant by him. One of the women was his alleged ex-wife, but I learned that they were still married and had five kids. In addition to using the money I gave him to house his women, Puegot also bought expensive cars and treated himself to a brand-new Porsche he was keeping from me.

I was livid and confronted him with the evidence. Sprawled out on my kitchen table were lists of the license plates on the new cars and the addresses of properties he'd bought.

Puegot hardly looked at the papers.

"What does any of this have to do with our relationship, Tanya? I love you. That's all you need to know. Why do you keep bringing up other women? Focus on us," he said. "We've already been through this."

"How can I do that when I'm sharing you with half of the women in Minneapolis and Gary? Why do you need all these women? I'm sure they all think they're special and that you love them. You're lying to all of us."

Cold as ice, he started walking to the door, saying, "You want to deal with me, you're going to have to accept that." He walked out and slammed the door behind him.

Left alone, I swiped all my evidence from the table and sent it whirling to the floor. He was giving me all he could and taking everything I had. I had to move on and never look back.

"Fuck that Negro," Randall said later when he and Terrell showed up to console me with bottles of Dom Perignon, salmon, cheese, and crackers. They even brought three matching kimonos and made me put one on, hoping it would cheer me up.

"He ain't shit," Terrell agreed.

"Church!" Randall applauded.

I tried to perk up, but I was too heartbroken. I couldn't believe Puegot had the nerve to do me wrong. I was insulted, angry, embarrassed, and scorned.

After a few days in bed with my curtains closed and eyes wet with tears, I decided it was time to get even. I could not let him get away with what he had done to me and all the other women he was probably lying to.

I focused my ire on Puegot. He needed to know unequivocally that what he'd done to me was unacceptable. I wanted to hurt him like he hurt me. The best way to do that was to hit him in his pockets.

"Internal Revenue Service. You've reached the tax evasion and property tax fraud hotline. How may I help you?"

"I need to report someone. I hate to do it, but cheating the government isn't right, you know?" I said.

The female IRS agent echoed me. "We don't like cheaters either. Do you have a name and an address?"

"I do."

When I hung up, the IRS knew everything about Puegot's extensive property list. With his "investments for our future," he was living far above his reported income as a group home counselor.

Within weeks, the IRS audited Puegot and slapped him with a giant tax bill. He called me.

"How could you do this to me? You are my girl. You are the special one."

Lying in bed and looking up at the ceiling as he groveled, I was amazed by how much his tone had changed from cold indifference to a desire to connect and understand. He wasn't mad. He was hurt.

I listened to him go on and on and then I said, "I did it because you lied and used me."

"I didn't—"

I cut him off. "Who are you? What kind of man has different women all over the place thinking they have a future with him? You don't have a heart. How could you do this to me and all those women who trust and probably love you too? You have a wife you don't even acknowledge. Don't you care about your kids? You don't even spend time with them. You kept them a secret from me for years. It's wrong, not only to me but to your children."

"It's not what you think. Please believe me." He begged.

I could hear in his voice he was serious, but it didn't matter anymore. "I don't want to be loved that way," I said. "Goodbye, Puegot."

When I hung up, I cried for a long time. I took residence beneath a blanket on my living room floor and listened to all our love songs until my eyes were swollen. I loved him from my heart and let my feelings guide me. From that point on, I vowed I'd never let it happen again. I would only love using my head. I would put myself first.

When I called his mother to tell her what I did and to say our final goodbye, she absolved me of wrongdoing.

"Tanya, I understand why you did it," she said. "And it's pretty funny. Don't tell him I said so."

10

MOVING ON

I came out of that relationship aspiring to a new level of dedication and purpose in my work. If I couldn't be with the man I loved, I would focus on my empire. The '80s brought a new era of advancement for women in the workplace. They were making power moves in power suits with shoulder pads. I considered myself one of them. In my own way, by doing what I was doing, I'd broken a glass ceiling.

I did not return to USC. I was no longer going to waste time sitting in college classes I had no interest in. I still wanted to make my parents proud, but I had to be honest with myself. I wasn't Ethel Payne. I was Tanya Smith, and what Tanya was good at, what Tanya had mastered, was doing transactions.

I hooked back up with Randall, Terrell, and some old runners. I stopped sending wires to the bank for Paid Upon Proper ID pickups. Instead, I had my runners open bank accounts armed with fake IDs and scripts I had crafted to ease future withdrawals. I coached them in staff meetings at my apartment.

"Dress well. Be cheerful and friendly. Tell the account manager, 'I'm moving here, so I'm having funds wired from my old bank. Over the next few days, I'll need a portion from the account for new housing expenses.'" They'd take notes and nod, carefully following my every instruction. Even Randall and Terrell, afraid I'd skip town again and their funds would dry up, tried to get in line.

The beauty of the new account structure was that I could wire any sum without triggering an IRS report, which happened whenever someone withdrew $10,000 or more. I could even shuffle funds between accounts. When I saw that the wires had cleared, I'd send the runners to present their fake IDs and withdraw cash, just as they'd told the bank manager.

For the sake of credibility, my runners withdrew only a portion of the funds in the account. Someone with $50,000 in the bank could reasonably be expected to withdraw $25,000 in one day. If that person soon needed an additional $19,000—never the entire balance—that was also plausible. "Always leave a decent amount of money in the account to avoid scrutiny," I advised everyone in staff meetings. "Don't worry. We will hit them until we've withdrawn all the money. Then—poof! I'll close the account. It'll be like it never even existed, and you'll be on to your next location. Let's get 'em."

I quickly discovered that for withdrawals of more than a couple thousand dollars, my regular crew wasn't cutting it. Randall, Terrell, and the others would come back to me with no cash.

"Girlfriend, that white fish was treating me like I was a criminal who crawled from beneath somebody's prison."

Randall and the others complained about the tellers insisting on multiple forms of ID or just flat out refusing to allow the withdrawals.

"It doesn't make sense. Nothing's wrong with the account. I wonder what tipped them off. Was it your skin color?" I asked.

Banks were far more suspicious of Black people, even of supposedly high-balance account holders. Tellers seemed to hate putting large sums of cash into Black hands. Sure enough, when I started using white runners, the transactions went through. The tellers blindly assumed they were legit.

Being back to work and leading my team was exhilarating—forbidden and dangerous—but also intellectually engaging. I was addicted to the transactions. They had my brain firing on all cylinders, tapping my powers of persuasion, my ability to impersonate, my capacity for split-second information processing, the need for careful emotional calibration, and the intense satisfaction of solving puzzles.

That summer and fall, I made more than two million in cash. I had cash stashed everywhere—in safe-deposit boxes, in a storage unit, and even under the floorboards of my Golden Valley townhouse. I kept a little bit in a bank account just to have walking around money.

With all the money coming in, it became a challenge to spend it. Right away, I made big donations to charity: tens of thousands here and there to the Salvation Army, the Red Cross, St. Jude's Research Hospital, the United Way, and the NAACP.

I also loved surprising people with extravagant gifts. One time, I slipped $10,000 into the pocket of a man who was begging for change. He started crying and praised God for his good fortune.

A few girls I grew up with had kids. I enjoyed helping them out by buying clothes, toys, furniture, school supplies, whatever they needed. Having seen how rich people lived across town and spent time in celebrity homes in Los Angeles, I saw how having fine things impacted people's emotional well-being, and I wanted my friends' kids to experience that. A hand-me-down shirt from the Salvation Army was nice, but a cashmere sweater from Bloomingdale's brought a new level of hope.

While I hardly spent money on myself and kept my appearance pretty basic—except when I hit the town—word got around that I was rich and that people could make money working for me. I was shocked when a complete stranger came up to me in the mall and said, "I need cash to get my son out of jail. Could I do one of your jobs?" It happened more than once. I was mortified. How many people knew about me?

I had to be more careful. I decided that I would never have personal contact with a runner, that I would work only through intermediaries. If Randall and Terrell couldn't be discreet, I'd have to find other runners and recruiters. As I dealt with larger amounts of money, I had to be that much more cautious about protecting myself.

I visited my parents one evening after finishing up at Pillsbury. We commonly had dinner together, and I wasn't surprised when Mom called the office inviting me over. But when I walked in, I didn't smell anything cooking, and they weren't in the kitchen laughing like usual. Dad led me into the family room, where Mom was sitting on the couch with a worried look. My thoughts immediately went to Taryn. Had something happened to her?

"Is everything OK?" I asked after sitting down beside my mother.

"What are you up to, Tanya?" my father asked, pacing in agitation.

"Excuse me?"

"I got a call from the chief of police today. He said you're under investigation by his office and the FBI."

"Under investigation?" I started feeling dizzy, like the room was closing in.

"Honey, do you need to tell us something?" Mom asked.

"Are you mixed up with someone who's stealing money from banks?" My father jumped in.

Hearing the words *stealing* and *bank*, I knew the chief, one of Dad's old friends, had real information about me. Enough that I couldn't lie to my parents and leave them completely in the dark. I didn't fully confess to stealing, but I did admit that I'd come to possess some funds not quite my own. However, I didn't say exactly how I came to possess them.

"Why, Tanya?" they asked. They weren't angry. They were grievously disappointed. Seeing their hurt was more crushing than any recrimination.

"You could do anything with your life," my dad said. "Now you could wind up in jail. What a waste of your intellect and opportunities. How could you just throw all that away?"

I would have said anything to ease their pain. I told them how grateful I was for all they'd done for me, even for the example they'd set. With tears spilling from my eyes as I held my mother's hand, I apologized over and over for having let them down. I assured them that I would work harder to get my life on track.

Walking out of my parents' house, I felt some shame that ignited into a fiery rage. My parents had come from little. They were the children of cooks and maids and worked hard to give their children a better life. The top echelon of society in Minneapolis embraced my father, but he was always on the outside looking in. He never even dreamed of enjoying the luxury and ease that his wealthy and privileged friends took for granted. But I'd found a way to get it.

I wasn't sorry for that, not one bit. I was pissed that my parents had been put in a position to see me as a common thief. I wasn't stealing. I was just skimming from the slush funds of institutions.

I wasn't going to let law enforcement, the guard dogs of the system, spook me. I was under investigation because of human frailty—gossiping, bragging. With the right network of runners, I would ensure my work would be less dangerous.

My dad made some calls to his friends—judges and politicians—to have my name erased from whatever list had me on the FBI's radar. I'm not sure it was effective, because I started to spot the same cars in my rearview mirror, tailing me wherever I went. When I turned, they turned, sometimes down alleys. When I got on the highway, they were behind me on the ramp. I was under surveillance, and the cops weren't even subtle about it.

One night, I invited some friends to dinner at a Mexican restaurant. We'd started eating when a sloppy drunk suddenly plopped down in the booth behind us.

"Time to go," I told them.

"We're not done." My friends protested. I packed up our enchiladas and queso and asked for the bill.

When we got outside, my friend Michelle demanded to know what was up.

"That drunk, the one who sat in the booth behind us, was an undercover cop," I revealed. "They've been tailing me for weeks. I've gotten good at spotting them."

"No way," she said, amazed. "But why would they be here tonight? We don't know anything about your work."

"I think they're just trying to scare me or something. Make me slip up," I said.

We all turned and looked through the window beside the booth where we'd been sitting. The drunk had vanished. At that moment, I realized I had to start protecting those around me. I didn't want the law getting that up close and personal with people I knew.

11

THE MASTERMIND

U ntil the investigation cooled down, I planned to lay off the transactions. To take my mind off the drama with law enforcement, Randall and Terrell invited me out for a night of barhopping. I wasn't in the mood to party, but I wanted to spend time with them. Working together had been difficult, and I didn't want our friendship to suffer.

"Don't be trying to go home at midnight like you Cinderella or something. We shutting this shit down tonight," Randall said as we walked into the Gay '90s, one of our usual anything-goes spots where people went to be whomever they desired.

"Speak for yourself, sister," Terrell shot back at him. "I need to preserve my beauty."

"Come on. Tonight isn't about you. Us girls are supposed to have fun. Isn't that what Cyndi Lauper said?" Randall sang. "Girls just want to have fu-un."

We laughed and went to the bar. Randall and Terrell got tipsy on the bartender's hefty double shots. After dancing to a few songs, we decided to leave and head to the Fox Trap, which was right around the corner.

Though I was feeling the music there, I was watching my surroundings. The Brothers, Puegot's old buddies, still hung out at the Fox Trap, and I didn't want to run into him.

Scanning the crowd, my eyes landed on a handsome light-brown brother dressed in a neat, button-up blue shirt and dress slacks. He looked classy and sophisticated. I'd actually seen him at the Fox Trap before, but we had never met. He seemed to be popular and always had a different woman with him. That night was no different. Dancing beside him was a thin, tall, blonde who looked like a model.

"That's Shawn Davis. You two would look good together," Randall whispered in my ear.

"If you don't want him, we'll take his fine ass." Terrell joked, but I knew he was serious.

"He's cute but not exactly my type. Plus, I'm not really trying to date right now."

"Girl, hush with that. Life requires orgasms. Get one," Terrell said. "No one's saying you have to marry him. Just have some fucking fun."

"Right!" Randall cheered. "You're a queenpin. You need arm candy. And that man is looking like a lollipop."

It had been a while since I'd been touched, and my body craved attention. While love was out of the question, enjoying the company of a handsome man could be an entertaining way of keeping my mind off the cops.

Considering all of this, when Shawn and the model parted ways on the dance floor, I agreed to be introduced.

Terrell went over to talk to Shawn and brought him back to Randall and me.

"Tanya, this is Shawn. Shawn, this is Tanya," Terrell said, adding an unusual bass to his voice.

"Hello," Shawn said, shaking my hand. He was dark skinned, of Nigerian descent, and stood at six four. He smelled good and seemed friendly.

We were hitting it off but then the thin blonde returned, and she seemed miffed that Shawn was talking to me. The way she spoke and grabbed Shawn, demanding that he cater to her, reminded me of Elvira, Tony Montana's girlfriend in *Scarface*.

Clearly not wanting to further annoy her, Shawn said, "Nice to meet you, Tanya," and walked away.

"Well, that was interesting," Randall said as we watched them walk away.

About an hour later, when the Fox Trap was about to close, most of the partygoers hung around outside mingling, showing off their cars, clothes, and women. It was the usual show after the party.

As I stood chatting with Randall and Terrell, someone tapped my shoulder. I turned to discover it was Shawn.

"I was thinking we could get something to eat somewhere," he said.

"OK," I agreed. "Where?"

"There aren't a lot of places open at this hour. But we could go to Denny's on Lake," he offered.

We went to Denny's and talked until dawn. Shawn was so easy to talk to. He was sporty and enjoyed martial arts. I told him all about growing up on Washburn and how I flew to Los Angeles to meet the Jacksons.

"You're bold," he said.

"Oh, you have no idea."

After that night, Shawn and I started hanging out a lot. Because he was active like me, we'd hit the park in the afternoon and sweat it out playing basketball or under the air conditioner playing arcade games like Pac-Man, Centipede, Donkey Kong, and Galaga. We also went roller skating at Roller Gardens in Saint Louis Park. He was the roller-skating king there. We'd also throw footballs and race each other, doing laps around the track. He was a great companion and a nice transition from all the drama I had with Puegot. By the fall of 1981, we were a nightlife power couple. When we hit the clubs, we were always stylish in head-to-toe coordinated outfits. I supplied our clothes, which in the brutal Minnesota winter came to include white mink coats.

"Where did you get these beautiful coats?" Shawn asked when I presented him with his floor-length mink. He'd slid it on and was modeling it in the dressing mirror at my place, eyes dancing with excitement. I smiled behind him, happy I could make him feel that way. Nevertheless, I remained true to my personal promise not to fall in love. Spoiling Shawn was just fun for me. I'd grown accustomed to nice things. Seeing someone new experience those things was one of my favorite thrills.

"I've been saving to treat you to something nice," I said, fixing Shawn's collar. I hadn't told him about my transactions, and he was becoming suspicious.

"Ain't that much saving in the world," he joked.

"Fine, I'll return it then," I said, trying to snatch the mink.

"Absolutely not." He pulled away. "I ain't crazy. Just asking questions."

Initially, I had primarily never been materialistic. When I was with Puegot, I gave him all the money. I lived in my small apartment and drove a Pontiac. Being in California, surrounded by the rich and famous, it heightened my appreciation for the good life and nice things, like designer clothes and expensive cars.

With the money I was making, it was a minor expense to buy motorcycles for myself and Shawn. I got a Ninja and purchased a Yamaha for him. We zipped around the city's scenic Chain of Lakes Park. We joined a group of Black motorcycle riders, and I was the only woman. I loved putting on my tight jeans, a cute top with boots or sneakers, and hopping on the Ninja. When I would stop at a light, men and women looked at me and gave nods that said, "You go, girl!"

One evening, I treated Shawn to dinner at a fancy steakhouse. It was our common Friday-night routine. When the waiter asked for his order, Shawn said, "I'll have the New York strip and a baked potato."

"You sure love a New York strip and a baked potato," I teased when the waiter was gone. I noticed that whenever we were out to dinner, he'd barely glance at the menu and always ordered the same meal. "You didn't even read the menu."

Shawn's face fell, and he was quiet for the rest of the night. Whenever I asked what was wrong, he'd say he was fine, but when we got back to my place, he said he wanted to talk and revealed that he couldn't read. He was too embarrassed to even try to decipher the menu.

The revelation was a turning point for us. It took great trust for him to open up about something he'd been ashamed of all his life. It touched my heart, and I had to help him.

I bought a bunch of elementary school books and had Shawn read aloud to me for practice. I kept pushing and drilling, and Shawn, being intelligent, quickly began to pick up skills. I then asked what subjects he was interested in and got books and magazines for him to read and learn more about the topics. After a few weeks, something clicked, and he got it.

I quickly noticed a difference in Shawn's demeanor once he could read. He seemed more confident and outgoing. One night, after we'd read the newspaper together, he said, "I can understand things I never thought I would be able to. I can make my own decisions now. I don't have to depend on other people. I'm independent."

Cheering him on, I said, "That's how you always want to be. Let's go celebrate."

"Celebrate what?"

"You. Your tenacity and resilience. I think it's amazing," I pointed out, sincerely proud of Shawn.

We went to the Classic Motor Club in St. Louis Park. The waitress handed us menus, and Shawn read out loud every single item on the menu.

"Tanya, you changed my life," he told me. Those words meant a lot, but I wasn't helping Shawn to hear nice things about myself.

Feeling more connected to Shawn, when my rich friend Natalie called me and asked if I would come to Los Angeles to host a party she was giving, I agreed and brought Shawn along as my date. As soon as we got off the plane, Shawn was in awe of everything about Los Angeles.

"Wow," he said about the palm trees.

"Wow," he said about the skyline.

"Wow," he said about the beach.

Wow about everything.

I thought he'd gotten them all out, but when we got to Natalie's house where we were staying, Shawn let out another, "Wow." It was earned. Natalie had redone her furniture, and it looked like a Parisian showroom with velvet draping everything and a collection of stunning paintings.

Natalie was excited to see me and meet Shawn. We were like best girlfriends hanging out as she caught me up on her fabulous Los Angeles life.

Her children, who were in grade school, were also happy to see me. They gave me the biggest hugs, started jumping all over me, and begged me to take them to the park, which I always did with them.

Shawn and I agreed to walk them to the park down the street. The sun was shining and the weather calm; it was a perfect day in Los Angeles. Before we were a block away from the house, cops pulled up and stopped us.

"We're gonna need some ID," one of the officers requested, looking at the children, who were shaken and hiding behind me.

"For what?" I asked. "We're just walking down the street."

"Did we do something wrong?" Shawn added as we handed over our IDs.

"That depends. Where do you live? And what are you doing with these children?" the second officer asked as the first one returned to the patrol car to run our IDs.

"I'm visiting from out of town. These are my friend's children."

He looked at the kids and asked, "Do you know these people?"

Fully terrified, they clung to my legs and nodded; however, that wasn't enough for the police officer who pointed at me and added, "What is her name?"

Both kids said my name. Instead of looking relieved that no crime was happening, the officer looked annoyed, like Shawn and I were pulling one over on him. His scowl didn't let up until his partner returned and announced that our IDs came back clean and we were free to go.

As we walked away, one of the kids asked, "Did we do something wrong, Tanya?"

Shawn and I locked eyes and shook our heads in disgust.

The trip had done a number on Shawn. Having been around my wealthy friends, he suddenly became insecure about how much money I had and how different we were.

I tried to fix it by buying a new car for us to get around town. To avoid creating a legal record of owning luxury automobiles, I didn't want to register the car in my name. Shawn had a trusted female friend who agreed to put the car in hers, and I gave him the down payment with the understanding that it was my car. We landed on purchasing a black Lincoln Continental with a black cloth top, which made it look like a convertible, and black-and-gray interior. It was top of the line, elegant, and classy. Moving through Minneapolis, the car immediately upped our status.

Initially, I kept it at my place and drove it all the time, but I noticed Shawn wasn't feeling that. He'd make snide comments about deserving to drive it as he'd helped me get it registered and claimed that I thought I was "all that" when driving it. To cater to his bruised ego, I started letting Shawn drive the Continental even more than me. Quickly, his attitude changed. He started getting cocky and bragging to his friends about his car and how he was the man.

My parents had many questions when they saw the Continental.

"How can you afford this?" Dad asked, fingering the black leather seats. "The insurance alone is probably higher than the payment on any car I've owned."

I laughed it off and said I was being frugal to afford nice things.

Mom was more suspicious. Before I got the Continental, I was getting different luxury sedans every week to see how they handled, and she'd commented on that. "Every week, a different car?"

"Mom, they're just rentals," I explained. She let it go, but when it was clear the Continental was an actual purchase, it was harder to convince her and my father that nothing was off.

Shawn was also becoming more open about his suspicions. The furs and the motorcycles piqued his interest, but the car pushed him over the edge.

"I've told you everything about me, but you're holding back. I can tell," he said one Sunday afternoon after we finished riding our bikes.

I didn't want him to know too much about my operation, but he kept begging.

Sitting in the Continental after roller skating, I described the broad strokes of my operation. Shawn was intrigued. Immediately drawn in, he said he wanted a piece of the action and volunteered to help recruit and manage runners; it wouldn't cost me a thing. He'd keep a cut of their share.

I wasn't excited about onboarding someone new and definitely not in such a critical role, but I continued having doubts about Randall and Terrell; not only were their runners getting turned down at teller's windows but Randall was spending a lot of time in California and Terrell was spinning out before my eyes in Minneapolis, spending all his money on cocaine and extravagant gifts.

I wanted a frontman to shield me from the runners. Shawn thought he could do that, and after more begging, I accepted his offer.

"You have to know there are risks. This is considered illegal, and if you get caught, you could go down. That's always a possibility," I explained to him.

"I know. And that doesn't change anything. I'm all in," Shawn reassured me.

Shawn was bringing in runners from all over the place. He had ten at one point, and they were difficult to keep in line.

One of the girls, a Latina who had just moved to Minnesota, was an hour late to a pickup. Another one of his runners, a guy he claimed he went to grade school with, but I wasn't so sure, brought his kid on a run. A third person was an ex-girlfriend who was still in love with him. It was too much.

"Don't worry about it," Shawn said every time I pointed out an issue.

I felt like his runners needed more training, direction, and observation. It seemed like Shawn simply told them what to do and hoped for the best. He had no knowledge of managing an operation like I did, but I didn't want to step in. The whole point of having Shawn was to allow me to orchestrate things from afar, not get too involved. But it wasn't working. Since everyone knew I was dating Shawn—and I had money—it wasn't hard to guess who he was working for.

An added complication was Shawn's popularity with the ladies. He seemed sincere for a little while, but like Whac-A-Mole, the women would just pop up here and there, especially when Shawn started working for me and had money to burn. He'd disappear for a day or two then call me to say he was handling some business. Still, having dealt with Puegot, I knew he'd been off somewhere with one of those girls. Honestly, I really didn't care. I wasn't in love. I wasn't even looking for love with Shawn. I knew our situation was temporary, and the other women would more than likely remain in his life longer than me. What was really eating away at me was what he was doing to my business. All his spending was bound to attract attention—and that attention would lead to me.

"Don't worry about it," Shawn repeated for the hundredth time when I explained that after one of his disappearances.

One afternoon, when Shawn had my car and I was driving a rental to the store, I suddenly heard sirens blaring behind me. I looked in the rearview mirror. There was a police cruiser, lights flashing. He was so close to my bumper and would've rear-ended me if I had hit the brakes. "Pull over," ordered a harsh voice over the bullhorn.

I nosed the car over to the curb, breathing deep to stay cool. My mind started racing. Had I been speeding? Did I run a stop sign? Was my taillight broken?

Two white male cops approached, one on each side of the car. They both had one hand on their guns and the other on their nightsticks. I looked out to the road, where traffic was light, but people were slowing down and looking at me as if I had done something wrong.

One of the officers tapped my window. I slowly rolled it down, careful not to move too quickly.

"Hello, officer," I said. "Did I do something wrong?"

"License and registration," he demanded, not even making eye contact. Out of the corner of my eye, I saw the other officer scanning the interior of the car.

As I handed over my license, he asked, "Whose car is this?"

"It's a rental," I told him. "What's this about?"

"Tanya Smith, we're going to escort you to the station."

"Why? What did I do?"

"We just want to talk to you."

"About what?"

"You know what," the officer standing beside my window said, looking grim.

"No, I don't." I tried to convey my surprise without sounding alarmed. "Am I under arrest?"

"Not yet."

"Well, if I'm not under arrest, I don't have to come. Do I?"

"You can come with us now, or we'll get a warrant. That will be a lot worse for you. What's it going to be?" the cop scanning the interior of the car said, glaring at me.

I followed them to the precinct in my car. *You knew this day would come*, I thought as we drove across town. To calm myself, I summoned the drill I gave my runners: *Stay polite. Don't argue. Don't act nervous.* Slowly, my fluttering nerves settled and were replaced by a serene restraint.

As I entered the chaotic police precinct, I repeated a mantra to sustain my focus: *Try not to talk. You'll get through this. You are in control.*

The interrogation room looked like a set designer's vision: stark and gray-walled with a long table and harsh fluorescent lights. Four fit and nearly identical white men sat on one side of the table—two local detectives and two FBI agents—and I sat facing them, alone. It struck me that I needed a lawyer, but at twenty-one, I didn't have one in my phone book. I could call my parents, but I wanted to protect them.

In the beginning, all four of the men were friendly. "We need your help" was their opening line. Someone was spiriting money out of banks. "They can see the money's missing, but they don't know how it's done. It's such a clever scheme that they can't track it," one of them said.

Not a word, I told myself. Listening, I nodded along but gave them nothing else.

My detached disposition soon rattled them, and their friendliness disappeared. Without a word, they regrouped and tried something different.

One of the FBI agents was low-key and played the good cop, while one of the Minneapolis detectives—fortysomething and aggressive—played rough. His obsessive fixation on me was apparent as he peered into my eyes.

"Now, we know it's not you who's doing this," the low-key FBI agent said. "We're pretty sure this is an inside job— someone at the bank who knows the system. But we think you can tell us who that is."

I was puzzled. If they believed it was an inside job, why did they think I was involved? Why was I even there? They revealed that someone who'd been detained for an unrelated crime—a runner or maybe just someone who'd heard the gossip—had fingered me as a bigger fish.

"We're not after you," low-key said. "We don't even need to know what role you played. The person we want is the ring-leader. We just need a name."

Seeing I wasn't budging, the bad-cop detective cut to the chase. "Who's your boss?" he asked me directly. "We need a name right now."

"I don't know what you're talking about," I said.

This pissed him off. He popped out of his seat and put his hands on his hips like I was an unruly child getting a lecture.

"You must not realize the trouble you're in. This is bank fraud, a federal offense with heavy fines and prison time. The exact charges will depend on how they got the money, which we don't know yet. But we'll find out, and when we do, we're coming down hard on this mastermind," he said.

Low-key added in a soft tone, "You don't want to be on the wrong side."

They went on, taking turns talking about the brilliance of the crime, how hundreds of thousands of dollars—no one knew exactly how much—had simply vanished from a slew of Midwestern banks. It took real expertise to pinpoint a hidden vulnerability in the national banking system. Bypassing all safeguards, the thief had moved the money in judicious incre-ments, leaving no footprints.

"This was no small-time heist," the stern detective noted. "This guy is a genius."

Guy? What "guy" were they talking about? This was my operation. My expertise. There was no guy. While I felt some latent satisfaction hearing these agents and detectives unknow-ingly identify my work as genius and me as a mastermind, their insistence that some guy was behind it irked me to near exasperation.

The detective turned a chair around, sat on it backward, and leaned in close to me. "You're being used," he said. "Do you think whoever engineered this scheme gives a damn about you? Do you think he gives a damn if you go to prison? Why protect him? If you don't cooperate, you're going down with him. I promise you that."

The agent added, "Just give us the name. Is he a boyfriend?"

"No. She doesn't have a boyfriend. It's just some guy who's using her," the detective said.

"Using me?"

"Yes. And he'll throw you away when he's done with you. He'll probably laugh when you get locked up. Move right on to the next brainless woman."

"Right. Because that's what you are by protecting him, a brainless woman," the agent said.

"No. I'm not," I blurted before I could stop myself. "I'm not protecting a man. I'm the boss. It's me."

My words landed with a clunk. A deafening silence followed. Then the men burst out laughing so hard their faces turned red.

When they were done, the stern detective noticed I wasn't laughing, and slowly, they all realized I was serious. Their tone sharpened.

"What do you mean, it's you? Quit jerking us around," low-key said, looking offended I had interrupted his dream of what kind of bad guy they were chasing. He sounded like I'd just told him Santa Claus wasn't real.

"I'm the one moving the money," I repeated. I already regretted my honesty, but it was too late to back down.

The officers refused to believe it.

"Look—we know you recruit people. We could arrest you right now, but we're giving you a chance to save yourself. You can get a good deal if you give us the name," the agent said.

"It's not you." the detective spat out the words. "Here's how I know: You're a Neeee-grro." He drew out the syllables, long and slow. "Neeee-grroes murder, steal, and rob, but they don't have the brains to commit sophisticated crimes like this. That just doesn't happen."

The other men smirked, making little attaboy snickers.

"No way are you smart enough to pull this off."

"So, as a Black woman, I'm incapable of being smart?"

"Now, Tanya, you don't honestly expect us to believe you're responsible," low-key said. "You just can't admit that some guy's been playing you. But think about this. What's going to happen when you're locked up? Will he be as loyal as you are? I've seen this go wrong for so many girls."

I was too angry to listen anymore. I let them bluster and threaten but didn't answer their questions. Eventually, they had to give up and let me go. They didn't have the evidence to hold me or arrest me; I knew that much.

When I reached my car, I was shaking with a fury I had never felt before. How dare they insult my intelligence.

Driving home, I questioned everything in my life that might have led to the officers hovering over me, deciding who I was and what I was capable of. "You're a Neeee-grro. Neeee-grroes murder, steal, and rob, but they don't have the brains to commit sophisticated crimes like this . . . ," echoed in my mind.

I was feeling exposed by runners I didn't know, who were being badly managed by Shawn. I was making money, but the process was messy and becoming more stressful than exciting.

I had to professionalize and bulletproof my operation. *Just wait till you see what this Black woman can do*, I thought.

12

THE FIREWALL

When I got home from the precinct, I decided playtime was over. To focus, I rented an apartment exclusively for the transactions. I called it my war room. I closed the curtains to block out the world, dusted off the computer, and took out a pen and pad to write down a bulleted plan of action. I had to clean house by getting rid of the old staff and set up a new superteam.

The first thing on my list was to hire a lawyer. After a spate of calls and a little research, I found an attorney named Julio Phillips. He'd just won a murder case I'd read about in the papers. His client had been caught in the act, but Julio got him off. I figured a lawyer who could get a perp like that acquitted would be more than capable of handling my prospective case.

"I need a shark who'll keep these cops and Feds off my back, is that you?" I asked Julio at our first meeting in his office.

He was of Mexican descent, impeccably dressed in a dark suit, and had perfectly manicured hands. This let me know two things: he had money and good taste.

"I love your case," Julio said. He was married to a beau-tiful Black woman, and after having a few run-ins with the criminal-justice system in his youth, he hated cops. "You never have to talk to the cops again. I'm here to keep you out of trouble. "

It was all I needed to hear. I kept Julio on a $5,000 retainer.

I fired Shawn.

I had purchased concert tickets to see Prince at First Avenue. The night of the show, I was expecting Shawn to pick me up.

Taryn called me. She was already at First Avenue. "Tanya, where are you?" she asked. "Shawn's here and guess who he's with?"

Taryn revealed that he was with Kelsey, the same model he had on his arm when we first met at the Fox Trap. "They drove up in your Lincoln, and you won't believe what she's wearing!" It was a white, floor-length mink coat that perfectly matched Shawn's.

I needed a partner and a friend I could trust. It was clear that wasn't Shawn.

Late that night, I had my friend Ron pick me up in his car because Shawn had mine. We drove by the apartment where I knew Kelsey lived, and sure enough, my Lincoln was parked in the lot.

"Pull up," I told Ron. The lot was pretty empty. It was late enough that no one was outside.

I unlocked the Lincoln using my key and hopped inside. Instead of starting the car and taking off, I started looking through the car for any evidence of the other woman and found

NEVER SAW ME COMING

a key ring in the glove box. "Bingo! A bonus," I said, jangling the keys.

Ron got out of his car and came over when he saw what was going on. "What are you up to, Tanya?" he asked, shaking his head. "Let's just get out of here."

I ignored Ron and went back to his car. From the passenger's seat, I hoisted the plastic bag I'd brought along. Inside was a gallon of paint.

"Hold it," Ron said, glaring at the paint. "Isn't that your car?"

"Not anymore. Shawn's been driving it," I told him. "He can buy his own bitchmobile."

I sloshed the entire can of paint onto the car—all over the roof, the windows and doors, the windshield, the hood, everywhere, until it dripped down onto the pavement. Ron couldn't believe what he was seeing. "Have you gone crazy?"

I dropped the paint can and headed toward the building, holding the key ring.

"Now what are you doing? We need to leave." Ron begged, peeking over his shoulders to be sure no one was watching.

"Not yet. I'm going in."

"No! Come on! Don't go in there. What if he has a gun?"

"He doesn't. He's a punk."

After fumbling with the keys, I found one that let me into the building. From my research, I knew Kelsey lived on the second floor in the corner unit.

"Come on! Let's go before the cops come," Ron insisted.

I left him downstairs stewing as I made my way up to the apartment.

Pressing my ear to the door, I didn't hear a sound. I turned the key and entered quietly. It was dark, but I could see Shawn and Kelsey asleep on the living room floor, cuddled up under a blanket.

"I'm finally seeing this with my own eyes," I hollered.

My voice startled them out of their sleep.

Kelsey screamed.

Shawn scrambled to his feet, and as our eyes connected, I told him, "I always knew it."

As he started to come at me, I took off running. Wearing nothing, his soft penis dangling, he tried to get ahold of me but couldn't. I ran down the hall, down the stairs, and out of the apartment building.

I drove Ron home in his car and went back to the apartment. I waited in the parking lot until morning. I wanted to witness Shawn walk out and see the newly painted car. At about eight that morning, Shawn and Kelsey emerged. Kelsey gasped and put her hands over her mouth when she saw the Continental. She acted like it was her car. Shawn fell to his knees and started screaming like he'd spent a dime on the car. Kelsey went over and wrapped her arms around him. He leaned into her and cried. I started laughing.

A few weeks later, he begged me to meet and talk.

I proudly picked him up in my post–Lincoln Continental, a sleek black Corvette.

"I see you're doing well," Shawn said, sitting in the car beside me. I could tell he was jealous.

"Better than ever," I hissed. "What do you want?"

"It's the police. I can't take it no more. They want to question me. Everywhere I go, they're on me," he said.

"Well, you could take it fine when you were making money. You knew the risks. Now you're breaking down?"

"I didn't say that. But it's tough."

"Listen—I could get you an attorney, but you don't need one. They have nothing on you. They're just trying to scare you into talking. If you don't want to go to prison, just do as I say," I offered.

"Which is?"

"Don't ever admit to doing anything or knowing what I was doing. If you let them scare you and you talk, they will control you and send you to prison. From now on, your favorite sentences are, 'I don't know' and 'I don't remember.' Got it?"

"I guess," he said sheepishly.

"Look—do you trust me? Have I ever lied to you?" I asked.

"No."

"Right. Well, do what I say, and you'll be fine. Trust me and not them."

Shawn was so shaken by the time he got out of the car I didn't know if he'd turn himself in or run off to Mexico. The Feds were putting pressure on him, his family, and friends, and I could see he was scared. I knew Shawn wasn't built to withstand the pressure, and I wasn't sure if he would remain loyal.

I went back to the war room to go about the business of building a more formidable team. Randall and Terrell were both begging to work for me, but I could not risk it. Terrell was mad because his lifestyle was changing without the money.

Randall, always more levelheaded, was more understanding
and apologized for his bragging and being out of control.

During a telephone call, he said, "I understand you don't
want to have contact with runners any longer to protect you and
this operation. I know someone you could trust. She'd be the
perfect recruiter."

"Who is she?" I asked.

"Her name is Livilla. She knows everyone, including people in high places."

"Where is she?"

"The Lou. St. Louis," he said.

"That's a plus. A little distance could help," I said after
thinking about it for a beat. "And she understands her position, right? She's a firewall. Her recruits would be completely
removed from me, with no clue who I am or where I live."

"Yeah, yeah, yeah. She gets it, mama," Randall said. "She's
all business. You'll love her."

After getting off the phone with Randall, I checked Livilla
out on the computer, and I was impressed. She was a former pros-
titute and ex-con with experience dealing with the police. I knew
she wouldn't cave under pressure if she got jammed up. I jotted
down her number and went to a pay phone to give her a call.

"I don't play games. You can trust and believe that I'll do as
you ask so long as you treat me right," she said after our initial
introductions. Her voice had a soft, soulful depth that let me
know she was an older Black woman who'd seen some things.
She went on to say that she viscerally valued a job that was
lucrative, smooth, and clean.

"I run a clean operation. I just need help with management," I explained.

"I got you," she said, and I could feel her smiling through the line. "I like your style. I've put in a lot of work, but this is my first time serving a real Black-woman boss. Let's make some money together."

After the first call, Livilla and I spoke a few more times to iron out the specifics of our engagement.

"Picture me like a mom," she once said. "I'll take care of you, and you'll take care of me."

For her services, she asked for 50 percent of the take, which she was to split with the runners she recruited. It seemed fair.

"Let's start out small," I told her. "We'll move twenty-five thousand at a time. Your people will do the pickups after I transfer the money and share the locations."

"Copy."

With Livilla onboard, I went to my war room to upgrade operations. It was time to streamline everything by going all digital. I'd been using the computer for research, opening bank accounts, and so on, but I was still arranging the actual wire transfers by phone. Finally, I had enough confidence in my knowledge of the computer network to try using it to transfer money as well.

Setting up the first few transactions with Livilla, I went the extra step and transferred funds to accounts from my terminal. It was easy. Just a few keystrokes and I was done. No more risky person-to-person telephone interactions. I went to the pay phone to let Livilla know it was time to send out her troops.

Randall was right about Livilla's connections. From prior experience, I knew that white, professional-looking runners had the best chance of making withdrawals. Not only was Livilla able to recruit people who appeared reputable but she also brought in a few celebrities—athletes and entertainers—and even a high-level bank official. I couldn't imagine how a hustler knew all these seemingly model citizens, but then, I didn't have to know. With Livilla handling her recruits and Randall acting as our go-between, flying to St. Louis to pick up the cash, to Minneapolis to drop it off, and then back home to LA, I was completely sequestered.

Livilla was also a master at handling her side of the business. She followed my directives to the letter and kept books that were scrupulously accurate.

When a runner was short a few hundred dollars according to her records, she ominously said over the phone, "We won't be hearing from him" and never mentioned the man again. When her tone got like that, it reminded me of Livilla's past—she was streetwise and experienced. It scared me a little. I suspected she was linked to a scary underworld, possibly the mob.

In time, Livilla and I became a powerhouse team, pulling in almost unimaginable sums—sometimes as much as a million dollars a month. With our new, more "respectable" runners, we could make bigger withdrawals, up to $250,000 or more.

"Send your guy to that bank downtown. I transferred three hundred thousand. Randall will be there to pick it up tonight," I ordered Livilla over the phone and then hours later, when the deal was complete, I'd be back on the line. "Let's hit them for another hundred and seventy-five. Do you have anyone else who can do it?"

"You know it," Livilla would answer.

Sometimes we'd do three pickups in one day. So much money was coming in I didn't do transactions every day because it seemed unnecessary.

"Take a break today. Get out and smell the roses or something. Don't you do anything else?" Livilla would say some days, breaking me from my constant desire to close big deals and hush the words of those cops still ringing in my ears: "You're a Neeee-grro. Neeee-grroes murder, steal, and rob, but they don't have the brains to commit sophisticated crimes like this."

What about now? I'd say, arguing with that ignorant detective and FBI agent in my mind. *You still think I can't commit sophisticated crimes?*

Sometimes I did take Livilla's advice to smell the roses. As I had in the past, I'd take sacks of cash and hand it out to people in need. I also gave large sums to charities, like children's hospitals. To stay under the radar, I kept my donations to charity anonymous by sending bank checks, purchased with cash, in sums ranging from $10,000 to $50,000.

Since I no longer had runners bragging and flashing their finery in nightclubs, the police had no pipeline to my activities. But they stepped up their game by harassing everyone I knew. One of my friends, Lisa, was a buyer for a big department store, a job she loved. Her boyfriend was pals with Shawn, and we used to double-date. But she knew nothing about my operation and was not involved. The Minneapolis cops, who evidently thought otherwise, badgered her constantly, even after Shawn and I split up. She kept telling them, "I'm not talking to you about Tanya."

Then, to turn up the pressure, they threatened her. "If you don't cooperate, we'll get you fired," they said. She didn't believe it, especially since she had nothing to offer.

One day, she called me in tears. "Tanya, I lost my job. The police told the store that I was mixed up in something illegal."

"That's a lie," I said, outraged.

"Of course," Lisa said. "But I want you to know that we're still friends. I don't blame you at all. What the cops are doing is crazy and wrong."

One morning, there was a boom at the front door. I put on my bathrobe and went to see who it was, though I already knew it was the cops. Who else would bang on someone's door like that?

"Tanya Smith, we have a warrant to search this residence," a detective said, pushing past me with two underlings behind him. He waved a stack of papers in my face and dropped it before I could take it from him.

I picked it up and went straight to the phone to call Julio.

"There's nothing we can do to stop this. Just be cool. You have nothing to hide," Julio said over the phone as I watched the officers rifle through my belongings.

At one point, a cop held up some children's books as if they were contraband.

"What are these for?" he asked.

I just shrugged, not bothering to explain that they were readers I used to teach Shawn.

After a few hours of tossing my things about, they left with nothing. Still, I was fuming that they'd used a court order from a judge to turn my place upside down. They were getting more aggressive, and I feared where the harassment would lead.

Later that night, I sat at my typewriter and typed a letter to all the Minneapolis police officers and FBI agents who had been investigating me: "Intelligence is not determined by race. You've underestimated this Black woman. How dare you ruin the lives of innocent people—costing them jobs, ravaging their homes, trampling their civil rights. Leave my friends and family alone! *I will always be ten steps ahead of you.*"

The next morning, I walked to the mailbox and popped the letter in. It was gratifying to give voice to my rage, to call those assholes out. I never signed my name. They'd never catch up. They'd never see me coming.

13

THE RETURN

With the police badgering everyone I knew, I left Minneapolis. I hoped the cops would lay off if I was out of reach. I returned to Los Angeles and rented a spacious townhouse with a gourmet kitchen in Encino, near Lake Balboa. It was five minutes from the Jackson compound. When I passed their gate in my new, black 911 Porsche Carrera, I laughed.

I loved being back in LA during the magical mideighties. I enjoyed driving to the beach and up into the canyons. I resumed my friendship with Natalie Trundy, made the rounds at my favorite jazz clubs, and went to hot spots, like Carlos and Charlies. There were celebrities and rich people everywhere. I met Stevie Wonder and Richard Pryor through my dad's friend H. B. Barnum. Many people had money, and I liked that I didn't stand out. If anyone wondered about my income, I implied that I came from a rich family with a father who "owned movie theaters" or was simply "a successful businessman." But most people didn't ask. It was enough that I fit in. Still, while I was enjoying myself from time to time, I was focused on my transactions and staying ten steps ahead of anyone who might be tracking me.

Shortly after I moved to Los Angeles, Livilla followed. Since we were in the same city, instead of using Randall, I worked out a plan to collect the money myself. Once a week, I booked a different hotel or motel room under a fake name. After leaving a key for Livilla at the front desk, I called her from a pay phone to provide the location and room number. I never let her know in advance where it would be. This way, she wouldn't have time to set me up or let others know where I was. I also wanted to be there before her to surveil her entry and exit.

I watched from a distance with binoculars to be sure she was alone for her drop. She drove a green Cadillac that was always freshly washed. She was dark-skinned and shorter and thicker than I imagined and wore big wigs with blunt bangs that nearly covered her eyes.

When she left the drop, I waited about fifteen minutes or more before returning to the room. If the drop was at a hotel, I sat in the lobby and pretended to read a newspaper while I waited to see if there was any suspicious activity. If it was at a motel, I observed the room door from my car and watched cars pulling into the parking lot.

Once the coast was clear, I entered the room and looked under the bed, where Livilla would usually stash a suitcase filled with $300,000–$500,000. In case someone outside the room was watching me, I never used Livilla's luggage. Instead, I moved the money to my backpack. I then put the room key on the dresser and walked out. For the better part of two years, we used this system to perfection.

Randall moved to Los Angeles and asked to start doing transactions again. I went to visit him. He lived in a beautiful house in West Hollywood. I was happy to see he was doing well, but soon I realized ten or fifteen other men lived there as well.

"We all chip in a bit, but an A-list actor pays the mortgage," Randall bragged while making me tea in the kitchen.

"Who is it?" I probed.

"He shall remain nameless. He's super straight and has kids and everything, but he loves the boys, if you know what I mean."

We giggled and sipped our tea. I spent the rest of the day at the house with Randall and his many roommates. All they did all day was drink, do drugs, and have sex. It was a wild house.

"Slow down," I tried to tell him before I left. "You can go too far and kill yourself with all these drugs and drinking."

"Leave me alone," Randall said. "I'm fine. I'm having the time of my life."

After leaving the house, I knew there was no way Randall could come back to work for me.

Livilla begged to meet me in person, but I resisted, determined to maintain the firewall. Still, she kept after me. "Come on, Tanya. You're like my daughter. Why can't we get together?" she asked over the phone after one of our exchanges. "Some of my people want to meet you. They're well-connected and want to see you happy. They want to protect you."

"No. I don't need any protection," I insisted. "I'm only dealing with you. I don't want to know anyone else."

"Your call. But if you ever need anything, we'll take care of it."

This conversation occurred quite frequently, and eventually, I popped up at her house. She lived in Inglewood, which was about thirty minutes from my house without traffic. After parking outside her quaint, Spanish revival bungalow, I knocked on her door a few times, but there was no response. I recognized the Cadillac in the driveway.

"Livilla," I shouted toward the front picture window, just loud enough for her to hear. "It's me, Tanya. Are you in there?"

I heard a click at the door, and it swung open. Livilla was standing there looking surprised. She smiled, pulled me over the threshold, and hugged me tight. Something about her smile and how she hugged me felt familial, like she was my aunt and I'd known her my whole life. Right then, it dawned on me how long it had been since I'd seen my mother. We kept in contact via a beeper I mailed her. The distance was wearing me down. I was lonely, and Livilla's smile and hug brought all that out.

"Tanya!" Livilla shrieked. "I was standing inside the door watching you and wondering who was on my doorstep. I thought you were a Jehovah's Witness or something." She started laughing and led me into the house. "Look at you. You're so beautiful I could eat you up! Get in here."

Her presence was imposing, but her voice was soft, audible on the phone but hard to hear in person without straining.

Contrasting her flawless logistics and accounting, her house was cluttered with knickknacks and pictures dating back to black-and-white. Her fancy living room furniture was covered in plastic. Even with the curtains open, the place was still dim. I preferred orderly, bright spaces, and I immediately felt claustrophobic.

"You want something to eat? Drink? There's a rib spot around the corner," she offered, but I declined. We sat in her living room and talked about life in Los Angeles and how amazing it was that we were making money together.

"I'm so glad you came by to meet in real life. See—I don't bite. Well, maybe if provoked," she joked. "Now, don't you become a stranger again. Hear?"

After the visit, I kept my guard up, still preferring hotel handoffs, but now and then, I would drop by Livilla's work at a college in central LA—her office cover job—for a chat or a quick bite and one of her hugs.

Things were going smoothly in LA, but missing my family and friends and wanting to witness the birth of Taryn's first child, I decided to go back to Minneapolis for an extended visit.

I was lucky to make it home in time for Taryn's delivery. I was by her side at the hospital when my nephew, Aiden, was born. He was sweet and cuddly. I held him and felt like he was my baby too.

"Hey, handsome boy. I'm your Aunt Tanya. I love you," I whispered to him.

Even more excited than me, my parents were over the moon about having a grandson. They got things ready for Aiden in their home. It was nice seeing them happy by stealing moments with Aiden and helping Taryn get adjusted to motherhood.

Though my parents were thrilled that I was home, they were worried sick. After my welcome-home dinner and some cuddle time with Aiden, they pressed me for updates, questions, and demands.

"The cops searched our home," Dad revealed.

"They keep asking us all these questions about you," Mom added.

Without waiting for me to respond, Dad went on, "You're going to get caught if you keep this up. You'll be in trouble so deep that I won't be able to help."

"You can still turn this around. Just get on the right side of the law, and everything will be fine." Mom advised me with tears in her eyes. "Why can't you just do that? Is something wrong? Do we need to help you?"

Hating their disappointment, I tried to reassure them. "No. I'm fine. I'm perfectly safe. Everything is under control. I promise."

It was all true. Business was good. But I knew that wasn't what my parents wanted. Getting back at those officers, surpassing every limitation they spoke over me, was my new agenda. I couldn't just quit.

One night, I went out dancing with some of my old friends. I bumped into Wesley, a guy from my neighborhood who went to school with my brother Mason. He was with the best-looking man I'd ever seen. He was about five ten, dark, and so handsome he nearly looked pretty. He was expensively dressed in a silk shirt and flowy slacks and had a gleaming gold ring on his pinky finger. I hadn't really connected with anyone romantically since my blowup with Shawn. It was time for a change and to have a little fun.

"Who's you're friend?" I asked Wesley when the guy went to mingle.

"J.D." he answered.

"He's handsome. What does he do?"

"He's big money. A businessman with real estate in Houston," Wesley revealed.

"Can you introduce us?"

"Sure thing." Wesley grabbed my hand.

"I'm J.D.," he said as he held out his hand to shake mine. He had a sophisticated air I'd seen more often in LA than Minneapolis. "I'm pleased to meet such a divine lady. What brings you to Minneapolis?"

"I'm from here," I said. "I live in LA now. I'm back visiting my family."

"Well, while you're here, maybe we can get to know each other. What do you like to do?"

"I love riding motorcycles," I said. "I have a Ninja."

It immediately piqued his interest. "I have a VMAX."

"Wow! That's a muscle bike."

"We should go riding together. Are you available tomorrow?" he asked.

"Sounds great," I said, though I was storing my Ninja in my parents' garage to keep it out of sight from investigators.

"How's Lake Calhoun? Noon?"

"I'd love that." I said, mentally shuffling my return plans. I was supposed to leave for Los Angeles the next day. "By the way, is J.D. your real name?"

He smiled and said, "I'm Jake Dixon."

"Perfect."

I committed the name to memory and ran a check on him on the computer when I got home. In addition to the banks, I'd gotten good at accessing mainframes for government agencies and could do basic research on individuals using their names and other personal information.

Jake Dixon was thirty-two. He didn't have a job or any record of previous employment. His name didn't pull up any property or business holdings in Minneapolis, Houston, or anywhere else in the country. Accessing the DMV portal, I discovered his name was associated with several residences in St. Paul, Houston, and Las Vegas. Most interesting, by cross-checking his addresses, I discovered that they were all rented by women. Researching them, I learned they were all beautiful. Like me, J.D. had secrets. Somehow, that was an icebreaker that made him more relatable.

We met at Lake Calhoun. He brought his brother, Phillip. The three of us went riding all over the Twin Cities and lakes. We stopped for lunch at an outside diner in Uptown. I was about to pull out my cash to pay, but J.D. grabbed the bill.

"I got it," he said.

His offer was refreshing. I was used to paying for the guys I dated. When we finished eating, we set out on the bikes again. J.D. pushed ahead of us, working the curves in the road like a pro. He was fearless and free on his bike. I liked what I saw.

J.D. asked me out again. Over the next few days, we spent a lot of time together, riding bikes, going out to eat, and talking.

I enjoyed being around J.D. We respected each other and had lots of fun.

After hanging out for a few weeks, I wanted to show him how much I appreciated his company. After he mentioned that he once dreamed of having his own boat, I gave him $100,000 to buy a custom-made speedboat. When the boat was completed, we took it for a spin. J.D. was elated. Driving the boat, I saw his inner child come out. It was magical seeing another person live out his dream.

One weekend, I invited my lawyer, Julio Phillips, and his wife, Trish, out to meet J.D. I took them to Lord Fletcher's, an upscale waterside restaurant with fine cuisine and specialty cocktails on Lake Minnetonka. It was owned by Dad's friend Bob Naegele, and we didn't have to pay for anything. At dinner, J.D. easily won Julio and Trish over with his wit and charm.

After dinner, we took Julio and Trish out on the speedboat. J.D. took command of the boat and raced around the lake, crashing into waves as we held on tight.

"Slow down, you crazy man!" I yelled, but J.D. kept going. I was afraid for my life but laughing the whole time.

One day, J.D. and I were riding in his Mercedes when the police pulled us over.

"Officer, can you tell me what I did wrong?" J.D. asked, surprised by what was happening. He wasn't speeding and hadn't violated any law.

"Just give me your license and registration," the officer demanded, though he kept his eyes on me.

After a few minutes, the officer handed the documents back to J.D. and told us to slow down.

"What was that about?" J.D. said, annoyed.

I was silent but felt I knew what the stop was about. The cops wanted me to know they were tailing me and knew where I was. I left Minneapolis later that day.

Back in LA full-time, Livilla and I resumed our transactions, and money was coming in.

I was shocked to get a call from Julio Phillips, one of the few people who had my real phone number.

"Tanya, they're about to charge you for bank and wire fraud," he said.

"What?" I couldn't believe it. "I thought they didn't have the evidence."

"They believe they do now, but I haven't yet seen the discovery."

"What's going to happen?"

"You have to come back and surrender," he told me. "If you don't, they'll obtain a warrant for your arrest, which means they can lock you up until the trial."

Oh my god.

"So, fly home, and come straight to my office from the airport. I've already negotiated with the AUSA. I'll take you right downtown to get booked, and a bondsman will be waiting to bail you out."

"Can we fight this?" I asked Julio.

"Absolutely. You are represented by the best," he said.

14

THE TWINS

When I landed in Minneapolis, I hailed a cab and headed to Julio's office as planned. Halfway there, I heard the head-splitting wail of sirens and saw the flashing of colored lights behind the cab.

"What's going on?" the driver complained to me before pulling over.

I turned to see a dozen cop cars in formation behind the cab.

Not knowing what was going on, the driver said, "I'm sorry about this. I don't know what they want."

My mind raced. How did they know where to find me? Were they staking out the airport? Had they wiretapped Julio's phone? Did the prosecution tip them off about my arrival?

The cops were out of their cruisers and slowly approaching the cab with their weapons drawn. It looked like they were trying to take down a major crime boss.

"Tanya Smith, you're under arrest!" one of the officers beside my window announced.

Alarmed, the driver looked back at me.

"I need to call my lawyer," I said. "We had a deal."

The cops acted as if they didn't hear me. I guess they were determined to deny me the dignity of surrender and to publicly humiliate me.

Within seconds, they pulled me out of the car and slapped handcuffs on me.

"Where are you taking me?" I asked as they put me into a cruiser. No one responded.

I found out later when we arrived at the FBI building in downtown St. Paul. There, they fingerprinted me and stuck me in an interrogation room where they asked questions that seemed banal, like "What's your favorite color?"; "Do you drink tea?"; "Have you ever taken an IQ test?"; "What TV shows do you watch?"; and "What books do you read?"

Between the inane questions, they told me that if I talked, it could lessen the charges against me.

"I need to call my lawyer," I repeated until they listened.

Julio, who'd been waiting for me at his office, was hopping mad.

"What the fuck? You got arrested?" He shouted over the line. "Those lying sons of bitches. Sit tight. I'm coming right down to get you out."

Julio arrived. "This judge is a sack. They're setting your bail at a hundred-thousand dollars," he revealed during our meeting in the interrogation room. "They claim it's because this is a serious charge. But it just feels like there's something more going on. Let me call the AUSA. Don't worry. I'm going to get you out. I'll be right back."

When Julio left, I was placed in what was called the holding tank. It was a bare room with no windows. I was told I could make one phone call.

When I reached my parents and told them I was being held, they were distraught. They didn't want me to spend one night in jail, and Dad started making calls to his powerful friends. One of them was Joe Goldberg, a bondsman whose office was right across the street from the Hennepin County jail. When he heard that my bail was set at $100,000, he called Julio to offer help, saying, "Smitty is such a great guy." Usually, defendants pay 10 percent of the bail in cash and put up collateral—like a house—against the rest, but Joe waived the collateral and asked for $5,000, which Julio paid out of a slush fund I'd set up.

When I was free to go, Julio dropped me at my parents' house.

"We warned you; we told you to stop," Mom said. "And now this. The FBI? Are you really a criminal? Do you want to spend the rest of your life in jail?"

Dad focused on comforting her. "Honey, don't get yourself too upset. You know it isn't good for you," he said and then turned to me. "You can't keep doing this to your mother and me. We've already been through too much."

They were dealing with Taryn's drug use, Ryan's illness, and now me.

"I'm not trying to do anything to anyone. The FBI is coming for me!" I exclaimed, outraged.

"What do they want? What are they charging you with?" Mom asked.

I told them.

"What? You robbed a bank?" Dad asked.

"I didn't rob a bank. I didn't rob anyone," I replied. "Listen—I'll explain it all one day, but right now, I have to figure this all out if I'm going to stay out of jail."

"OK," Mom said. "Let us know how we can help. We're still your parents. We love you and will always support you."

Over the next few weeks, Julio and I scrutinized every angle of the charges against me—one for bank fraud and three for attempted bank fraud. They referenced transactions made when I was starting out. The sums seemed minuscule—basically several thousand dollars here and there—compared to the money I was moving recently. Of course, the size of the smaller withdrawals didn't make them any more legal.

Trying to come up with a strategy, I spent days holed up in the University of Minnesota Law Library, reading case law and winning defenses. Julio, the seasoned pro, certainly had the skill to craft his own strategy, but I wasn't convinced that his ideas would work, and I had to take ownership because it was my future at stake. Those legal texts were thick with nearly incomprehensible jargon. As when I learned about computers, I meticulously looked up words in the dictionary and reread page after page until I understood the cases and taught myself how to Shepardize them.

The charges rested on the testimonies of some former runners and some bank employees who claimed they had personally seen me arrange transfers and make pickups, which was impossible. I never once did a pickup and always worked alone while organizing transfers. The witnesses were either lying or confused. It got me thinking about the courtroom instruction "beyond a reasonable doubt." In a criminal trial, the judge tells jurors not to find the defendant guilty if there's another reasonable explanation for the evidence presented. "Beyond a reasonable doubt," in my case, meant that no one but me could have moved the money.

But in my case, eyewitness testimony was unreliable because I have an identical twin sister. No one who didn't know us well could tell us apart. If the witnesses couldn't be sure that it was me they'd seen and not Taryn, that would constitute reasonable doubt. Plus, Taryn had a potential motive, a history of drug use, defined by the constant need for cash.

When I presented this as a possible strategy to Julio he was doubtful. "The jury is never going to buy that," he told me.

"It will work," I insisted. "I'm the client, and it's my life, so it's my decision. I'm paying you to do as I ask."

Julio wasn't happy, but he had no choice.

It was easier to persuade Taryn. Being twins, we had an indelible bond, even if our lives had diverged. I knew she'd do anything to help, but I had to make sure she felt comfortable.

I brought along my research materials to show her the overriding importance of reasonable doubt.

"We hear that phrase on TV, but it's for real. It means that the jury has to be 100 percent convinced I did it," I explained.

"So you're saying that since we're twins, the witnesses can't be positive who they saw. That's clever." Then she looked worried. "Will I get arrested?"

"No, because the witnesses and evidence say it's me. The Feds can't suddenly change the evidence to point to you. And the witnesses can't tell us apart to say who really did what."

"How does that affect you?"

"If a juror believes 99 percent that I did it, but there's a 1 percent chance that I might not have, they can't convict me."

"Wow. I get it," she said. "So, what do I need to do to help?"

"Just leave town during the trial," I told her. "They won't be able to subpoena you to testify if you're gone."

"Got it. Let's do it!" she said.

I went to trial in late April 1985. It was a cool spring day. I wanted to look respectable and proper and wore a white blouse, black skirt, sheer hose, and black pumps. Apart from my lawyer, I was alone. Afraid the stress of the trial would be too much for them, I told my parents to stay home.

When I entered the courtroom, I was surprised to see it was pretty packed. The rows of seats were filled with FBI agents and journalists. Nearly everyone was white. They all stared at me as I walked to take my seat beside Julio. I could tell they were curious about me. They watched how I walked, how I sipped water, how I talked to Julio.

"Don't pay them any mind. They're just attempting to try the case in their minds," Julio said.

The jury looked the same—a lot of white people.

After an hour of courtroom preparation where the judge was seated and the jurors and spectators were provided instruction, Assistant US Attorney Horace Fitzgerald, chief attorney for the criminal division and the toughest AUSA in the office, laid out the case against me.

"The gist of all the charges," he said, "is that the defendant arranged for acquaintances to pick up cash at various banks where she had induced them to believe that there had been a wire transfer to support the payment, but there had not been such a transfer."

Fitzgerald detailed the amounts of money involved: $6,500 at First Bank Grand, St. Moses; $4,000 at Southwest Bank of Edina, Minnesota; and $3,000 at First Bank, Minneapolis. Because I'd masterminded those pickups, they were charged as attempted bank fraud. The single, more serious charge of actual bank fraud applied to a withdrawal from St. Paul's American National Bank, which they claimed I planned and then collected myself. It was nerve-racking to hear.

The jurors were glaring at me. It got worse when Fitzgerald started calling witnesses—bank employees and runners Randall and Terrell recruited. They all corroborated Fitzgerald's claims. By then, the jurors' eyes were fixed on the AUSA, without even a peek at me. I felt sure they had decided I was guilty.

Fitzgerald's attitude also stoked my anxiety. He seemed confident, even cocky, in his presentation. He was white and fit. He looked like a former college frat boy. When he looked at me, it was with triumph and contempt, as if to say, "You're going down."

When it was my turn to testify, the reporters sprang into action, snapping pictures as I took the stand. The spectators got loud, and the judge, an older white man with a head of gray hair, banged his gavel.

"Settle down, everyone," he said. "This is a court of law, not a television studio."

Once I sat down, Julio walked me through the preliminaries before asking, "Tanya Smith, are you guilty of these crimes?"

"I am not," I told him.

"Do you know who is?"

"My twin sister, Taryn," I said softly.

A hubbub ensued. People whispered, "She has a twin?" The AUSA, caught off guard by that piece of information, looked like his eyes could pop out of his head. The reporters were writing furiously on their notepads, comparing information.

"Order in the court!" the judge demanded. "I will have order in my courtroom." He banged the gavel again.

When everyone hushed, I started to cry, surprising even myself, as I testified, "My sister is a drug addict. She did this because of her drug addiction. I don't like drugs. They make her do things she shouldn't do."

I told the court how Taryn and I were often mistaken for each other. "People get us mixed up all the time," I said. "That's been the case since we were children."

As I spoke, the jurors peered into my eyes.

The obvious next step in the trial would have been to put Taryn on the stand, but the court was informed that "she could not be found." Instead, I insisted that Julio recall the witnesses to demonstrate how few people could tell us apart. I told him to ask them if they were sure which one I was.

While pointing to me, Julio asked each witness, "Are you sure that's Tanya and not Taryn?

One by one, they looked at me and said, "I'm not sure. I can't tell them apart."

One witness who would have been able to tell the difference was Shawn.

When he was called to testify, I was nervous, wondering if he'd cut a deal or wanted to get even with me. He wouldn't even glance in my direction as he took his seat beside the judge.

When Fitzgerald questioned him, each time, he responded with three words: "I don't know." When Fitzgerald got annoyed and pressed him, Shawn switched up his wording to "I don't remember." After thirty minutes of this, Fitzgerald was done with Shawn, and Julio had no reason to cross-examine him.

The next day, Fitzgerald strutted into the courtroom, practically crowing. He'd learned that I have a small, almost imperceptible, scar on my forehead, which I got when I fell off my bike when I was ten years old. Two tellers from American National Bank testified that they'd seen the scar, proving the person who picked up the money was me. In fact, it wasn't. It had been Taryn, who was visibly pregnant at the time.

When Julio questioned the tellers, he asked, "Was the woman who came into the bank pregnant?" None of them could say whether that was true with any certainty.

Before closing arguments, I told Julio, "You must make the jurors understand reasonable doubt. They have to be 100 percent sure it was me to vote guilty. They can't do it if they're just 99.9 percent sure. It has to be 100 percent."

AUSAs don't divulge the legal standard to juries, because their conviction rate would drop. Judges share the information, but they don't break it down for the jury, everyday citizens, to wholly understand it. In that way, it seemed the judges were somehow in bed with the prosecution. My freedom was in Julio's more-than-capable hands.

He said, "I know, Tanya. I know what to do."

In his closing argument, Julio repeated my explanation of reasonable doubt word for word. As he spoke, the jurors leaned in and seemed to fully get it.

Not long after the lawyers rested their cases, the jury was sent off to deliberate, and court was adjourned until they returned with a verdict.

"Whatever you're feeling, whatever you think is about to happen, let it go," Julio said to me as we walked out. "Anything is possible. I've learned not to predict an outcome."

I tried to remain calm. If I were found guilty, I would face years behind bars. Considering this possibility, my heart began racing, and I felt lightheaded.

The jury did not return with a verdict that day.

Julio reached out to shed light on what might be happening. Over the phone, he said, "Short deliberations usually mean guilty. Longer ones mean there are some issues between jurors—some wanting to acquit and some wanting to convict. Be patient. We will get word soon."

The next day, there was still no word. I couldn't sleep and was extremely nervous. I lay in bed for hours, only leaving to go to the bathroom or down for dinner when my mom came up to demand that I eat.

More days passed.

Finally, Julio called and said, "Tanya, get down here. The jury has reached a verdict."

The courtroom was full. All eyes were on me.

I showed no emotion when the judge said, "Can the defendant please stand?"

I stood, and he looked at the foreman, saying, "Has the jury reached a verdict."

The foreman said, "Yes, your honor, we have."

I expected him to keep talking, but he stalled, and those seconds of waiting for him to read the verdict felt like years. A furious storm of emotion raged inside of me. It only subsided when the foreman read the verdict. On all charges, the jury voted *not guilty*.

Later, the foreman reported that they "had five different charges . . . we are dealing with a set of identical twins, and when that is presented to a jury, you need to show some pretty conclusive evidence that it was one and not the other who committed the crimes. We just feel like we did not see that conclusive evidence."

In the pandemonium that followed, Julio and I hugged, whispering to each other, "We did it." When I turned back around, the judge hit me with an unwavering stare, like an x-ray.

AUSA Fitzgerald came over to me and Julio, looking furious, but said, "Congratulations." He shook Julio's hand. He turned to me and said, "Tanya Smith, job well done."

He lowered his voice and said with venom, "Don't think this is over. You're not home free. We're going to get you."

15

THE CLIFF HOUSE

Legally, I was free to go live out the rest of my life however and wherever I chose. But after I was released, the Minneapolis police department and the FBI stepped up their antagonizing surveillance of me and everyone I loved. They continued to stake out my parents' home. Whenever I went out, they tailed me. If I was driving, they'd pull me over just for the hell of it. If I was on my motorcycle, a prowl car would creep behind me. If I went out to eat, a cop would follow me into the restaurant. They were putting pressure on me and wanted to see me sweat. They wanted to make me pay. In addition to outsmarting their banking system, there I was, a Black woman who'd now outsmarted a federal AUSA's office that had a 95 percent conviction rate.

One day after going for a ride on my Ninja, I returned to my parents' house to find everything in disarray and my mom and dad, both crestfallen, in the middle of the mess, trying to clean it up. I got down on the floor with them and started picking up papers.

"We can't keep living like this," Mom said. "It isn't right. When will it stop?"

"I'll contact one of my buddies at the precinct and ask if he can get them to back off," Dad said.

"We've already done that. They won't stop." Mom looked at me. "They want you. They are not going to stop until they get you."

"I know, Mom. There's nothing I can do about it, though," I said.

"Something's got to give. You can't work without them harassing your employer. You can't be with your family without them searching their homes. You can't even hang out with your friends. No one wants to be followed and stalked by the cops."

Mom was right. All of my friends had backed away from me. "Tanya, I'm scared to hang out with you," they'd say, or, "I'd rather you didn't call," because they worried about phone taps. The cops actually did a sweep at my neighbor's house, where they found my black Corvette hidden in the garage.

"We're worried. We can handle the cops coming in here and searching our home, but we don't want to find out where this is going with you," Dad said.

I trembled, knowing what Dad meant by "where this is going." Minneapolis was nothing but a glorified small town. The police could spirit me away in the dead of night and then barely pretend to be curious about how I wound up in a creek somewhere. My parents could clean up a house, but they couldn't stand the thought of identifying a body.

When I was being tailed one afternoon while driving a rental car home from the grocery store, I pulled over on the side of the road. I sat there waiting for something to happen.

Finally, the officer tailing me got out of her cruiser and approached my car. It was a white female officer I'd seen before.

When I lowered my window, she said, "What did you do? At every roll call, all we hear is 'Tanya Smith.'"

"Really?" I asked. "Why?"

"You tell me. With so much crime, how come they're hot for you? Weren't you found not guilty?"

I shrugged.

She looked off like she was contemplating what she was about to say or making sure another cruiser wasn't observing us. "Look—you better watch out," she said. "You aren't safe here." She went back to her cruiser and pulled away.

Sitting in the car, I realized I had to get out of Minneapolis right away. I started thinking about how I could get out of town undetected. If I booked a flight, they could probably stop me at the airport. At the very least, they'd know my destination. Driving was the only option.

I drove to a pay phone and called the only person I knew who might help me.

"Hello?"

"Hi, J.D."

"Tanya."

"Yes, it's—"

"—good to hear your voice. It's been a while," he said.

"Who you telling?" I asked, and we laughed because I knew he knew what had been going on with me. I was all over the news and in the papers. There was nothing to explain. "I need help."

"Then you've called the right number."

"I need your car," I said.

"OK. Then you have one. Let me know how to get it to you."

"Thank you," I said. "I really appreciate this. I'll pay you back."

As a precaution, I had J.D. drop his car off a few blocks from my parents' house. I was glad I did because, when I turned onto their block, there was a cop car parked at each corner. I waited until sundown, threw some clothes into a small bag, and packed the money I'd collected from various caches into a briefcase. It was slightly over a million dollars.

My parents weren't home, and luckily there was no one to question me as I slipped out the back door. I dashed across the alley behind the house and entered our neighbor's backyard. After crossing the property, I crept to the front yard and looked up and down the street in search of more cop cars. When I saw everything was clear, I ran across the street and padded between two houses to another alley. Carrying the bag and briefcase, I was weighed down and out of breath when I entered the back of another property and exited the front. I finally emerged two blocks away from our home, where the cops were in position.

J.D.'s Mercedes was waiting right where he promised to leave it. I quickly hopped in, threw my stuff in the back seat, pulled the key from under the floor mat, and took off. The car had a big center console sporting a car phone.

When I was an hour out of town, I used J.D.'s phone to call Julio Phillips. I told him about the surveillance, my encounter with the policewoman, and that I was on my way back to LA.

"Tanya, don't run," he said. "We can fight the harassment."

"It's just too much," I explained. "Not just for me but for my parents. With those cops on the corner, for my sister, for my friends . . . the pressure isn't worth it."

"Goddamn cops," Julio said, "You know they're hassling you because you're Black and a genius. They don't even hound murderers like this. I know because I represent really violent and bad people. It's racially motivated intimidation, pure and simple. Let me file a complaint."

"Not this time," I told him. "It's better that I leave."

The next person I called was my mother.

"Tanya, leave all this mess alone," she pleaded. "Just come home and go back to school."

When I told her that I couldn't right now, she cried. After we hung up, I did too.

Finally, I called J.D. to thank him for the car and told him that I'd call when I reached my destination. "Then you'll know what a lifesaver this has been."

Minneapolis to the West Coast is about a thirty-hour drive. With the Los Angeles skyline streaked a pink and calming gold, I reached Van Nuys on Sepulveda Boulevard and was heading into Sherman Oaks when suddenly the car slowed down. I pumped the accelerator, but nothing happened. I managed to steer the car to the curb as it rolled to a stop and died.

There was a strong mechanical smell of friction and smoldering wires. I was too tired and could barely react. It wasn't until I noticed smoke leaching out from under the hood that I jumped out of the car, half panicked. There were no flames, and the smoke subsided.

I grabbed my bag and briefcase and stood on the curb to catch my breath. As a wave of exhaustion hit me, I realized that my only choice was to walk and find a motel where I could rest.

I was on a busy commercial street. Early risers, morning joggers, and workers were out beginning their day.

As I approached Ventura Boulevard, I spotted a hotel.

I checked in, went into my room, and collapsed on the bed. Before I closed my eyes, I called the Mercedes dealership in Encino to describe the disabled car and asked them to pick it up.

"I'll be in tomorrow to talk about the repairs and buy a brand-new one," I said. Even if I didn't have to replace J.D.'s car, the comfort of the ride over those long, grueling hours had sold me on the brand.

I resumed my Los Angeles life in a black, sporty two-seater Mercedes-Benz that I bought straight off the showroom floor. J.D.'s car, it turned out, could be saved. Its engine had blown out because I didn't realize that, on such a long drive, I had to top off the water and oil. "It was bone dry," the mechanic said. "I'm amazed it didn't conk out sooner. You were lucky."

I flew J.D. to Los Angeles in first class. In case I was being followed by federal agents, instead of coming to my place, J.D. stayed with his friends Bradley and Maurice in Pomona. Since their place was an hour's commute from me, even in light traffic, I checked into the nearby Century Plaza Hotel. In the parking lot of the ABC Entertainment Center, I presented J.D. with his thank-you gift, a bright-red Ferrari GTO with a red bow on top. He was thrilled.

"Really, Tanya? You really got this for me?" he kept saying.

"You didn't have to help me," I said. "I just hope you like red."

"I love red. You done good."

A few weeks later, after J.D. had taken the car back to Minneapolis, he called me frantic.

"I was leaving my apartment, and these strange guys who always dress like utility workers and are set up in an empty apartment down the hall walked by staring at me," he said. "It was so weird. Then I got a knock at the door, and a guy introduced himself as a Secret Service agent. He started asking questions about you. He asked if we are dating and if I knew where you were."

"Secret Service? Why would they want information about me?" I asked with my thoughts spinning. The Secret Service sounded like a big deal. "Don't they protect the president?"

J.D. said the agent revealed that the Secret Service also conducts financial investigations to secure the integrity of the country's currency. Since they believed I defrauded the banking system, the FBI pulled the Secret Service in to investigate me.

"More help and intelligence," I said.

"Before he left, he gave me a warning. He said, 'If you know what's best for you, if you know or hear anything about Tanya, let us know. It may be best to keep your distance from her if you don't want trouble,'" J.D. recalled.

I was stunned into silence. The Secret Service investigating me made me feel cornered, more alone than ever before.

"I don't think they know you left Minneapolis. They seem to think you're still here and still with me," J.D. said. "I think that's why they set up a surveillance operation here." His voice was growing more grave. "Listen. I don't—"

I cut him off. "You don't have to say it, J.D. You've helped me enough," I said. I knew this was a lot for him. He liked ease and fun, and being with the woman Minneapolis's media had labeled "America's Most Wanted" was no fun.

Though J.D. and I went our separate ways, I remained friends with Bradley and Maurice. Bradley and I, especially, grew close. As a business owner, he was always looking for new ways to make money. When I opened up about my transactions and everything that happened in Minneapolis, he said his friend Jack could help me move money through Vegas.

"You can wire him any amount, and there won't be any questions, not like at the banks. The casinos just want you to spend the dough. They don't care where it comes from," he said. "Trust me."

Wanting to see if Bradley was right, as a test, I wired $100,000 to Jack in Vegas. I sent $50,000 to MGM and $50,000 to Caesars Palace. Within hours, Bradley was off to the airport to meet Jack for our take. I split the money with Bradley, and over the next few weeks, we made over a million dollars running wires through casinos. We only stopped when Jack's bosses wanted to meet me to see how we could make more money together.

"I don't work with people like that. I don't know them," I told Bradley, who agreed and added that he thought Jack might be connected to the mob in Vegas.

"You get in with them and you'll never get out—not alive." Bradley had said what I was thinking. We decided to cool off with Jack and stop working through the casinos.

Bradley was also an amazing R&B singer. He spent a lot of time working on his music at the same studio as the Deele, an up-and-coming music group he loved. When we started making money in Vegas, he asked me to financially back the group and invited me to the studio to hear them sing.

The Deele included Antonio "L.A." Reid on drums, bassist Kevin "Kayo" Roberson, vocalist/percussionist Darnell "Dee" Bristol, guitarist Steve "Tuck" Walters, and the phenomenal Kenneth Edmonds on vocals.

I had money to fund the Deele and other artists, but it would have led to too much exposure, and I couldn't risk it.

A serial killer was also terrorizing LA County. Known as the Night Stalker, he would break into homes—six in July alone—and rape and brutalize his sleeping, mostly female, victims. Living alone in a big house in Encino, I was terrified, sure that every creak in the floorboards was an intruder. I moved to a gated community of multimillion-dollar homes called Country Estates in Diamond Bar, East Los Angeles County.

The city was built on the site of a vast cattle ranch—one of the largest in the West—and took its name from the ranch's branding symbol, a diamond over a rod. A vestige of its history remained in Diamond Bar's many equestrian centers, where residents boarded horses. I commonly saw people on horseback.

I rented an elegant Tudor-style, four-bedroom house, cantilevered over a hillside, with a magnificent panoramic view of the mountains. On the entry floor were a living and dining room, kitchen, and family room, which had a spiral staircase leading down to my spacious, well-stocked wine cellar. It took me months to decorate the house. I wanted everything to be top of the line, modern, and bespoke. I had imported Moroccan rugs, marble sculptures, custom marble countertops, and glass fixtures. Each time my interior designer presented a collection of new pieces, it reminded me of my mother carefully decorating our home and how much pride she took in keeping everything picture-perfect. It made me feel closer to her.

I also got a smaller place nearby to serve as my office, which is where I kept my computer. Livilla and I reconnected and started doing bigger transactions than before.

"How about moving a million," she proposed during one of my lunchtime pop-ins at her cover job.

"Sure, I can transfer the money, but who could withdraw that much cash?" I'd grown to trust her instincts and her ability to close deals.

"I got just the guy," she said. "He's a big shot at a bank. No one will ask him questions about a big withdrawal."

"Let's do it," I said. I wanted to ask her how she met this person and how she knew many different kinds of people, but I knew not to cross the line. The less I knew about her, the better.

The next day, I moved the money into an account, and Livilla's contact did the withdrawal. Livilla dropped $500,000 for me at a local motel.

Looking to invest the large sums of cash coming in, I started purchasing gold and diamonds. I'd read on the computer that smart investors were buying precious stones and metals. I contacted a jewelry broker to learn the ropes and then I started wiring money directly to dealers in Antwerp, Belgium, for gold and Botswana for diamonds. They'd then ship the gold and diamonds back to me in the US.

One time, I got a shipment of diamonds delivered to a broker. When I got the box, I was excited and opened it in my Porsche in the parking lot. Inside, I found a handful of uncut, D-color, internally flawless diamonds. They looked like frozen teardrops, exquisite and alluring.

"Excuse me!" someone shouted.

I looked up to find a middle-aged, puffy Black security guard at my car door. I must've looked as surprised as I felt because he apologized for scaring me.

"I'm sorry. I just wanted to let you know that your lights are on," he said.

"Thank you," I said, switching off the headlights.

I drove home and stashed the diamonds in a lockbox with the rest of my treasures.

My investments would continue to diversify.

After closing another big transaction, Livilla asked, "Can you get cars?"

"Yes," I replied, remembering how I bought my black Corvette via wire transfer when I was still in Minneapolis. "You thinking luxury cars?"

"Yes. Let's try a Rolls. I have contacts in New York and Florida. They can do pickups there."

After that, I used bank accounts to wire funds to dealers to purchase Rolls-Royces, Lamborghinis, Aston Martins, and Ferraris. All of the purchases were easy, with no flags or questions asked. Livilla and I gave the cars to friends and connections. I didn't keep one for myself, because it was safer to pay in cash and have legitimate paperwork. Aside from the black Mercedes from the Encino dealership, I bought myself a red Ferrari Testarossa and a super sporty Aston Martin.

The Ferrari was a definite asset in nightlife. The best velvet-rope clubs had gatekeeping doormen to filter the clientele. I'd pull up in the Ferrari dressed in runway couture, hand my keys to the valet, drop $100 bills on him and the doorman, and then sweep into the club, leaving those waiting in line whispering, "Who is she?"

In the late '80s, the clubs in Los Angeles were heavy on techno and house music. People danced until they dripped with sweat and snorted cocaine right there on the dance floor before dancing some more.

I often encountered famous men, many of whom hit on me. While I enjoyed the attention, I never took them up on it, figuring that all they wanted was novelty. Male celebrities felt entitled to sex with whoever caught their eye, and plenty of women were happy to oblige.

Once, I was dancing at a velvet-rope club on the Sunset Strip with my friend Amelia. She was beautiful and always had celebrity men salivating over her. A Black comedian who'd had a top comedy special and then turned into an A-list actor asked his security to bring her into VIP, where he was. I went with her since we were together. He ordered bottles of champagne and treated us very well.

At the end of the night, she pulled me to the bathroom where girls were doing lines of cocaine on the sink counter and said, "He invited me to a hotel. I'm going."

"Girl, no. Don't be so easy. You know how these guys are," I said, but really I could tell it was no use. She'd been clinging to him all night and loved all the attention she was getting for being in VIP.

"No. This is different," she said. "I can feel it. The way he's looking at me. He really likes me. A girl knows, Tanya."

She went to a hotel with him, and they slept together. After spending two nights with the comedian, she referred to him as her boyfriend.

"Really? You think he's your *boyfriend?*" I asked, repeating the word so she could hear how ridiculous it sounded on her tongue.

"Oh yes," she gleefully confirmed. "Look—he gave me this gold chain."

I fingered the beautiful rope and smiled to let her off the hook.

Their affair went on for two more days and then . . . *poof* . . . he disappeared. She never heard from him again. She was confused, but I wasn't surprised. It wasn't a big deal for him to purchase her a necklace. It was lunch money to him. Since I had my own cash, none of that impressed me.

I enjoyed hanging out with my friends Bradley and Maurice. Since they knew about my operation, I didn't have to worry about them getting suspicious about how much money I was spending and snooping around. Carmen, one of Bradley's girl-friends, became a runner. She was an airline stewardess and could easily do pickups in faraway cities.

One night, Maurice and I went out to a club called the Gas House in West Covina. I always parked my Ferrari right out front. On the dance floor, I spotted a guy who was really working it—swiveling, twisting and turning, gyrating like a gymnast. He was already sweating. I liked guys who danced with cool, smooth control, and he was not my style. But in his skin-tight jeans with his white T-shirt clinging to his well-muscled chest, he was certainly sexy. With his mustache and shiny, loose curls on his head, he looked like Philip Michael Thomas, who played Detective Rico Tubbs on *Miami Vice*.

Maurice noticed me watching him. "Oh, you like the pretty boys," he teased.

I ignored him and managed to catch the pretty boy's eye, but he quickly looked away. Most men I sought the attention of easily flirted back.

"Maurice," I said, "please go ask that guy if he'll come and talk to me."

Maurice went over to the guy. I watched as they chatted. The guy glanced at me a few times as Maurice whispered in his ear. Seeming displeased, he shook his head, and Maurice started walking back.

"He's not interested," Maurice said, baffled.

"Really?" I laughed, surprised. I knew I looked good. I knew I could get any guy in the club. Why was he playing hard to get? A challenge? I found it irresistible.

"Forget it," Maurice said when he saw the intrigued look on my face. "There's all kinds of guys here. Some look better than him."

"Not to me," I told him. I was locked in. "Go back over there and make him interested. At least get his phone number."

"Tanya, leave him alone. You're wasting your time. He isn't interested."

Just then, I noticed that the guy seemed to be saying good night.

"Maurice, quick! Go talk to him. He's leaving," I said.

"Come on, Tanya! Stop!"

"I'll bet you a thousand bucks that you can't get his phone number."

"What!" Maurice laughed. "You can't be serious."

"You heard me."

He took the bet and caught the guy at the door. Maurice grabbed his shoulder and whispered something in his ear while pointing at me. The pretty boy quickly stopped in his tracks and turned to look at me, his eyes suddenly widening with interest. I started nodding along to whatever Maurice was saying in his ear. Then he took the pen and paper Maurice held in his hand and wrote something down. When he was done, Maurice gave him dap, and the guy walked out of the club.

Moments later, Maurice, now beaming, returned waving the slip of paper.

"Here's the number!" he said. "And I gave him yours. So, where's my thousand dollars?"

"How did you convince him?" I asked.

"I told him you were the richest girl in here, that he was crazy to say no to you, and that he'd never get the chance to meet a woman like you again."

"You didn't!" I giggled.

"I sure did. Then I said, 'Man, you know that red Ferrari out front? Well, it's hers.'"

The red Ferrari sealed the deal. We had to laugh at that. In plastic Los Angeles, things like that mattered to people. While the sudden interest would've vexed most women, I was tapping into my queenpin energy. If rich celebrity guys could pick up beautiful models for fun on the strip, why couldn't I? I wanted to play.

He called a day later and introduced himself as Jim. His voice wasn't as appealing as I expected, but he made me laugh. He asked me to meet him for lunch at Sizzler. I had never been to Sizzler and said yes.

Everything looks different in daylight, but Jim was the exception. He was just as handsome as when I first spotted him at the Gas House. He wore jeans again but with a collared shirt that had three or four buttons undone. I liked what I could see of his chest. The only obvious difference was that his daytime clothes, while neat and clean, were a little worn—not out of style but on the cusp. His car was also battered. It was a beat-up Pinto, a car they stopped making back in 1980, when they were labeled as firetraps.

Over lunch, he charmed me with his sense of humor.

"LA is cold in the summer and warm in the winter. Sometimes, I have no idea what to wear when I leave the house. I put on flip-flops with a parka. A wool hat with shorts. It's too confusing," he joked.

As Jim and I got to know each other, I found myself laughing harder than I ever had on any date. His sense of irony and timing was impeccable.

"Do you have any children?" I asked.

"Yes. Two," he said proudly, listing names and ages. "But I'm not with their mother. I'm a single man."

"No ex-wife or anything lurking around?"

"Not unless you know something I don't know," Jim joked.

As we continued talking, I learned that Jim also didn't have a job. He spent most of his time at local gambling houses in Pomona Valley and San Bernardino. He preferred gambling in Vegas but didn't have enough cash to play to win big.

At twenty-five, I'd never been to a casino, but I admitted it sounded fun.

"We're going to have a lot of fun together," Jim said. "You have to meet my mom. She's going to love you."

"Really?" I said, amazed. We were on our first date and Jim already wanted to introduce me to his mother. It felt like high praise.

We hung together regularly. He took me to a few gambling houses in Pomona to roll dice. He said I was sure to bring him good luck. He was in his element, but it wasn't my scene. There were older, unsavory men, drunks, and people talking a lot of crap that could lead to violence. Jim promised things would be better if we ever made it to Vegas.

*   *   *

Each time Jim and I stepped out together, I couldn't help but note the difference between my couture and top labels and his uniform of jeans, a shirt, and the same pair of tattered Converse All-Stars. I'd really begun to like him and was enjoying a Pygmalion fantasy of outfitting this beautiful man. Livilla and I had a lot of dough rolling in. I could drop a million on Jim over lunch and move on to the next guy. It would be a fun project.

I started by asking, "What's your favorite car?"

"I like the one you have, the Ferrari Testarossa."

"Oh, and what's your favorite car color?"

"I like red, just like yours."

"So if you could have any car, you'd pick a red Ferrari like mine?"

"I love your car," he oozed. "I've always loved Ferraris, and I'm amazed to know someone who drives one."

"Well, let's go buy one for you," I said.

Jim got quiet and said, "No. No way you're buying me a Ferrari." He was in total disbelief and remained so even after we reached the Ferrari dealership and purchased his new car right off the floor.

As we pulled off the lot, Jim was quiet, like he was in some kind of trance. I'd grown accustomed to throwing large amounts of money around and forgot how unimaginably extravagant it might seem to purchase a Ferrari on a whim.

"Now," I told Jim, "let's go buy you some clothes."

I took him to one of the most exclusive men's shops on Rodeo Drive.

"I've never owned a suit," he said.

"Never? Well, let's get a few then."

We made a rainbow, picking out suits in every color. The tailor took Jim's measurements. Along with the suits, which would be for evenings, I had them bring out some nice shirts, slacks, and blazers for everyday wear, along with coordinating shoes and belts. Everything looked good on him. He was such a stunning man. The king to my queenpin walked out of the store sporting a pair of bespoke, crocodile, Italian shoes.

When we finished shopping, Jim wanted to call his mother. He began their conversation by saying, "Mom, I've met an angel . . . " He went on to describe everything I'd bought him that day, from the car to the shoes. I could hear squeals of excitement coming through the line and then he turned to me. "My mother wants us to come over. OK?" he asked. "She really wants to meet you."

On the way to her house in Rancho Cucamonga, a suburb about an hour from LA, Jim kept thanking me.

"Nobody ever did anything like this for me," he said. "Not even my family. It's so generous that I just can't believe it. It's like a dream, and I don't want to wake up. Why are you so good to me?"

"Because it makes me happy," I told him. "I know I'm lucky and sharing gives me joy."

As we continued driving, Jim told me about his family. He'd grown up in Bakersfield with three siblings. When his father abandoned the family, his mother married a chef.

"My stepdad worked for the school system. He moved our family out to the suburbs and bought us a big house," he said.

"That's great," I said but then Jim revealed that his mother didn't really love her husband.

"She was just trying to survive," he revealed. "Sometimes people have to do whatever to survive.

Jim's mother lived in a modest New England–style ranch. When we arrived, the whole family—including his sister, Ava, whom his mother had invited over—came running out to see the Ferrari. I could see where Jim got his looks. Ava was nice looking, and his mother, Angela, still attractive, clearly had been a great beauty. They all had the same ringleted, jet-black hair. Everyone *ooh*ed and *aah*ed over the car. Jim's mother had tears in her eyes as she said, "You did this for my son?"

Ava, who was a little younger than me, praised my generosity and teased her brother: "How did you come to deserve this? You better be good to this girl." She also asked, "You got the kind of money to buy my brother a Ferrari? What do you do?"

I smiled. Jim's mother had us all come inside for a meal. She'd been cooking ever since Jim called. Sitting around the table eating with Jim's family, I missed being with my own. How long had it been since we were all gathered around the dining room table, laughing and talking and enjoying a meal? I was alone in California. I was also lonely, secluded, seques-tered, and shut off from everyone I loved. My wonderful exis-tence of transactions had become a kind of prison that cut me off from the rest of the world. I was starving to let someone in.

After meeting Jim's family, I invited him to my home. He'd been to my "office," the smaller place where I kept my computer. I'd never before brought a lover to my business apartment.

As we pulled up to the guard booth, he was silent, as if he hadn't ever gotten into a complex that way. It surprised me since Southern California is full of guard-gated communities. Immediately, the guard recognized me and waved. The gate opened, and we began to wind our way up the road lined with white fences to the top of the hill.

"Wow," Jim said "This place is amazing."

My house was at the very top with the valley spread out below.

"This is yours?" Jim asked, a little breathless.

"Yep," I casually confirmed.

From inside, the view of the valley—the velvet darkness, the twinkling lights—was even more dazzling. Jim, the lively conversationalist with a great sense of humor, was mesmerized and could barely speak. "Let me give you the tour," I said.

I led him through the sprawling ground floor living and dining rooms and then into the family room with its dedicated bird-watching nook.

"You have your own wine cellar?" Jim asked.

"Yes, I'll show you."

The wine-scented air in the cellar was sensual. As Jim ran a hand over the bottles, I chose one to bring upstairs.

"What's behind this door? The basement?"

I told him that it opened onto the hillside, which had a pretty steep slope. I didn't have a backyard.

*   *   *

Upstairs, we toasted the view with a glass of wine before finishing the tour with the second-level bedrooms. In my bedroom was a huge walk-in closet. After getting dressed that morning, I'd left the door open.

"Oops," I said, moving to close it with Jim beside me. As I did, I realized that, in choosing my jewelry for the day, I'd also left the door of the large floor safe ajar. Jim got a glimpse of some gold bars and bundles of cash. I made a mental note to place the goods elsewhere.

"What's all that?" he asked, "Is that real money? Is that gold?"

"Of course not," I told him. My heart was pounding with self-reproach for being careless. After a minute, I managed to catch my breath and change the subject, "Well, do you like my house? What do you think?"

He hugged me and said, in an exaggerated, joking voice, "Oh my goodness, I am falling in love with you."

"With me or my house?"

"Both! Well, no—you! But, seriously, your house is incredible. I've never seen any place like it in my life."

16

MY HERO

I won Sexiest Man at the dance club when I jumped on stage and did a striptease for the ladies."

"Excuse me?" I questioned Jim's confession after we'd enjoyed a fabulous lobster dinner and went to my place to relax and watch the sunset over the canyons.

He didn't laugh at what I thought was a joke. He grinned while looking deep into my eyes. "I'm serious. The girls went crazy and voted me the winner."

I burst out laughing and then he popped up from my couch and started reenacting his sexy dance moves.

We leaned into each other like we'd been looking for a relationship like this our whole lives. He catered to my every need, showering me with kisses and compliments. Anything I could ever want from a man, he would figure it out and become that thing. If I said I needed space to do some work, he went on his way. If I said I wanted to spend some time together, he'd show up at my gate. He never questioned me. He never complained. He was perfect.

"I was thinking, I want you to meet my brother. Mom and Ava said such great things about you that Randy wants to meet you too. Could we invite them over?" Jim asked.

"Them?"

"Yes. Randy and his wife, Rita. They may want to bring their baby girl as well. Is that OK?" Jim looked at me like a puppy trying to get a biscuit. It's how he looked whenever he wanted something—a second lobster, a new pair of shoes, gas money. He'd look like I could break his whole heart if I said no. It wasn't the most attractive trait in a man, but I liked that he was humble and didn't assume things about my money or my time.

"Of course. It would be nice to have your brother and his family over," I said. I was flattered that Jim's family seemed to be fond of me and wanted to socialize with us. I was also pleased that he wanted to invite them to my home. Showing off my house—the expression of my taste, the fruit of my achievements—felt like a reflection of his pride in me and the promise of our future together. Family dinners at his mom's house and quality time with his brother and his sister-in-law at my place all hinted at belonging.

Friday night, Randy and his wife, Rita, came over. When they walked in, I immediately noticed that, like Jim and his sister, Randy was good-looking, and his wife was beautiful with long curly hair and light-brown skin. They were dressed nicely, like we were going out to dinner and had grocery store flowers for my table. It was a nice gesture. They raved about the house and the glorious view, calling it "spectacular."

"See—I told you my baby has good taste," Jim said proudly while holding my hand.

"She sure does," Randy agreed, eyeing my twinkling crystal Baccarat chandelier. "Amazing taste. Ain't nothing in here under five-thousand dollars."

"Thank you," I said. "Are you both hungry? I ordered some Chinese. I don't cook," I admitted.

Rita laughed. I loved it. "No need to apologize. You're a businesswoman. It's 1985. A woman's worth isn't in the kitchen."

"Yeah. It's in the bedroom," Randy added.

We all laughed, and Rita pinched his arm.

"No, that's where a man's worth is," she said.

After eating, we settled into my screening room to watch television on my Sony big screen.

"It's so bright and clear. It looks like the people are right here in the room with us," Rita pointed out.

"That's what I said when I first saw it. We've been holed up in here watching *Miami Vice*," Jim said.

"That and my *Dynasty*," I added.

"Me too. I just love Diahann Carroll as Ms. Dominique Deveraux," Rita said.

"Girl, remember her first episode?" I lay back on the couch like I was Dominique and said her iconic lines: "It's burned! The champagne was obviously frozen in the bottle at some point."

Rita played Alexis: "If the champagne is too burned for your taste, don't drink it. The caviar I trust is not burned."

I closed with, "I really wouldn't know. You see that is Ostatrova, and I prefer Petrossian Beluga."

We fell out laughing, and Jim couldn't help but chuckle at how much we adored television's first true diva.

"Randy hates when I watch *Dynasty*," Rita said. "Right, babe?" She looked over her shoulder, but Randy was gone.

Figuring he got lost, I volunteered to go looking for him. He wasn't up in the bedrooms or on the ground floor, which left only one place: the wine cellar. When I got halfway down the spiral staircase, I saw him getting ready to climb up.

"There you are!" I said.

Beyond him, I noticed that the cellar door leading out to the hillside was slightly ajar.

"Did you go out there?" I asked.

"Out where?" he said. "I was just looking at all the wines. Having a cellar like this is a fantasy of mine."

"Well, the sales office is right near the security gate. Pop in, and the dream could become reality," I joked before shutting the cellar door and leading him back upstairs.

A few days later, Randy called to thank me for the evening. "Rita and I enjoyed it so much. We also appreciate how kind you've been to Jim. We'd love to thank you by taking you out to dinner," he said.

I was surprised.

Randy insisted, "This one's on us. Treating you will be our pleasure. And don't tell Jim about it. We'd like to get to know you."

While I was delighted that they wanted to get to know me, I was curious about why they didn't want Jim to know. It seemed that they wanted to tell me something that I needed to know about Jim or the family, and I agreed.

We planned to meet at my house and then head to a nice restaurant in West Covina.

"The guard will call me from the gate, and I'll tell him to send you up," I told Randy when we finalized our plans.

They arrived early. Rita had their adorable daughter in her arms. I asked them in for a few minutes while I finished getting dressed.

"I'm so sorry for bringing Madison. Our sitter fell through, and I didn't want to cancel," Rita said.

"But our little sweetie is quiet, and she won't be a bother," Randy added.

"It's absolutely fine," I said, looking at the two-month-old clinging to her mother. Rita was a few years younger than me and said she wanted more kids.

I went upstairs and rushed to put on my heels and a little makeup. When I came downstairs, Randy was coming up from the wine cellar.

"You need to get a wine cellar really soon. This one already has an owner," I said with suspicion.

"I'm working on it," Randy said.

When we walked outside, Randy announced, "Hey, I'll drive." We all piled into his sky-blue Cutlass, bypassing my Aston Martin.

Randy and Rita took me to a pizza joint, and we stuffed ourselves with lasagna and slices of pizza. Halfway through dinner, they explained why they invited me out without Jim.

"If we're going to be family soon, we want to make sure we know you as an individual," Randy said. "And that you could get to know us personally too."

"Thank you. I thought maybe you had something to tell me about Jim," I said.

"Oh, no. My brother is great, and he really likes you a lot. All arrows point to nobody but you."

On the freeway, as we headed back to my house, a car started riding our tail. It was dark, and there weren't many cars on the road. The high beams were blasting through our back window. It was way too close.

Sitting in the back seat, I yelled, "Randy, they're trying to run us off the road!"

I turned to see the car just an inch or so from us. I braced myself for the jolt—*slam!*—that came as it smacked our bumper.

Madison started crying beside me in her car seat. Rita put her arms around her to try to comfort the little girl. "It's OK, baby. Everything is OK," she kept saying to her.

"What the hell is going on?" Randy shouted. He punched the gas, trying to lose the car. But it pulled alongside us, trying to squeeze us onto the shoulder.

Randy had no choice but to slow down.

"Don't stop!" I screamed. "Who is this? What do they want?" Peering into the night, I glimpsed the driver, who looked like Rambo, with a bandanna tied around his forehead.

"I don't know!" Randy said. Then the car rammed us from the side. "What the fuck?"

"It's Jim!" Rita screamed.

Then with moonlight shimmering over the car, I recognized the Pinto. "Jim, what the hell!" I cried out.

Through his open window, Jim shouted, "Pull over! Pull the fuck over, you punk ass motherfucker."

Both cars swerved onto the shoulder. Jim and Randy got out. They started hollering at each other, waving their arms. Jim threw a punch, and Randy started swinging too.

I jumped out of the car, yelling, "Stop! Just stop it! What's going on?"

Jim looked like a madman, cursing, sweating, and out of breath.

"Tanya, get back in the car," he ordered. "Stay there and don't get out."

Considering his tone, I was afraid to argue and did as I was told.

He turned to Randy. "Remember I'll be following your punk ass. Don't try anything."

When Randy got into the car, I asked, "What's wrong with Jim?"

"He's crazy," Randy said. "He's jealous that we took you to dinner. He wants you all to himself."

As Jim said, he tailgated Randy all the way to my house. I was growing suspicious and scared about what Jim was alarmed about. I planned to jump out of Randy's car at the security gate, but when the guard saw me in the car, he assumed all was fine, opened the gate, and waved us in.

When the car reached my house, I stumbled out, shaking. Jim screeched to a stop, leaped from his car, and grabbed me, commanding, "Don't go in the house!" All I wanted was to rush inside.

"Why? What's going on!" I begged.

"Call off those motherfuckers," he shouted at Randy, who was getting out of his car. Rita and the little baby stayed inside, watching us. "Do it now."

Randy argued. "Man, you ruin everything. You're greedy."

"What? Ruined what?" I demanded.

Randy was trudging up to my front door. He banged on it, yelling, "Come on out."

The door opened, and two strange, angry men emerged from the house. I tried to holler for help but couldn't catch my breath.

"We're gone," Randy said. "Get in." The men got into the backseat of Randy's car, cursing, "Goddamn," and "What the fuck?" Randy sped off.

"Jim!" I cried, finally catching my breath. "Oh my God! Who were those men? What just happened?"

"It's OK," he said, pulling me to his chest. "I've got you now. I'll tell you everything."

We went into the house, which, to my horror, had been ransacked. In my bedroom, drawers had been dumped out on the floor. My clothes and jewelry were everywhere. Some stuff was missing.

"Why?" I asked Jim, sobbing. "Why did this happen?"

"They wanted valuables," he revealed. He said that Randy had asked me to dinner and sent his men to rob my house. When Randy came to pick me up, they were crouched in his backseat. He opened the wine cellar door for the men to enter when we left.

Their main target was the safe. They'd lain in wait for my return to force me to open it. "My God," I said. "How would they do that?"

Jim's look was grave. "They had guns," he said. "And they wouldn't have left you alive. They kill people."

I was distraught, shivering with fear. "Rita was in on it too? I can't believe it."

"I found out just in time. They were working together. That's why I stopped you on the freeway," Jim said. "Randy's crazy. He jacks people. But when he asked to meet you, I never dreamed he'd pull this shit. I believed he'd respect my woman. I found out just in time."

"You saved my life."

"I had to protect you," Jim said. "I never would have let him hurt you."

"What if they come back?"

"I'll stay with you tonight," he assured me.

Of course, I couldn't call the police to report the home invasion. Minnesota law enforcement had no idea where I'd gone, and I couldn't take the risk.

Jim helped me secure the house and then he lay with me in bed. My mind was spinning. Jim held me tight and eventually, feeling safe, my eyes closed.

After the near robbery, I was afraid to be alone, especially once I recognized that, in case of trouble, I was defenseless. I had nowhere to turn.

Except to Jim, whom I sweetly called "my hero."

Still, I had questions: How did Jim discover the plot "just in time?" Why didn't he warn me not to trust Randy? Why did Jim ask me to entertain his brother at my home, where he could case it, knowing that Randy, in his words, "jacks people," and may even "shoot people?" And how did Randy know where to find the safe?

After staying by my side day and night for a few days, Jim started asking me questions. He was grateful that I wasn't going to file charges on his brother, whom he said he'd handle, but he seemed suspicious about why I didn't call the cops. It was out of character for the coddled rich girl I claimed to be.

One day when I returned home from my office, he asked, "Do you really come from money?"

"Of course," I'd said. "How else could I afford this house and the cars I drive?"

"But what does your family do?"

"I told you. We own theaters in the Midwest."

Jim left it at that, but I could tell that he didn't believe me.

That night, I woke up to an empty bed. After a while, I went looking for Jim and found him rifling through my desk.

"What are you doing?" I asked.

"Oh, I was looking for a pen and paper," he said.

I knew he was lying.

After getting word about what happened with Randy, Jim's mother called to empathize.

"I'm mortified," his mother said. "I can't account for what Randy did except to say that he has problems. Please don't hold his craziness against the rest of us."

"I won't. I'm just so happy Jim has been by my side. If he weren't here, things could've gotten bad," I said.

"Why don't you come over so we can talk things through?" she asked. "I don't want you to think we are all thieves. We really like you, Tanya."

I said I'd think about it, but she begged and promised me an amazing home-cooked meal. Twenty-four hours later, I found myself at her house.

Ava answered the door with her son Isaiah, who was about five years old, by her side. "Tanya, come on in." She welcomed me with a big hug. "I'm so happy to see you again."

Inside, I found a Thanksgiving-level feast laid out on the table just for me. I was salivating and humbled by Jim's mother's efforts.

As we ate, I told them my side of the story. They seemed genuinely shocked and apologetic. As I talked, Jim's mom held my hand and teared up.

"My heart just weeps for you. To have your space violated in such a way, no one deserves that," she said, and I could see in her eyes that she was sincere.

"We are here for you, sis. We have your back if you need anything," Ava added.

The dinner sealed my connection with Jim's mother and sister. Little by little, they won me over. Being with them felt warm and comfortable. Soon, I was hanging out with them several days a week. They welcomed me into the family, almost as if Jim and I were already married.

The closer I grew to them, the deeper my romantic connection became with Jim. Though we didn't live together, he was always at my house, and on weekends, we were either with his family or hanging out together. He confided in me about challenges in his life—including "old" girlfriends he was trying to shake. *At least he's honest and not sneaking around*, I thought.

As we grew closer, Jim circled back to his original questions about my money and my past, saying it was time for me to come clean.

"Something's up with you," he said. "I just know it. You say your family is wealthy, but the stuff you have is too much for that. They would have to be billionaires to afford all this. And where are they? Can I meet them?" He kept poking and prodding, finding new interrogation angles and hoping to trip me up and spark a confession. It was exhausting to field all his questions and keep my lies straight.

My pride in my work was at its peak. My system seemed airtight and boundless in its potential. I longed to revel in my incredible triumph instead of keeping it a deep dark secret from the person in my bed.

One night, as Jim and I lay in bed, I opened the conversation by saying, "I'm ready. But let me say everything before you comment or ask questions. It's a lot."

Jim nodded, and I told him all about my transactions, how I made money, and the trial.

He smacked his palms against his temples and cried out, "I knew it! I knew you had some hustle going! Whoa, girl, you better tell me how it works."

I filled him in on the operation—the runners opening accounts and withdrawing funds—explaining, "Using the right people, I can transfer and withdraw any amount of cash. But I'm not just limited to bank withdrawals. I can buy anything—really, I can do anything I want."

Jim was overjoyed. "You're a genius!" he cried. "You cooked this up all by yourself, and look at all the money you made! Damn, girl, you're bad! You're blowing my mind!"

He was hyperventilating. He hopped out of bed and started pacing around, too excited to hold still, repeating, "Damn, you bad! You. Are. Bad!"

Jim had a gleam in his eye that I now had the ability to recognize. It was greed. It was I-struck-it-rich jubilation. I'd seen it in Puegot. I'd seen it in Shawn. I saw it every time I entrusted a man with my secret. It was what I was afraid of.

"Listen—I've had some bad experiences with men when I tell them about this. That's why it took so long for me to tell you," I said.

"Don't worry about me. I'm not here to bring you any harm. I want to protect you. I'm your hero, right?" Jim reassured me. "You just keep being a badass, and I'll have your back. You can trust me, OK?"

I agreed to let go of my anxiety, but it wasn't long before Jim tried to wheedle his way into the operation.

My interest in diamonds was growing. I purchased an exquisite emerald-cut diamond ring from Harry Winston in New York. When Harry Winston received my $50,000 wire to pay for the ring, they asked me who was coming in to pick it up.

Not wanting to lead anyone to me in Los Angeles, I asked the salesperson, "Can someone fly to Oklahoma to meet my assistant at the airport?"

"We haven't done that before," he said. I could tell the unusual request put him off. After a long pause, he added, "But since you already paid for the ring, I suppose it could be arranged."

When Jim realized what was going on, he insisted that I use one of his friends to do the pickup.

"This is easy. My friend Elijah can handle it. He'll go to the airport right now if I tell him to," he said.

"But he has to know how to play the role. You have to teach him. He's picking up a fifty-thousand-dollar ring. He needs to be classy and relaxed; otherwise, the salesperson will be suspicious and may alert authorities. Then he'll be arrested," I explained.

"Let me handle that. You just make sure the diamond is on the way."

Hours later, Elijah was on a flight to Oklahoma to meet the delivery person from Harry Winston. Before he left, I told the salesperson my assistant would be wearing a blue suit and black shoes. He said the jewelry delivery person would be a woman in a long, tan, cashmere trench coat. They were to meet at three thirty near the lunch counter.

Jim and I waited at the pay phone for word. When it rang, we thought it was Elijah calling to say the deal was done, but it was the salesperson at Harry Winston in New York.

"My delivery person just phoned. She's quite nervous, it appears," he said.

"Why? What happened? Did she see my assistant?" I asked.

"Yes. I believe so. She spotted the gentleman in the blue suit with black shoes, but there was one problem. Is he Black?"

"Yes."

"Oh. I see. So he's picking up the diamond?"

"Yes. That's what I mean."

"Sure. I'll let her know everything is fine."

That evening, Elijah flew back to LA with the diamond. I gave Jim $5,000 to give him as payment for the run.

When Jim returned to my house with the diamond, I was blown away by how beautiful it was. I wore it around the house and kept looking at it all night.

"Come on now. You can't wear a ring that big. Someone will rob you," Jim said. "Let me take it so I can store it somewhere safe."

I protested, but I knew Jim was right. People were getting killed in LA for wearing gold chains. A diamond that big was an invitation for drama. After staring at it a few more times, I handed the precious stone over to him.

Off the success of the Harry Winston diamond run, Jim wanted to try to manage bank transactions. He started by criticizing my split with Livilla and the runners.

"You're nuts to give away half," he insisted. "I know people who'd do those pickups for five or ten grand."

"The split is fair," I told him. "It's super risky to go into banks to open accounts and take out cash. Only a special kind of person—cool, confident, and professional—can pull that off. They have to be reliable. And Livilla is a genius manager with a million connections. She's worth every dollar I pay her."

"I could try my friend Leon—I'd trust him with my life," Jim pitched.

I vaguely remembered bumping into Leon with Jim. I was sure he wouldn't fit the "professional" profile. "Would he know how to play the role? To talk to the bank manager about opening the account, expecting a wire, and all that?" I asked Jim.

"Sure," Jim said. "No problem."

Jim's idea would pierce the all-important firewall between myself and the runners—since Leon, knowing him, could implicate me—but he kept begging.

Finally, afraid my ambivalence would lead to a split, I told him, "OK, I'll do one transaction with Leon. But it can't be for a lot of money," hoping it would be disastrous, and Jim would let it go and move on.

Leon opened the account, and I transferred in $10,000.

When I heard nothing, I asked Jim what had happened.

"The cash didn't come through," Jim said.

"What?" I checked and double-checked the account on my computer. Everything was in order. The money was in the account and then withdrawn.

When I told Jim the money was in the account, he said, "I mean he couldn't do the withdrawal. They wouldn't give him the money."

"That makes no sense," I replied. "I can see the account debit right on my screen. I can always check, you know."

Jim said, "Well, that's what he said."

"OK." I didn't want to suggest the obvious. "I'm not wasting time on Leon again. These little deals are not my thing."

Jim didn't argue. But a short time later, he proposed a new scheme. He knew another guy, Reggie, who owned an auto-body shop with a constant inflow and outflow of cash. "You could deposit money right into his business account, and no one would ever question it," he said.

I was growing annoyed with Jim's insistence on getting in on my action. I couldn't help feeling degraded—as if my clean, well-oiled Rolls-Royce of an operation was being pressed into service hauling garbage. He clearly felt there was no way I was capable of handling and growing it on my own, that I must need some new ideas from a man. Though I felt this way, I understood why he kept pushing the issue: Jim, who didn't have a job, wanted to generate his own income to feel manly. Transferring funds to a business account and then pulling out cash was a decent idea. It would look like a payout to a vendor. This time, I wired in a more substantial sum, $100,000. Again, I waited to hear the outcome.

"Oh, he got the money," Jim reported when I finally asked two days after the wire. "That son of a bitch denies it, but I know he has it. The motherfucker just won't hand it over."

"I'm sorry, Jim. That's a big loss," I said, with some empathy and again dropped the conversation.

When Jim came up with a third guy, a pawnshop owner who could receive a wire and pay out cash, I said no. "It's just not working," I told him. "I'm taking chances with these shady players, and you're not even getting the money. It's too much risk with no upside."

Jim was determined to prove himself. He pleaded and nagged until I finally broke down and agreed to put through a transfer. He announced right away that he had gotten the cash. He said, "It came through, just like you said!"

But there was a catch. "I gave the money to my mom and stepdad to hold," he added. "That way the money will be protected if something happens. I'm saving it for our future."

I sighed, thinking of how often I'd heard the words "our future." I also noted that Jim kept the whole sum, minus whatever he paid the pawnbroker, without handing over my split.

Bringing up his rationale for stashing all of the take at his mom's house, I asked, "What do you think might happen?"

"Well, you're doing something illegal. You get busted, the cops could take what you have. You need to have money hidden away someplace safe," he explained.

With my parents, the money would have been safe too, but they would never even dream of touching my ill-gotten gains. As I was coming to learn, Jim's family was different.

17

THE GAMBLE

Jim and I were making a lot of money doing transactions. It was time for us to have some fun by visiting his favorite place: Las Vegas. I saved a million dollars for the trip and made sure Jim packed his most expensive suits to match my couture dresses.

When we hit the strip, I was awestruck by the glittering lights, round-the-clock revelry, and the sheer excitement of gambling, which included throwing a lot of cash around. Women were unapologetically glamorous and sexy in heels and curve-hugging dresses. Men were cool and collected in debonair suits and shiny shoes. It wasn't all Dean Martin and Frank Sinatra, though they were a strong presence. There were also younger performers and spectacles, like Siegfried and Roy, who did an incredible magic act with white tigers. While I'd grown accustomed to the spectacular beauty and riches of Los Angeles, Vegas's adult playground atmosphere brought out the wonder of the small-town girl in me.

When Jim and I arrived at Caesars Palace, we didn't pause in the smoky, bustling lobby, where small timers worked the slot machines for hours on end. We headed straight for the high-stakes salons, where there were wooden felt-topped tables and a hush of respect for the money at risk. Jim, donning his expensive suit, let the pit boss know we were there to spend lots of money. After Jim whispered a figure in his ear, the pit boss who was the acting manager took it on himself to escort us to a VIP suite that the casino would comp. He then walked us to all the major VIP lounges and let the dealers and staff know we had all access.

When we entered the high-roller lounge, celebrities were everywhere. We saw sports star Michael Jordan and rapper Heavy D. I could feel Jim's excitement at finally being on the inside.

Jim knew his way around and showed me the difference between blackjack, poker, and the more complicated baccarat, along with the spinning roulette wheels and the communal-feeling craps tables.

"What do you want to play?" he asked.

"Let me watch for a while," I said. While the scene was interesting, I knew I wasn't going to be a big-time gambler. I was into making money, not losing it.

Jim was itching to blow some cash. We settled at a black-jack table next to up-and-coming boxer Mike Tyson and baller Michael Jordan, who were trash-talking each other. Ever confident, Jim put up the same hefty bets as Jordan and Tyson. But the cards—and the dice since Jim loved shooting craps—rarely fell his way. Over the next few hours, he lost every dime he walked in with. Unbothered, we ended the night making love in our VIP suite.

After that weekend, at times, I would accompany Jim to Vegas. Taking pointers from the transactions Bradley and I did with his Vegas friend Jack, I started wiring large sums to the casinos to finance our getaways. We'd enter the high-rollers lounges with $250,000, and Jim would spend it in one sitting. I never picked up gambling, but the scene and risqué behavior were fun, and I enjoyed getting dressed up to enjoy the party spirit where people would watch me like I was a celebrity or royalty.

Sometimes Jim would head to Vegas alone. Often, I didn't even know he'd gone. He still claimed to be squirreling away funds for our future, but he almost certainly gambled away as much as he saved. He'd have me do a transaction using one of his runners. As soon as the money came in, he'd vanish, inevitably coming back broke. Then I'd have to let him arrange yet another pickup just to keep him afloat. It was a crazy cycle.

I was so deeply involved in my transactions with Jim that my work with Livilla slowed. She and her people were not happy. Livilla's partner Lucas, who kept asking to meet me, stepped up the pressure to connect, insisting that we talk on the phone. Since I refused to give them my number, Livilla arranged a three-way call.

After Livilla sent the number for the conference call to my beeper, I dialed in from a phone booth near my house.

"You're phenomenal," Lucas told me. "We can do so much together. It's a shame to waste this opportunity." He sounded well educated and classy, older, maybe in his fifties. The deep, cold intonation in his voice brought back my suspicions that Livilla was in bed with the mob. Nervous about making that kind of connection, I told Lucas I was flattered he thought highly of me and that I'd consider his offer, but now wasn't a good time—maybe later. He accepted my position, and we ended the call on a good note. But once I told Livilla about Jim's brash behavior, the three-way chats with Lucas grew more pointed and frequent. Like Livilla, Lucas would lay on the compliments and then shift to asking about Jim: "Who is this man? You must really like him. What's his last name? Where does he live?"

I never offered any information. I said Jim was a private sideline and that I'd be back in business with Livilla soon. But with each call, I could sense that Lucas's exasperation was growing. Clearly, he wasn't used to hearing words like *no* and *later*—and it was obvious that he was ready to make a move with or without my consent.

To calm him, I continued doing certain transactions they requested—mostly sending money overseas—but I didn't resume my old routine with Livilla. She kept warning me about Jim. "He's going to get you caught."

Jim was getting increasingly jealous of Livilla. Having arranged some successful pickups, he was convinced that he could fill her shoes. He loved raking in money.

"Damn, girl, we're rich!" he once said. "There's only one person I'd leave you for: Christina Onassis."

He was also determined to control the runners and collections—to pay out a small split rather than half, keeping the lion's share for us. Unfortunately, "for us" still meant "for himself" or, really, for Vegas.

To try to ease the tension in my relationship, I decided it was time to make a move. I popped up at Livilla's job at the college.

"Tanya," she said, surprised but as warm as ever. As usual, she hugged me, telling the staff I was her daughter.

"Can we go someplace to talk?" I asked.

"Sure," she said, "let's go eat."

When we sat down at a nearby café, I laid it out: "I can't keep dealing with you, at least not for a while."

"But we got all these accounts set up. People want to get to work. We got to keep making money till we can't do it no more. Then we can relax because we'll be rich."

"I'm telling you I want to stop."

"Oh, Tanya, what's wrong? You know I've never cheated you."

"It's not that. You've got to understand that now I'm working with Jim."

"Fuck Jim," she said. "That dude is no good. He's dirty. Mark my words."

"What do you mean 'dirty?'" I asked. "You don't even know him."

"I mean I'm sure he's got other women. He's the type. But worse than that, he's messing up our crew, and he's got you messed up too. You ain't in your right mind."

"Jim is the man I could see myself having a future with. He wants to do this with me," I said.

"Look, Tanya, my people are pissed. They say he's got to go. It's time to take him out," Livilla said flatly.

I couldn't believe what I was hearing. Was she serious? Were they willing to kill him? I was shocked.

"Is that why Lucas kept asking me questions on the phone?" I asked.

"Just tell me his last name," Livilla whispered. "If something did happen to Jim, no one would connect you."

"Who the hell are you people?"

"Oh, honey," Livilla said in a conciliatory tone. "I'm trying to look out for you. Just think about it. How much money does he give you?"

The question stung. I was chilled to the bone. Embarrassed. "I've got to run," I told her. "Let's just say we're on hold. I'm sure I'll be back in a month or two. But right now, I need a break. Please understand."

I was lying about coming back, but with her talk about killing Jim for his transgressions, Livilla had me too afraid to insist on pulling out.

"OK, honey," she said. "I hear you."

I was in way over my head working with Livilla. I couldn't imagine anyone but the mob who could "convince" high-powered executives, celebrities, and politicians—and everyday people—to commit illegal acts. The runners must have been people working off debts or otherwise under the thumb of the mob. What would happen if I crossed them? If they were that willing to take Jim out, surely I was in danger too. I was scared and planned not to take Livilla's calls going forward.

I hung out with Jim's mother and sister, especially when he was off on his solo Vegas jaunts. When I was visiting, strangely, Randy and Rita started dropping by. The first time it happened, I tried to leave, shaken and outraged that Randy would show his face.

"Wait, Tanya, please," Randy begged, chasing me out the door. "Let me apologize. That incident was months ago, and I didn't know you back then."

"Months ago? You can't be serious."

"I am. Look—my family loves you a lot. You're a nice person to do what you have done for them. Can you ever forgive me? I'm so sorry."

I shrugged him off and kept walking to my car. Behind me, I could hear Randy's mother and sister rebuking him, saying, "You better apologize. You shamed our whole family! What you did was so wrong!"

The next time I stopped by, Jim's mother and sister tried talking to me about Randy.

"He's not a bad man," his mother said. "He was just in a tight spot. He's always been jealous of Jim. I think that's what this is about."

"Everyone knows Jim is Mom's favorite and that's always bothered Randy," Ava added. "Making matters worse, Rita actually wanted to be with Jim but had to settle for Randy instead. Randy knows it too. It makes him do ugly things."

"Tanya, our family has to accept Randy—flaws and all. He's one of us. You are too," Jim's mother said, taking my hand and rubbing it softly. "Please understand. It was a lapse in judgment. That's all."

One Saturday night, when Jim had slipped away to Vegas and I was feeling lonely, I went over to his mom's house for dinner. His stepdad and Ava were there, and his mother had prepared a delicious soul food feast, including ribs. When Randy and Rita showed up, I stayed planted in my seat. I wasn't prepared to accept either of them, but I decided not to reject him. Maybe I could give him one more chance. He kept his distance and waved from afar as he fixed a plate.

"You are just amazing. Truly an angel on earth. Jim is so blessed. No one has ever treated him so well. He should be grateful for the new life you gave him," said Jim's mother.

When Jim's mother and sister got busy playing with the children, Randy, now carrying a plate piled high with ribs and macaroni and cheese, plopped down next to me at the table. He took a few bites of his food before turning to me.

"Tanya, I want to tell you something you might not want to hear," he said in a low voice that only Rita, who was standing nearby, and I could hear. "Jim planned the whole robbery. He told us about the safe. He was in on it 100 percent. Once you started buying him cars and clothes, he figured he could get more money from you just pretending to be your boyfriend. That's when he called it off."

I rolled my eyes and started to get up, but Randy stopped me. "Please, listen to me. When all of this was going on, I didn't know the type of person you were. Me and my boys, we were broke and just trying to hit the jackpot. We thought Jim wanted everything for himself and was cutting us out, so we decided to do it anyway. Right before it was supposed to go down, one of the guys who didn't know Jim tried to cancel the job. He called him to find out where to meet. That's how Jim found out we were going through with it."

"Randy, I'm not interested in anything you're saying, so you can stop right there," I said. While much of what he said made sense and cleared up some of my questions about the robbery, I remembered Jim's mother and sister insisting Randy was jealous of Jim and would do anything to take him down a notch. After listening to him, my stomach turned. I got up to toss what was left of my food into the trash.

Randy got up with me and kept talking. "I'm telling you this because Jim is not who you think he is. And he has other women too. He's using you."

"Fine. Whatever." I couldn't think straight and needed to get away from these people quickly.

I put distance between Jim and me by leaving Los Angeles for a little while. I needed time to clear my mind and get back on track business-wise.

I settled on Atlanta as a possible escape. Carmen, Bradley's cute airline stewardess girlfriend, who was based there but lived in Los Angeles, offered to show me around. "I'm heading back there in a few days," she told me. "Why don't you fly out with me?" I was intrigued by the idea of moving South.

Since I'd need money to start my new life, I took bundles of bills from my safe-deposit box. Figuring I might need more cash, at sunrise, I drove to a nearby canyon where I'd buried a stash of emergency money and dug it up. Sadly, the stash, close to $500,000, which I had buried in plastic bags, was soiled and decomposing.

To get my computer to Atlanta, I called Duane, one of Puegot's best friends, and asked him to come to Los Angeles to load the computer and some of my furniture into a truck and drive it across the country. I offered to pay him $50,000 to help me out. The next day, I flew him and a friend to LA. They arrived at my place with a rental truck. Duane owed me big time because I did a $100,000 transaction for him to get his family out of a financial bind.

"Wow, Tanya, you are living large," Duane said, looking at the house and my fine furniture as they loaded the truck. His friend, a chubby guy I hadn't met, was carrying a desk with $100,000 stashed inside. "I mean I knew you were doing it big, but this is magnificent."

I smiled, proud to have someone from back home see I was doing OK for myself. After the trial, there were lots of rumors floating around about me. The FBI and the cops in Minneapolis were still hot and heavy, constantly surveilling everyone I knew to ferret out my whereabouts. They were using forceful tactics, like popping up at people's jobs. During one of their searches of a friend's house, they said if anyone knew where I was and didn't tell them, they could be charged as a conspirator.

*　　*　　*

"You know Puegot still talks about you to this day? He swears you are the love of his life and got away," he said. "He still thinks of you as his woman."

"That's the past. I don't even think about it anymore." I lied.

Duane went on, "You know he never wanted any of us to talk to you without him around? He would have a fit if he knew I came to help you without getting his approval. I didn't tell him anything, though. I need the money, and I want to help you. I didn't want Puegot to tell me not to come out here, not because he wouldn't help you himself but he would be upset that you didn't go to him. You know how he is."

"I do," I said. "But don't worry about Puegot finding out. I never talk to him, and I don't plan on changing that. I never go back once I'm done for good. It's one of my rules," I explained. "Your secret is safe with me."

When they finished loading the truck, I checked to be sure the computer was properly stowed and concealed. I couldn't risk it breaking during the days-long journey. It also had to be well hidden in case Duane got pulled over. If the Feds got ahold of the computer, there would be enough data on it to send me away for a long while.

Once the computer was on the road, I shut the house down and called a cab to take me to the airport.

When I got to LAX, I asked Carmen if she could carry the suitcase with the cash onto the plane since she was a stewardess and didn't have to go through the metal detectors and security. She didn't know what was actually in the luggage, but she knew it was something I didn't want anyone to see.

"I'll do it. Don't worry," she said.

Relieved, I handed her the bag, and we both floated through security. The airport screeners hardly looked at it.

When the plane touched down in Atlanta, I took my first deep breath in weeks. At last, I could put everything behind me. Atlanta was like no place I had ever been. It was alive with a kinetic energy.

I checked into a hotel on Peachtree, got all dressed up, and met Carmen to hit the town. She'd grown up in Kansas City with Cliff Levingston, a power forward for the Atlanta Hawks. We joined him, Dominque Wilkins (the team's star slam dunker), some other major players, and the coach for dinner at a glamorous restaurant in Buckhead. When we walked in, everyone was looking at us, saying hello to the players, and asking for autographs. The staff took us to a private dining area to avoid interruptions. Over dinner, the ball players discussed deals they were making, businesses they'd opened, and ventures they were pursuing. They were making power moves. Carmen and I were the only women there.

"You love it, don't you?" Carmen teased, seeing my eyes wide with wonder as we left dinner. "Don't trip. I was the same way when I first got here. This place makes you feel like you can do anything."

I found a cozy townhouse to rent in Dunwoody, a historic village north of the city proper where a lot of the old-money families lived. I got the keys right on time to meet Duane, who arrived with the moving truck carrying my computer and furniture after being on the road for nearly three days. After he and his partner unloaded the truck, I paid Duane for his service, and he handed me the receipt for the rental.

Once my place was set up, I purchased a black two-seater Benz to get around. I drove around Atlanta to get to know the city. There were all-Black areas, including the West End, which was home to six Black colleges, with campuses that were all interconnected. Nearby was the Cascade area, where Black doctors, lawyers, entrepreneurs, and politicians lived in beautiful mansions. I visited dozens of Black restaurants and clothing stores.

In Atlanta, unlike any city I'd ever been in, African Americans dominated. The birthplace of Dr. Martin Luther King Jr., it was even on its second Black mayor, Andrew Young, who'd been elected to his second term with 85 percent of the vote. Now that's Black Power. Soaking it all in, I thought my dad would love to see Atlanta.

After I met the Hawks players, I got invited to a few fabulous parties, but I didn't really know anyone in town. Carmen introduced me to her stewardess friend Vivian, thinking we could be friends. However, after hanging out a few times, I realized Vivian had a serious cocaine addiction. She tried to hide it and I tried to overlook it, but eventually, it was too obvious to deny. She'd disappear when we went out—just, poof, be gone and not return. She was always broke. She had massive mood swings. And she rolled with a seedy crew of outliers. All of this reminded me of my sister.

Eventually, I befriended my neighbor Susan, a white woman in her thirties who worked out twice a day. We chatted often at one or the other of our adjoining townhouses.

Eventually, I called Livilla to see if her people were still gunning for Jim and if our old relationship could be salvaged.

She was thrilled to get my call and delighted to hear that I'd left Jim.

"You were right about him," I said, standing in a phone booth on Peachtree Road.

"Oh, honey, no need to say that. I'm just glad you moved on. You deserve much better," she told me. But she added ominously, "He knows all your business. I still say he's got to go."

"Don't talk like that," I said. "It scares me. If we're going to work together, you can't hint at doing things like that. Jim is the past. Let's move on."

"OK, no more talk," she promised. "Let's make some money. Let me know when you're ready to start."

While I'd gotten used to setting up shop in a different place from where I lived, I decided to set up my computer in the townhouse. I wasn't sure if I was staying there long and thought if I moved the townhouse could become my office. Right away, I did a transaction for $150,000 with Livilla. She volunteered to bring my cut to me, but I didn't want her to know where I was, so I declined.

It was just like old times. After all the sketchy arrangements with Jim, I'd forgotten how seamless and effortless working with Livilla could be. I racked up another million dollars of transactions in just a couple days. I didn't really need money at the time and asked her to stash it.

Atlanta was good to me, but as Christmas approached, I grew lonely. I wanted badly to spend the holidays with my family in Minneapolis, but the sniffing pit bulls had made that impossible. One sad night, surrounded by bundles of $100 bills, I poured my frustration into an angry letter, lambasting the cops and FBI for harassing innocent people. I folded it and stashed it with the cash.

Meanwhile, Jim had been frantically hitting up my beeper with his code: 6969. I ignored him, happy to let him sweat. He didn't know where I was or if I was coming back. I was sure his money had dried up and that was why he was anxious to get me back.

After weeks of this, his mother and sister started beeping me too. Thirsty to hear a familiar voice, I returned one of the beeps with a call to his mother.

"Tanya, I'm so glad you finally called me. Where are you?" she asked.

"I can't tell you that," I said, watching light rain fall outside the phone booth. "Not right now. I just wanted to call to wish you a Merry Christmas. How have you been? How's the family?" I tried being casual, but she went straight to talking about Jim.

"We are OK, but Jim misses you so much. He really loves you," she said. "He's been a mess with you gone. You sure taught him a lesson."

"That's too bad," I said, as I felt myself softening. Deep down, I missed Jim too. The separation had stoked my affection for him. I let his mother arrange a time for Jim to be at her house to take my call.

"Baby! It's you!" Jim said when he picked up. "I been hoping that you'd call. Where are you?"

I told him.

"Come home," he pleaded with tears in his voice. "I need you. We're gonna get married. Have some kids. I have all our money. We can get us a big, fine house."

"I wish I could believe that," I said.

Jim continued begging and asking me to come back. He said I was the only woman in his life, the only one he ever really loved, and so on. Finally, I agreed to come back, just for a visit, to meet him in LA and then we'd drive to Las Vegas for New Year's Eve.

"Wow, that sounds fun," Susan, my neighbor, said when I shared my plans. I didn't tell her a lot about Jim, but I wanted her to know I was away in case something came up while I was gone. I gave her my beeper number and said to use the code 9-1-1 if anything came up.

"Don't you worry about a thing. Just enjoy yourself," she said. "Good luck in Vegas and good luck with Jim."

"Jim is a gamble that could go either way," I told her. "Luck is what I need."

Before leaving Atlanta, I took my computer and everything associated with my transactions to a storage unit for safekeeping. I packed stacks of cash, nearly $300,000, in an overhead bag and left for the airport.

When I put my bag on the x-ray scanner at the airport, the agents, two Black guys, were glued to the screen. Their eyes wide with shock, they looked from the bag to me and then back at the bag again. Knowing they saw the money, I froze. I looked ahead and saw a sea of airport security agents. I looked at the two guys like, "Give me a break. Please don't tell." Without blinking, one of the agents picked up the bag and handed it to me with a look that said, "Girl, what are you doing with all that money?" The other screening agents waved me off, and I walked away. My brothers came through for me. It felt good.

18

THE DELUGE

f I had a New Year's wish, it would be for a prosperous but, more importantly, peaceful 1986. I hoped it could include Jim and that everything would be what he was promising. It was high-risk, but I was in the high-risk business.

Jim and I met up at LAX to catch our flight to Vegas. The first thing I asked about was Randy and the robbery.

Jim laughed and parroted what his mother and Ava told me. "That fool is so jealous of me he will say anything to ruin what I have. I swear. He has no limits." He turned to me. "Wait. Are you serious? Are you really asking me this?"

"What he said made sense. How did they know I had a safe?" I asked.

"You said it yourself. Randy went walking around your house. He was snooping. Oh my God. I can't believe you let him come between us. Is that why you left?"

I didn't say anything.

"Tanya, you're my woman. I wouldn't do anything to hurt you. I know I can be fucked up, but I'm always here for you.

I'm your protector. Randy wants to pull us apart. That's why he said those things. Please believe me," he pleaded. Jim grabbed my hand and looked at me intensely. "Are you ready to focus on us?" he asked. "Can you at least try to give me a chance?"

"Yes," I said.

With my confirmation, Jim and I boarded our flight to Vegas for a glamorous New Year's celebration.

When we arrived, we were shown to a penthouse suite with mirrored walls and spectacular views of the strip. On the casino floor, Jim was greeted like a rockstar, and I was right beside him, his beautifully dressed consort. It felt like old times, everything I'd been missing and more. Because while Jim was focused on his gambling, he was proud to have me on his arm and kept telling everyone I was his future wife. I felt appreciated.

From Las Vegas, we returned to my cliffside house in Diamond Bar and settled back into our old routine for the next few months—romantic evenings, dinner with his family, and weekend trips to Vegas.

On one of those Vegas romps in early March, we got ringside seats to see Marvin Hagler, the world champion, take on the Ugandan star John Mugabi. Alone, waiting for Jim in the high-rollers lounge before the fight, I spotted Fred Williamson, the Hammer, the football hero turned star of the movies *Black Caesar* and *Hell Up in Harlem*.

He looked as handsome as ever. He looked over at me, and our eyes met. I was wearing a black evening dress that hugged me like a second skin, curving in at my small waist and then flaring out slightly at the knee. Fred grinned and walked over to me. He took my hand, raised it to his lips, and kissed it. "You're the most beautiful woman I've ever seen," he said.

I was speechless. And Fred knew it.

I couldn't wait to call my mom and tell her about it. Fred Williamson had been one of our heartthrobs for years.

When it was time to go to the fight, I was worried that it would be canceled. It had been raining all day, rare for Vegas, and the bout was to take place in an outdoor arena at Caesars Palace. Miraculously, right on time for the middleweight champ to defend his title, the sprinkles from the heavens ceased, and Jim and I were seated ringside in a crowd of fifteen thousand.

When Marvelous Marvin knocked the Beast out in the eleventh round, Jim and I cheered and hugged like we'd won the match ourselves. Jim whispered in my ear, "I'm the real winner here because I have you."

While I told Jim firmly that I was returning to Atlanta, moments like that ringside embrace and his Boy Scout behavior had me wavering. Jim kept pushing.

"When are we planning this wedding? We could just get married in Vegas, but my mom would be crushed. You know she wants a big wedding. She loves you," he said one night as we were lying in bed.

I was debating whether to entertain Jim's plans and give him one more chance when my beeper went off—9-1-1.

"Oh my God," I told Jim. "It's my neighbor in Atlanta. Something's wrong."

I jumped in my car and sped to the nearest pay phone to call Susan.

"Tanya, the pipes burst in your house," she said. "Water leaked through the walls and flooded my house too. You better get back here quick."

"I'll grab the next flight," I told her.

"Good," she said and added, "All the fire trucks . . . it's a mess. Your stuff must be totally destroyed."

My body froze with alarm. All I could think about was all the money I had there.

I immediately called Vivian, Carmen's stewardess friend, to see if she could help. She promised to go right away.

I sat in the car beside the pay phone to wait for her to beep me. An hour passed and then another. I started pacing outside the car, but I couldn't take the suspense anymore and dialed her number.

"Girl," she started, "I just got back and was about to beep you."

"What did you see?"

"There are fire trucks, all right, and police all over your house. Cars parked every which way. What's going on?"

"I don't know," I said.

"Well, I chatted up some of your neighbors, and they're saying it's a drug dealer's house. They heard the police called in the DEA."

Not wanting to get Vivian too involved, I didn't push for more information. I immediately hired a private investigator.

The investigator discovered that a cold snap had led to the pipes bursting in the house. Since I changed the locks, the landlord couldn't get in and the fire department broke down the door. Inside the house, there was about two feet of water. Floating in the water were $100 bills, totaling about $50,000. They assumed whoever lived in the house was a drug dealer; that's when the DEA was called in.

As usual, I rented the house under a fake name. But once they lifted my fingerprints, they discovered that I was the tenant. As further proof of my identity, they discovered the letter I had written to the FBI complaining about the harassment of my Minneapolis friends. The Feds also got my beeper number, thanks to my overly helpful neighbor Susan.

I told Jim I was back in Los Angeles to stay. The DEA couldn't arrest me for what they found in the townhouse, since there were no drugs or anything else illegal. Merely possessing cash, dry or wet, is not a crime. But now the FBI knew I'd been in Atlanta, which meant that I could never go back.

Jim was delighted—and so was Livilla. Both of them kept urging me to get to work. But I needed time to pull myself together. I was feeling unlucky. At the moment, cosmic conditions were against me. In every way possible, the universe was telling me to slow down.

"Jim, I need my share of the money you've been saving for us," I said, though I had more than enough hidden in numerous places. "And what about the Harry Winston diamond you're holding for me? Where's that?"

"Don't worry about all that. I got it. I have everything," he promised and switched the topic to the wedding he was planning.

* * *

I got a beep from my mother. She seldom beeped me because I regularly checked in. When I saw her number, I rushed to a pay phone.

"Puegot came by," she said. Though she didn't know Puegot well, she and my dad had met him and knew how much he meant to me. "He gave me his number and asked me to tell you to call him."

"For what?" I asked. "Did he say?"

"No. But it sounded important. I told him I'd be sure to pass the message along."

After my mother gave me Puegot's number, we hung up and I stared at it, wondering if I should call. It had been years since we last spoke. I worked hard to move on and erase the pain of being betrayed by my first love. Every man who came after him was just a placeholder, a shadow of what I truly wanted, of what even Puegot couldn't be. Something had to be going on for him to stop by our house. Before I could stop myself, I quickly dialed the number.

"Hello?" As soon as I heard his voice, my heart melted, but I knew I had to remain emotionless.

"It's me. Tanya."

"Tanya, my girl, how are you doing?" He sounded happy, like all the things that happened between us were nothing. Gone away.

"I'm fine," I said cooly. "I'm calling because you stopped by my parents' house."

"I did. It's because the damn Feds came to my house again," he revealed. "They've been coming by since you left. I read about your case."

"What did they say?"

"Wait a minute. Don't you want to hear what I said first?"

"I don't care what you said. I only need to know what they said."

My insistence that we keep the conversation focused on the Feds and not him seemed to disturb Puegot, but he told me they were up to their usual antics: asking where I was and if he could help them.

"Good. If they're asking those types of questions, they don't know much," I said and chuckled.

"Oh, you think this is a game," he said.

"You can say that. I've been playing cat and mouse with them for years."

"I guess that game is what led you to Atlanta. Had my boy move your stuff and everything."

"Who told you that?

"The Feds," he said. "When they went into your spot in Atlanta, they found the rental van receipt with his name on it. They told me everything. I ain't even mad at you. I just don't know why you wouldn't come to me for help. But him and me? We done. Sneaking around with my girl?" His voice was stern. "He's dead to me."

"I'm not your girl, and we didn't sneak around," I said. "Please don't let him doing me a favor ruin your friendship. Y'all were best friends for a long time."

"I'll never forgive him."

"Puegot, don't block him out. You're a good person. Loyal. I know that. That's why I didn't have to hear what you said to the Feds. I know you'd never rat me out. You're a good friend," I said. "Duane is too."

Puegot ignored me. He warned me to tighten up.

"They ain't playing with you. One wrong move, and they're going to get you. Protect yourself." His words felt like harbingers.

"I got it," I said. "Don't worry."

After that, Puegot started trying to sweet talk his way back into my life, but I cut the conversation short. I had gotten what I needed.

A few weeks later, I got another beep from my mother.

"It's Taryn," she started. "She's been arrested."

"What?"

"In Chicago. It's a whole mess." Mom went on to reveal that Taryn had been living in Chicago and got the notion to try doing transactions on the phone, the way I used to with her sitting beside me listening in. Something had gone wrong, and she'd gotten caught. "I think they want you too," Mom added.

"For what?" I asked.

I called my lawyer, Julio Phillips, to ask if there was a warrant for my arrest.

He said there wasn't. To be prepared in case I needed to defend myself, I removed millions of dollars, jewels, and gold from safe-deposit boxes and storage units and put them in my home safe. I considered leaving America temporarily. Barbados seemed appealing, or some other island, but deep down, I wanted to stick around to help Taryn. I could not go to her, but I could pay for a good attorney.

*   *   *

I had no inclination whatsoever to do any transactions, even when I got a call from my dear friend Maurice, Bradley's room-mate. He was in a bind and desperate for quick cash. As Maurice and Bradley were close, Maurice knew about the money Bradley and I made in Vegas and that I could get lots of cash fast.

"Look—let me just give you some money," I offered. "How much do you need?"

"Too much to borrow," he insisted. "I doubt that I could ever pay it back. And I could never accept money from you as a gift."

"How much?" I insisted.

After more pressing, Maurice revealed that he needed $150,000 to get out of a jam. Saying this, he sounded fretful, like violence could be involved if he didn't produce the funds quickly.

"Please, Tanya, just do one transaction for me. There's a guy I trust, Lou, who can do the withdrawal," he begged.

I wanted to help Maurice. I couldn't imagine allowing something awful to happen to him if I could stop it. As we talked, I decided to do this last transaction and then shut down the operation altogether. I'd take my treasure and leave for Barbados.

After agreeing to help, I figured the casino would be the easiest and quickest way to move money without attracting attention.

Considering this option, I questioned Maurice closely. "Do you really trust this guy to do a big transaction like this?" I asked. "Can he handle himself?"

"Yes. He's discreet and trustworthy," Maurice said. "If you want to check him out yourself, I can get him on the phone."

"I never, ever talk to runners," I reminded Maurice. "It's too risky. I learned that long ago. I also stopped working with friends. But I want to help you."

"OK. But how will Lou know what to do? Will I need to train him? I need you to tell me what to tell him," Maurice said.

There was simply no quick way to explain everything about dispatching runners to Maurice to convey to someone else. Hoping Maurice thoroughly communicated everything I told him to the new runner was a game I wasn't willing to gamble on. I agreed to direct Lou through it myself.

Lou was sitting right beside Maurice as we spoke, and he passed the phone to Lou.

"We're gonna hit Caesars Palace," I said to Lou. "I'm wiring one-hundred-and-sixty-thousand dollars. With that amount, they'll consider you a high roller. Do you know what that means?"

"No," he said.

"They'll roll out the red carpet. Give you a VIP suite on the house. Bring you anything you need. Anything."

"Anything?" Lou said.

"Anything. And you won't pay a dime," I said.

"That sounds great."

"It is. But the trick is that if you're a high roller, you have to act the part. You have means. You're rich. Privileged. That means you're kind and expect nice things. Never seem surprised when they give you something. And you're there to gamble. You can't just get the money and run. Do you understand?"

"I do," Lou said. "I can do it. Count me in."

I went on, "The overall plan is this: After you check in, you're going to buy ten thousand in chips and hit a few tables. Have some drinks. The good stuff, top shelf only. And enjoy yourself. Talk to the girls who'll gather around to watch you gamble. Be smooth. The dealers are watching. So are the guards. They'll be looking through cameras, which are everywhere in Vegas. When the ten thousand is gone, you need to get upset about losing. Only then, when I tell you it's OK, can you take out the cash."

"Copy," he said. "This will be fun. And I get to help our friend. Trust me—I'll do just fine."

"I'm glad to hear that. The most important thing is that you have to check in with me at every step and do exactly what I say. Don't just try to wing it. I'm here to support you," I explained.

"For sure," he said casually.

"OK, pick up your ticket to Las Vegas at the airport. Beep me one-one-one-one with your pay phone number when you get to the casino."

The next day, as planned, when Lou got to Caesars Palace, he beeped me. I went to a pay phone and called the number he sent.

"Thanks, now go to the cage and confirm that your wire has arrived," I instructed him. "Then check into your room, send me the number, and wait there for my call."

"OK," he said. "Got you."

On schedule, Lou beeped me the room number. I gave him a few minutes before calling. There was no answer.

I waited half an hour. No answer. I tried again fifteen minutes later and then after another fifteen, I called again. I confirmed with the hotel operator that it was the right room number and tried again. No answer. I began getting anxious. I was about to call Maurice and abort the mission when, finally, Lou picked up the phone.

"What happened? Did you get the money?" I asked. Given the amount of time that had passed, I knew he must've skipped ahead and completed the transaction. Certain men don't want to take direction from women.

"Yes," he confirmed.

"Did everything go OK?"

"Yes, fine. I did just what you said. Exactly what you said." He was short. No excitement. No sense of triumph. I also noted that he kept saying, "You."

"Where's the money?" I asked.

"I have it all right here."

I was getting impatient with Lou's flat answers—and uncomfortable.

"You have it all? How did they give it to you?"

After a long pause, he said, "They gave me the cash in a brown paper bag."

Hearing that, I knew something was wrong, very wrong. No casino would hand over $150,000 in a brown paper bag.

"Is everything OK?" I asked.

"Yes. You will get your money."

*   *   *

The following day, Lou checked in for his return flight home. Maurice called to tell me he couldn't do the airport pickup, because he had to rush back to Minneapolis for an emergency. As I never met runners at airports, I was trying to figure out how I'd get the take from Lou without being personally involved.

"I can get it," Jim volunteered when I told him about my predicament. "It'll be easy. I'll meet him there and get the cash. Nothing's going down at the Orange County Airport. Ain't nothing but old white people there."

I didn't accept his offer. I was sure Jim wanted the money for himself. While I had a stash, he was flat broke. Annoyed, Jim proposed, "Well, why don't you do it then?"

Lou and I picked a place to meet. He told me what he'd be wearing and that he'd be holding the brown paper bag.

Before heading to the airport, I called Maurice. "Are you sure this guy's for real? Something feels off."

"He's cool, Tanya, I promise. Don't worry," he said.

Planning for a quick pickup, I had Jim drive me to the airport in his brand-new, custom-painted blue Mercedes.

"Jim, this is no good," I said as we neared the airport. "The guy sounded funny."

"Girl, relax. You always get like this when we are closing a big deal. If something happened, you would know by now."

"I know it's not right. I can feel it."

Aretha Franklin's voice came on the radio: "We're goin' ridin' on the freeway . . ."

To calm me, Jim started singing along in a high, funny voice, "Of love, winds against our backs . . ."

We were "ridin'" on the Orange Freeway.

I had to laugh.

"Come on, Tanya! Sing it with me! We gonna get some money!"

Singing eased my mind for a while. But at the airport, my intuition went on high alert. I felt like a door had closed, and I was stuck inside. I couldn't breathe.

"Drop me off," I ordered Jim before we reached the meeting place.

"I'm not coming with you?" he asked.

"No, just idle in a spot where you can see me and watch. If something weird happens—like someone grabs me—don't get out. Just pull out and drive away."

"Come on," he said. "It's gonna be OK. You're just anxious."

"It just doesn't feel right."

I walked to the meeting point with all my senses tingling. I passed a guy standing at the curb, facing away from me, who quickly swiveled his head in my direction as I passed. Though I was spooked, I stayed purposeful. I spied a red-haired woman sitting on a bench. She was reading the newspaper but, as I approached, shot me a hard glance.

Something deep inside of me hollered, *Turn back! This is a trick!*

Up ahead, I saw a guy holding a brown paper bag. He started toward me. *How does he know who I am?*

"Tanya!" he said and, without giving me a chance to answer, shoved the paper bag into my hands.

The moment I took it, the guy from the curb and the red-haired woman were on me, shouting, "FBI." More agents came swarming as they yanked my arms behind my back and cuffed me. Standing there in cuffs, everything slowed. It was like a dream. I watched the agents, jubilant, excited, congratulating each other and saying, "We got her!" as if I were the most wanted criminal in California.

One of the agents called out, "Check the cars. Look for an accomplice."

"Look for a Rolls! A Ferrari! A Jaguar! Check the parking lot," another voice shouted.

Out of the corner of my eye, I saw Jim's Mercedes roll right by us, heading out of the airport.

I hoped he'd go back to my house, where I had the resources to hire a lawyer and post bail.

The Feds took me to the Orange County Central Women's Jail, which was like a holding facility.

I called my parents to let them know what was going on. As if she, too, sensed that my luck was running out, my mother answered on the first ring.

"No. No!" she said when I broke the news. She sounded heartsick and tired.

Dad was even worse. He was quiet.

Both of their youngest daughters, their beloved twins, were now in custody.

"Don't worry about me. I just want you to know where I am. I'll figure out how to get out of this mess," I said before hanging up and crying.

When I received the indictment, I learned the Feds hadn't discovered that I'd lifted funds from a bank to wire to Caesars Palace. Apparently, Lou freaked out and ignored my instructions. When he went to the cage, instead of getting $10,000 in chips, he demanded the whole sum in cash—$150,000. The cashier, surprised, asked, "You're not gambling?"

"No, I just want the cash," he insisted.

"Why would you wire money to a casino if you're not going to gamble?"

Flustered, Lou's dumb ass blurted out that a girl named Tanya had told him to pick up the money. Of course, that triggered an investigation—first by the casino supervisors, who called the local police, who in turn brought in the FBI.

When Lou was missing for two and a half hours, he was being grilled by the Feds. They were there with him in the room, feeding him lines, when he finally answered my call and set up the arrest plan.

After learning all this, I asked the agent, "So, what am I being charged with?"

"We're transferring you to the Sybil Brand Institute. You'll find out there," he said.

As promised, hours later, when I was transferred to the Sybil Brand Institute, the women's jail in Los Angeles County, I was made privy to what I was up against. Once again, I was being charged with bank and wire fraud, but not in LA or even Las Vegas. Instead, I was being sent to Chicago for indictment.

"What the hell?" I protested. "Chicago? For what?" I immediately thought of Taryn.

19

SOPHISTICATED LADIES

At about 3:00 a.m., the US Marshals came to pick me up from Sybil Brand to transport me to the airport. I waived the extradition hearing and consented to voluntarily being transferred to Chicago.

We ended up at an air force base about a mile away from LAX, which was inmate transport protocol meant to keep traveling prisoners away from civilians. Moments later, I was out of the van and escorted to the tarmac in handcuffs. As we approached an off-white Boeing 737, I saw other male and female prisoners in handcuffs and leg irons waiting to board the plane. There were about 20 women and 125 men. Dozens of marshals held guns, guarding us.

Before boarding the plane, a female marshal checked everyone for contraband. She patted me down and made me open my mouth as she peered inside. She made me separate my

NEVER SAW ME COMING

hair down to the scalp. I even had to remove my shoes for close inspection.

The female prisoners boarded first. We were seated in the front four rows of the plane. The cold plane had a stale, mildewed smell, like clothes left in the washer too long.

We took off on a circuitous journey that reminded me of a bus route. For hours, the plane made stops in different cities around the country, picking up inmates and moving them to different locations for court appearances, medical emergencies, and facility reappointments. Throughout the flight, we were given a bag lunch and brief bathroom breaks.

By the time the plane landed in Chicago, I was exhausted by the state-hopping journey. The sun was setting outside, and a crisp chill attacked my skin as soon as they opened the door of the airplane.

When I arrived at the Metropolitan Correctional Center, the receiving guard, a tall Black woman, came out to get a look at me. Smiling and looking me over, she said, "Wow, you look just like your twin."

Hearing "twin," my thoughts immediately went to Taryn. I couldn't wait to see my sister.

After I removed my clothes, one of the guards checked every part of my body for weapons and other forms of contraband. They also took my fingerprints and a mugshot.

When they were done, a guard escorted me to the female inmates' floor, where Taryn was at the door waiting for me.

We fell into each other's arms, and tears sprang from my eyes. I was relieved she was OK and no longer felt alone in the world.

"Taryn! It's you!" I said.

"Tanya, I'm so happy you're here."

I hadn't laid eyes on Taryn since I fled Minneapolis a year before. She looked great, having gotten sober, and seemed just like her old self.

The guard told me to quickly take my things to Taryn's room because lockdown would be in a few minutes.

The MCC was a new facility and looked almost like a no-frills dorm instead of a jail. Taryn's room was carpeted. It contained a built-in hardwood bunk bed and a desk. In the common areas, there were microwave ovens and pool tables. There was a TV area.

The other floors were reserved for men. Male and female inmates lived separately but worked together in common areas, like the kitchen and laundry. Taryn had a laundry job and had already gotten herself a boyfriend.

I had no intention of settling.

"They are not gonna let you out of here," Taryn said when I told her my plan one night after dinner. Instead of hanging out in the common area with the other inmates, sometimes we'd sit in our room and have deep conversations, almost like we were back in our bedroom on Washburn Avenue. It was a small comfort.

"Why not? Bail is only denied if you're a flight risk. I never missed a single hearing during my last trial, so there's no reason to consider me one," I said.

"You came up with the defense that got you acquitted. You beat the Feds. No one beats the Feds. And then you fled

Minneapolis and they could no longer monitor your movement. They didn't like that. You know how they are. They'll find a way to keep you in here."

"I had the right to leave Minneapolis," I said. "I was acquitted, innocent under the law, not charged with any crime. I only left because of the surveillance and harassment."

After I finished stating my position, Taryn simply said, "We'll see."

When I went to court for my arraignment, I was assigned a public defender as I hadn't retained a lawyer. The AUSA presented my charges to the court. Most of the people mentioned in the complaint were from Taryn's circle in Chicago, friends I'd never heard of. But two names jumped out—Randall and Terrell. My public defender requested bail, stating that I wasn't a flight risk and needed to be free to be with my family and build my defense. Within seconds of hearing the request, the judge said, "Bail denied."

The words echoed through my soul. I couldn't move. I was frozen in disbelief. My stupor was shaken by the bailiff, who grabbed my arm to escort me out of the courtroom. Suddenly, I felt my legs giving out. She held me up. "Come on. Let's go."

When we got out of the courtroom, she said, "Don't you repeat anything I'm telling you, not ever. You hear me?"

"Yes," I said.

"I've been working here over twenty years, and I've seen it all. That wasn't right. Word is the Feds got to the judge. They leaned on him. Told him you'd bankrupt the country if you got out," she said. "I'm only telling you this because you need to know what you're up against. You need to get ready because what you're fighting—it's going to be hell."

When I got back to the MCC, I ran to the bathroom and vomited up everything in my stomach until golden bile came out. Taryn followed me to the latrine and pat my back sympathetically.

"You feeling OK?" she asked.

We locked eyes. Nothing needed to be said.

"Have you been to the doctor yet?" she added.

"No," I said. "I mean I just haven't really admitted it to myself yet. I'm having his baby. I can't believe it. I can't have my baby in jail." I told her all about Jim.

I called Julio Phillips.

After my last trial, with Julio's encouragement, I'd given him money for safekeeping.

"I want that rainy-day money!" I said when I got him on the phone.

"Calm down, Tanya. I'll defend you," Julio said.

"No, I need a top Chicago lawyer, someone here who knows the system, the AUSAs, and the judges. You have the money, and I need it."

I went on a bit, stressed by his pushback.

"Tanya, don't you know that they're listening?" he said. "They're recording every word you say."

I got quiet.

After a beat, Julio said, "I'll come to Chicago and represent you. It won't cost you a dime. Don't worry."

*   *   *

Learning the Feds were listening in on all of my calls, I avoided calling Jim directly. I didn't want him pulled into the conspiracy and forced to testify against me. I'd also lose access to whatever money he'd stashed. I called his mother. She knew about the transactions, and I was sure Jim had told her about the arrest. She was hip, and I wouldn't need to say anything that would implicate me.

"I'm in Chicago. I need help so I can get a good lawyer," I told her.

"Help?" Jim's mother repeated, sounding clueless and distant. "I'm not sure we're in a position to do that right now."

"You are," I said. "Just get things in order. Use what you have."

"We don't have anything."

Those words felt finite and were repeated by everyone else in the family every time I called.

On one of the calls, Ava, Jim's sister, said, "We don't think it's safe for us to be taking these calls. My mom is scared."

I replied, "I'm scared too. I'm pregnant."

"What? Is it—"

I cut her off. "It is."

A few days later, Randy and Rita came to visit me. We met in the visitation room, a glassed-in area visible to all inmates on the floor, with the guards standing watch. When they entered, they greeted me like loving family members. Rita wrapped her arms around me and held me tight.

"I've been worried sick about you. How have you been? How's the baby?" she asked, looking at my flat stomach. I was just a little over a month and not showing yet.

"I'm taking it one day at a time," I said, not wanting to give them too much. "My focus is on getting out of here. I'm due in December. You two have any word?"

"We haven't seen him much," Randy said as we sat at the table. "He hooked up with Vicki right away when you got arrested. She's pregnant. He took your money, and they bought a big house. They also bought two smaller houses."

"They're driving fancy cars and spending your money like crazy," Rita added. "She's even wearing your clothes, and Jim's gambling almost every weekend."

"And that Harry Winston diamond you had. He sold it," Randy said.

My heart sank.

"Some of the furniture he kept and some he sold," he said. "That includes everything else you had in that house. He cleared it all out. He's a very rich man now," Randy went on. "My mom and stepdad got in on it too. They bought a new house. Ava and her husband did as well. Everyone is living it up on your dime."

I could hardly bear to listen but didn't want to break down and reveal my despair. I let him go on. This was how Jim's family operated. They were all opportunists who'd stop at nothing to get what they wanted, even if it meant hurting another family member.

Finally, Randy got to the windup, the real purpose of their visit. "So, Tanya, the nitty-gritty is my brother is no good. He ain't gonna come through. Let us help. I know you got cash stashed away someplace. You just tell me where it is, and I'll take care of you. I'll get you a lawyer, get you some money in here."

I couldn't believe how stupid Randy thought I was. Why would I give him anything?

"Thank you for that information, but if you really want to help, get my money from your brother. That's what I need. Tell Jim I need my money. These Feds will put me away forever without the right representation, and I'll never be able to raise our child. My parents are getting up in age, and they're not in the best health. I need to get out to help them. Please figure out a way to get Jim to help me."

"He won't do it," Randy said flatly. "He won't give up what he has to help you."

"Well keep trying. And if you can get any of my money, I'll reward you for it," I said, using a promise that I knew would activate Randy and Rita.

Once I got back to my room, I sank into a blue funk as deep as any in my twenty-six years. It was one of the few times in my life that I'd ever felt helpless—locked up, facing charges too trumped-up to counter, with no resources to research a way out, cut off from the fortune that could get me a great lawyer; my hands were tied in every way.

While locked up, I got word that my older sister, Babs, had died under suspicious circumstances in Europe. Her boyfriend had her body cremated without even talking to my parents.

There was a certain camaraderie among the inmates, and Taryn and I were popular.

Still hoping to fund my defense, I reached out to Julio a few more times to ask about the money I'd given him. He always redirected me and repeated that he'd represent me "for free." I still wasn't keen on that and wondered if he had blown the cash.

The Feds, who were listening in on our conversations—violating attorney-client privilege—were curious too. Two agents I didn't recognize came to see me. In a meeting, they said, "Tell us why you're mad at Julio Phillips. You know he's a bad guy. A dirty lawyer."

"I know no such thing," I said, unwilling to help them divide and conquer. They were clearly getting at something concerning our relationship.

"Is he working with you?" one of them asked.

"He's my lawyer," I said. "He represents me."

Julio informed me that they wanted to charge him as my conspirator—or, at the very least, use my words against him. The AUSA had filed a motion stating it was a conflict of interest for Julio to represent me. To stop this, I had to file papers waiving the conflict of interest and noting that I'd spoken in haste on the telephone, that Julio was not a conspirator, that he was my attorney, and that I waived the right to another lawyer. While I still wanted to find a local attorney to represent me, I had no choice. I filed the papers and let Julio take on the case.

Taryn and I went to trial in September 1986. In the months leading up to it, we talked about how to play it and what we should say and do.

"Why don't we just plead guilty?" Taryn asked one night in our room. "At least we'll get less time. Or maybe if you tell them how you're doing all of this, they'll be even more lenient. That's what they really want to know. They want to stop it."

Taryn had a court-appointed attorney, Jack Ferguson, and I wondered if those words were coming from him. There was no way I would plead guilty or that Julio would advise me to do so.

"I won't plead guilty to something I didn't do. I'm going to fight this as hard as I can. I'll never bow down to the Feds. I'd never give them that satisfaction."

While Taryn and I told our parents not to come to Chicago to sit in on the trial, fearing it would be too hard for them, our mother sent us slacks and blouses to wear to court. As I was six months pregnant and showing, mine were maternity.

From the first day, our courtroom was packed, with people standing in line, hoping to get in. The identical twin angle proved irresistible to the media. The *Chicago Tribune* ran a story that began: "One of the weirder TV shows of the 1960s starred Patty Duke as wacky identical cousins, one British, one American. Well, Chicago is hosting a financial melodrama worthy of prime time, starring bona fide but allegedly crooked identical twin sisters."

Other news accounts noted that we not only looked exactly the same, with matching clothes and our hair pulled back the same way, but also had identical reactions, like crossing our legs or folding our arms the same way at the same time.

Assistant US Attorney Seymour Kennedy laid out the case against us: We'd been indicted for spiriting about $50,000 out of Chicago banks—the charges they thought they could prove—and "possibly as much as $400,000" in other cities that we had no charge for. In other words, they were beating us with a big stick for small offenses because of "possibly" more serious ones. Nine people were indicted along with us for serving as runners, including, of course, Randall and Terrell.

Kennedy described how the phone system worked, calling it a "sophisticated, clever scheme." He claimed that the previous trial, when I was acquitted, left me "too sure" of myself. He told the courtroom that I wrote to the FBI and the Minneapolis cops "bragging about how neither are smart enough to catch me." He was referring to the letter found in my flooded Atlanta townhouse. Kennedy depicted me as hard-core—conniving, defiant, and arrogant.

Then came the parade of witnesses: Taryn's friends. One of them claimed, falsely, that Taryn and I had sent him to make a pickup. I knew the Feds were behind the testimonies and feeding lies. The only factual information concerning me was that I'd sent Randall and Terrell to do pickups at banks in Chicago. But those transactions had nothing to do with Taryn or the other witnesses. They were separate transactions.

All the lying in the trial was getting me down. The Feds weren't playing fair. Even Julio seemed dispirited, as if he sensed that it was a lost cause.

When Randall was called to testify, it was sad to see him struggle to the stand. He was emaciated and frail with full-blown AIDS. I didn't blame Randall for testifying. I always cut people slack for what they do under pressure.

Sometime later, my mother told me that Randall testified only because the Feds threatened him with dying in prison. He told her he couldn't face dying alone.

Even Terrell, who was a smart-ass, with a "bitch, please" attitude, acted cocky and rude on the stand. The Feds are intimidating.

Kennedy kept calling Taryn and me "sophisticated." It was his code word, telling the jury we were more cunning and dangerous than a couple of twenty-six-year-old Black girls might seem. Our sophistication was the reason he cited to introduce an investigative tool never before used in the history of the federal court: voiceprint analysis. The technology was new and its admissibility was uncertain. In Kennedy's words, there was "little dispute" that false wire transfers were phoned in. "The only dispute will be about which twin did it."

The Feds had pulled voice tapes from the banks and had hired an expert, Dr. Hirotaka Nakasone, to compare them in court with recordings they'd made of Taryn and me.

Nakasone constantly affirmed that he could never be 100 percent sure which of us was talking. But as they played each tape, he'd say, "It's highly probable that this is Taryn's voice," or, "It's highly probable that Tanya is speaking."

Watching the jurors' faces, my heart sank. Taryn's lawyer challenged Nakasone's testimony, and the unprecedented use of voiceprint analysis was allowed to stand.

The trial lasted two and a half weeks. Neither Taryn nor I testified for fear that it might do more harm than good. When the jury returned from deliberations days later and we were called back into court, I was sick to my stomach and prepared for the worst.

On thirty-seven counts of wire fraud, bank fraud, conspiracy, and attempted credit card fraud, I was found guilty.

On thirty-one counts of wire fraud, bank fraud, conspiracy, and attempted credit card fraud, Taryn was found guilty.

When the foreman was done, the courtroom erupted with cries of joy from enthusiastic spectators, shouting questions from reporters who jumped over each other to get to Taryn and me and the jostling commotion of photographers snapping pictures.

Even in that chaos, Taryn and I stayed focused on each other as we did when we were kids.

We fell into a long embrace.

"Oh no," Taryn cried.

"Somehow, I'll get you out of this. I promise," I told her.

"We're in this together," she replied as the officers pulled us from our lawyers and escorted us out of the courtroom.

As the journalists and FBI agents crowding the courtroom continued ogling us, I told myself it wasn't over yet, not for me. They used their power to build a case using trumped-up, false conspiracy charges. No matter what it took, I was going to prove I could beat them at their own game.

I rubbed my bulbous belly and whispered to my unborn child, "Come hell or high water, we will be free."

After the ruling, Taryn and I were transported back to the MCC to await sentencing. Soon after we arrived, a guard came to my room to escort me to the visitors' center.

"That was fast," I said, following the guard. I assumed it was Julio visiting to rehash the trial and reveal a plan to get me out.

When we reached the visitors' center, the guard opened the door to one of the private meeting rooms. I entered to see three FBI agents.

I looked back at the guard. Was this for me? He shrugged, motioned for me to take the only seat left in the room, walked out, and closed the door behind him. Left alone, I felt like I was back in Minneapolis being interrogated by aggressive cops.

"Tanya Smith," one of the agents said, drawing my name out like it was a mantra he'd repeated in bed each night. "We gotcha!" He laughed and his face distorted into a demonic caricature.

"You're in deep trouble now," another agent taunted me, "We can lock you up for as long as we want. Got you all to ourselves."

The third agent snickered and leaned in close to my face. I could smell donut-shop coffee and Marlboro cigarettes on his breath. "So, do yourself some good. Tell us how your scam works, and maybe we'll help you at sentencing," he said before looking down at my belly and added, "You're young. Just twenty-six. It'll be a shame if you spend the rest of your life in federal prison. Won't it?"

I adjusted my body in the seat—pregnancy was doing a job on my back—and told myself to block them out, build a thick invisible wall between myself and them, and there would be no way they could see the rage burning within me. That's what they wanted—for me to break, for me to cry and throw myself at their feet. I wouldn't do it. Yes, I was terrified. I didn't want to have my first child in prison. I didn't want to go to prison at all. But the rage overshadowed any trepidation I had about my fate.

With the third agent's noxious breath still burning my nostrils, I looked him right in the eyes and produced a hint of a smile to let them know they weren't getting anywhere. I wasn't giving up any information about my operation.

His voice oozed with annoyance at my demeanor. He said, "You know you could turn this around if you just help us out. Otherwise, deal's off."

"There's no deal to call off." I laughed. "We're done here."

I got up and signaled for the guard to let me out.

20

SENTENCING

A few months later, Taryn and I were headed back to court for sentencing.

As usual, they woke us up at three in the morning to get showered, dressed, and fed to be ready for transport at five.

The marshal charged with driving us in the prison van was funny. He'd be all official when the agents were around, but as soon as they turned their backs, he'd laugh and joke like we were old friends. We could've been.

When Taryn and I got into the van, he turned on the R&B station, and Patti LaBelle and Michael McDonald sang "On My Own" to us.

"Hold on tight, sisters," the marshal said. "I like a bumpy ride."

We half laughed at his joke. He was trying to make things easier for us.

It was freezing in the van. The icy chill in the Chicago air reminded me of Minneapolis. Thanksgiving was in a few weeks. I was nearing the end of my pregnancy and finally accepting that my child would be taken from me soon after birth. I wouldn't see my baby beyond prison walls. I couldn't let that happen.

In the courtroom, federal judge Paul Plunkett, a stoic man with big ears and slender, almost invisible lips glared at Taryn and me like we'd done something really bad to him and now he was in a position to ensure we'd never be able to do anything like it ever again.

The judge pretended he was trying to be fair and not send us away for the rest of our lives. Part of his trickery was allowing my father to speak before sentencing.

Taryn and I didn't want him or Mom to come, but our lawyers thought it would be a good idea for them to ask the judge for leniency and show that we'd come from a good home and with solid parents who could look after us once we were released. Hoping it would lower our sentences, Dad insisted on attending.

I hadn't seen him in nearly two years, but Smitty looked the same as he walked to the podium to address the court. He was in his sixties, his short Afro was more salt than pepper. He wore a blazer over a nice white shirt and trousers. Though he looked like something was weighing heavy on him, he held his head high and his shoulders back. He'd always been a proud man. As he glanced over at Taryn and me, he nodded and smiled to let us know he wasn't angry with us. Quickly, his eyes welled up. By the time he reached the podium, his cheeks were wet, and he had to remove his glasses to wipe away his tears.

He described Taryn and me as children—the smartest of his six kids, the best in school, and the happiest. "Tanya would wake up every day with a smile on her face," he said. "Taryn is daring and sensitive." He talked about how proud he'd always been to show off his twins, saying, "Everybody loved them. They'd say, 'Smitty, bring those adorable twins back around here.'"

At one point, he cleared his throat and said, "I was always sure these girls would accomplish great things, your honor. And I did my best to make sure they had support. But then they got involved with the wrong kind of guys, and their lives began to change."

My heart ached at the sadness in his voice. He was searching for an answer. For how we, his baby girls, ended up here. I was the reason he was here. Yet, here was my father, steadfast and caring—despite how badly I'd let him down—pleading with the judge to have compassion, given my youth and impending motherhood, for what he called "destructive" choices. "I love my daughters, no matter what. And I'll always be here for them," Dad said, catching my eye.

Suddenly, cries from deep down in my gut pushed their way out of my mouth, and I started sobbing uncontrollably. I'd broken my father's heart, strayed far from the example he tried to set for me, from the path he laid out for all six of his children. Memories of the life Dad created for us flooded my thoughts and made my head feel heavy. "I'm still your baby girl," something within me wanted to shout to my father, but no sound came out of my mouth.

When my father was done and had returned to his seat, the judge said, "That was the most heartfelt and moving plea I've ever heard." He then looked at Taryn and me, and we were ordered to stand. "But my hands are tied," he said. He read our sentences.

For misappropriating some $50,000 and "possibly"—not verified—"as much as $400,000," I was sentenced to thirteen years in prison, and Taryn to eight.

The sentences far outweighed common rulings for what we were convicted of. According to a US Department of Justice report, 93 percent of those convicted of wire fraud at the time got less than five years.

"Really, considering everything you've done, this sentence is too lenient," the judge concluded, singling me out. "You're a one-woman crime wave, Tanya Smith."

I let his words roll off my back. At that moment, all I could think about was my father, the things he'd said and how he looked with those tears streaming down his cheeks.

The sadness on my father's face when they ushered me out of the courtroom made me wonder how things had ended up like this. In the beginning, I had just wanted to help people. I wanted to be like my dad. But step-by-step I'd gone elsewhere, and now we were both paying for it.

It was December 7, 1986. Taryn and I were still at the MCC, waiting to be transferred to the prison where we'd serve our time. I'd been moved to my own room. Less than a month after I was sentenced, I went into labor. The first contraction hit hard. It felt like a mule was kicking its way out of my belly.

The pain was intense, aggressive, each time it hit. I grabbed the sheet beneath me on the bed and twisted it up in knots in my hands to mitigate the waves radiating through my core. The jail provided no real maternity care. For them, my pregnancy was a burden I'd somehow planned to get special treatment.

"I gotta get out of here. Let me out. Let me out now," I screamed at the guard in the bullpen outside my room. "My baby is coming."

"What you in here hollering about, Smith?" the guard, a thick woman who wore her uniform too tight screamed back, though she was right at my door. We were locked down for the night; most of the inmates were fast asleep, and she was annoyed that I'd woken her from a nap.

"My baby is coming. Now!"

I found my way to my feet and hobbled over to the door, gasping for air. The pain was taking my breath away.

The guard rolled her eyes and sucked her teeth.

"Could you at least let me out of here so I could walk around. The doctor said it could help," I asked.

"Fine." She opened the door and backed up just enough for me to step out of the room.

"Please," I begged.

She hissed and stepped back again, giving me more space. "Better not be faking." She returned to her desk in the bullpen, which also had a television and a few phones that were usually turned off at night.

The doctor was right. Pacing the hall helped for a while. I rubbed my stomach and took deep breaths as the contractions came and subsided in increments.

As I passed Taryn's door, I knocked on the window.

"I think it's happening. The baby is coming," I reported.

She popped up off her bed and raced to the door with an eager smile. Every ugly thing around me melted away. Though she was just three minutes older than me, suddenly, she became my big sister who was helping deliver my first child.

"How far apart are the contractions? Your water break? You feel the baby moving?" She had many questions. Having had a child, she knew the routine. I could hardly keep up. All I knew was I wanted her beside me, holding me up, keeping me safe from whatever was to come. "I can't believe my niece or nephew is about to be born. I'm about to be a twin auntie!" Taryn squealed.

"What y'all talking about?" the guard asked, stepping between me and Taryn's cell door. Her suspicious eyes slid from me to Taryn behind the glass like we were planning an escape.

"Isn't it obvious? The baby," Taryn answered.

"She's just making sure I'm OK," I said.

"Fine. She sees you're OK, so keep walking." The guard gestured for me to move on.

I turned to start pacing, but right then, another contraction hit, and I cried out in pain.

"Tanya!" Taryn yelled before hollering at the guard, "Let me out of here. Let me help my sister."

"No. No one else is getting out. You wanna walk to help with the pain, you walk alone," the guard said.

I started walking again.

"I'm here," Taryn said. "Right here. I'm watching you, sis."

I made my way to the end of the hallway and turned back to the guard, who was on the phone at her desk.

I was starting to feel worse, and the contractions were getting closer together.

I trudged to the desk and pressed the guard, "I think it's time. I need to go to the hospital."

"It ain't been long enough. You fine," she said, barely looking me over.

"Please do something. At least let my sister out so she can help me," I begged.

She got up like she was doing me a huge favor and went to let Taryn out of her cell.

Taryn bolted to my side just as I fell into a chair in the bullpen. She grabbed my hand and stroked my back. "Hang in there," she kept saying. "Everything is going to be fine." She turned to the guard, who was standing over us. "What about the hospital? She needs to go."

"I've called. I'm waiting for word," the guard said.

"Word? What do you need 'word' for? She's obviously about to have a baby."

"She's OK. It's probably just false labor."

I started crying because of the pain. "I can't have my baby in this prison," I said, looking into Taryn's eyes. "I have to get out of here before it's too late.

"Call them again," Taryn barked at the guard, who picked up the phone and spoke low to someone on the other end. She hung up and shrugged.

"What? What did they say?" Taryn demanded.

"It's out of my hands. I have to wait for word."

"Taryn, I'm going to have my baby right here," I said.

"No, Tanya, you're going to the hospital. Fuck this."

Taryn jumped up and, without permission, went to one of the inmate phones and dialed 911. "I need help. My sister is having her baby, and these people are playing games," she said to the operator and hung up. "They're on the way," she added, glaring at the useless guard.

The next thing I knew, there were paramedics on the floor, loaded down with equipment. The other inmates were stirring.

"Where's the lady in labor?" the paramedics asked. "Someone called it in."

After a brief checkup, they strapped me onto a gurney. "We're taking her out," they told the guard. "Her baby's coming."

Hours later after pushing, breathing, and enduring pain like I'd never known, I delivered a nine-pound, eight-ounce son. I was between worlds. Depleted. When the nurse put my son in my arms, the haze of exhaustion lifted, and an unimaginable bliss filled my heart.

I stroked his perfect, delicate hands and feet, kissed his forehead, and took in his new-to-the-world scent. It wasn't sweet as I had imagined. It was earthy and raw, like putting my nose to a fresh wound. Still, I took in long, deep breaths of him and promised myself I'd never forget the moment—how he looked, felt, and smelled.

"It's your mommy," I whispered to him, though he was sleeping like he'd done all the pushing. "It's all right," I said.

"Get some rest, little baby. Just know Mommy is here and she loves you."

Staring down at that sweet, innocent soul in my arms, I was hit with guilt. What kind of world was I bringing him into? What kind of life would this be? His mother is a prisoner. His father, whom I only dated for six months, was in the wind. I couldn't believe I hadn't heard from Jim. I didn't want to be a mother without a husband. I always thought when I became a mother, I would focus on my children, like my mother did. Stay at home. Cook for them. Dress them up. Teach them right from wrong.

After a few hours, my baby boy, whom I named Justin, was pulled from my arms, and I was transferred back to the MCC, my body still wide open and raw from labor.

A few days later, my parents came to see me in the MCC. I was nervous. Any misgivings I had about the reunion quickly dissipated when I saw my mom. She greeted me with the biggest smile. She said she was proud of me. I'd created such a beautiful baby and knew I'd be a good mother. My parents agreed to raise Justin until I was released.

We met in the visitors' room. Taryn came along to spend time with our parents and see her son, who they also brought along.

"He already looks just like you," she said, doting on Justin.

I nodded, but I wasn't convinced. Just days old, he was still mushy in the face and his color hadn't come in.

"I'm going to put pictures of you up in his bedroom," she said. "And we'll start practicing saying, 'Mama,' so it'll be his first word."

"That's all right by me," I agreed.

Aiden kept darting his tiny eyes between Taryn and me. He couldn't figure out why two people looked just alike.

"I don't think he's ever seen twins before," my father said. "Boy, that's *your* mama right there." He pointed Aiden in Taryn's direction, and we all laughed.

Something clicked once he got to his mother, and he leaned into her. Though he hadn't seen her in a while, he knew.

The sweet reunion was a good distraction. Time was running out. Soon, our parents would have to leave with our children.

We weren't a churchgoing family, but my father gathered us together for a prayer. We held hands and bowed our heads.

"Lord Jesus," my father began, his voice solemn and dripping with a paradoxical mix of sadness and hope. "Watch over my daughters. Let them know they can always come home. To me. And to you. Watch over their children. Bless them as you have blessed all our children. Fill their hearts with love and joy."

By the time the guard knocked on the door, indicating it was time to go, we were all crying—even Justin, who was hungry for milk.

Holding him in my arms, I tried to memorize every corner and crease on his face, to take a picture with my heart.

As my parents packed up to go, taking Justin from my arms and wrapping him in a thick blanket to brave the Chicago winter outside, I felt the same mix of sadness and hope I'd heard in my father's voice during his prayer.

I was hopeful because I knew my mom and dad would cherish Justin. They'd been ideal parents for the six of us, unconditionally loving, giving, and empathetic. But I was also sad because none of this would be easy for them. Though they were putting on a brave face, beneath their excitement and prayers, they looked somber and careworn, shattered by sorrows. They were supposed to be enjoying their golden years, sitting on their porch, reflecting on good times.

As the guard escorted Taryn and me back to our cells, I refused to let one tear fall from my eyes. I used the raging emotions to fuel a plan to find a way out of this. I had to leave prison and hit the reset button on my life, to unburden my parents and nurture my son to manhood.

In my cell that night, I wrote a letter to the judge who presided over my case to request an early release due to excessive sentencing. Prisoners have the right to protest if they feel their sentences are excessive, which I certainly did. To bolster my case, I researched white-collar verdicts. There were plenty, including high-class grifters like Ivan Boesky, who was found guilty of making millions of dollars through insider trading. In lieu of prison time, white-collar offenders were fined millions of dollars in deals crafted by high-powered lawyers—fines that were simply the cost of doing business, the price of taking financial risks with huge upsides. For his crimes, Boesky was sentenced to three and a half years; he only served two.

The disparity in our incarceration time—years for me, months for people like Boesky—was shocking. I included all of this and more in my letter and sent it off, hoping it would reach an open ear.

21

ALDERSON

I f you're going to survive this, you have to learn how to keep your mind busy and focused on something other than where you are," another inmate told me, referring to prison. The unrequested tip came right on time. After giving birth, all I could think about was my baby boy and when we were going to be reunited. His birth presented an indelible time marker in my life—before Justin and after Justin. I was determined that everything would be different and everything would be for him.

Thoughts of Justin inspired me to get through Christmas without breaking down. Instead of being depressed and angry as New Year's Eve ushered in 1987, I was anxious and eager to set things in motion.

Everyone at the MCC made the time pass easier. Our pasts made us a family of sorts, for the time being anyway, and creating good times together was the easiest way to comfort each other. We exchanged gifts during the holidays, told old stories about our childhoods, and shared resolutions. While we enjoyed those pleasant moments of escape, there were also bad times. One was the day Taryn and I learned we were being split up. The Bureau of Prisons has the sole responsibility of determining where an offender will serve their sentence. While we begged to be sent to the same prison to do our time, they thought it would be a security risk because no one could tell us apart.

During our tearful goodbye in the elevator, I repeated my promise to Taryn that I'd figure out how to free us both. I didn't know how yet, but I'd do it.

"I promise," I cried into Taryn's chest. "I will do it."

"I know you can, but don't focus on that. Just be strong for me, OK?" she said, wiping my tears. "We've been apart longer than this. We can do it." She looked into my eyes. "We will survive this."

"I know, sis. I know."

When the elevator doors opened, the US Marshals peeled us apart. They ordered Taryn to get in line with a group en route toward an inmate-only ConAir flight headed to Pleasanton in Dublin, California, otherwise known as the Federal Correctional Institution or FCI: Dublin, where Taryn was to complete her eight-year sentence. Pleasanton was a so-called low-security prison for women that shared a campus with a men's detention center—effectively coed like the Chicago MCC but with more sex and drugs. The institution was also known for drastically reducing popular inmates' sentences. Patty Hearst, who was sentenced to seven years for bank robbery, only served twenty-two months at Pleasanton. In the 1990s, Heidi Fleiss, the Hollywood Madam, was released from Pleasanton after doing twenty months of a seven-year sentence for tax evasion and money laundering. Later, Michael Milken, whom the government claimed stole some $4.7 billion, only did twenty-two months of the judge's sentence reduced from ten years to three. Hopefully, Taryn would get the same breaks.

When Taryn was gone, the marshals took me to Midway Airport, where I was to board a flight to Las Vegas to face charges for the failed money transfer with Maurice's friend. At the airport, two marshals helped me out of the van. I was confused because we were at the main terminal, and I'd commonly boarded inmate flights at private terminals and bases.

"Why are we here?" I asked.

"You're flying commercial," one of the marshals replied.

I looked down at my cuffs. "Can we take these off?"

"No way."

As I was escorted through the airport, people gawked and pointed fingers in my direction. They looked like they imagined I was a serial killer or drug lord. I was embarrassed.

"Can we at least cover the cuffs?" I asked.

"No" was all I got.

We boarded the flight first. I was taken to the back of the plane and strapped into the very last row between the marshals.

By the time I got to Las Vegas, I decided I wouldn't fight the charges. I was caught in the act and didn't have access to my money to pay an attorney. Using a public defender, I pleaded guilty to fraud by wire and conspiracy and received a sentence of two years running concurrently, which means serving at the same time as the thirteen-year sentence from Chicago. I wasn't happy about it, but at least I didn't get more time.

About a week later, I was back on ConAir headed across the country to the Federal Reformatory for Women in Alderson, West Virginia, to do my time. Deliberately set in the middle of nowhere, the prison is a five-hour drive from Washington, DC. Its famous prisoners included Billie Holliday, who did ten months for drug possession in the 1940s, and Martha Stewart, who served six months for insider trading in 2004. During Martha Stewart's tenure, the press called the place "Camp Cupcake," which suggests that the inmates were all nonthreatening offenders. In fact, the population had the full range of prisoners, from violent ones, like killers and kidnappers, to white-collar ones like me.

When I arrived, I was sent to receiving and discharge, or the orientation unit, where I was greeted with whistles and catcalls from the other female inmates: "Hey, baby, I like you," and "Oooh, you're cute." Prison felt more permanent and walled-in than jail. Erected in the 1920s, Alderson was America's first all-female federal facility. It was designed to look more like a boarding school than a prison, with two-story "cottages" outlying two large dormitories. Its 150-plus-acre grounds were enclosed by a fence, without guard towers or barbed wire, on the theory that the remote location would make escape unlikely. Observing the terrain, I immediately felt cut off from the rest of the world, like I was in an alternate universe and it would take a rocket ship or a time machine to get me back to civilization.

As a newcomer, I was placed in what they called the dorm, a big room with maybe ten beds. I lived there for about a week, until a space freed up and I got my true placement. I was assigned to the "long-term cottage."

The cottage was a large structure with about thirty-five rooms, each holding two or three inmates. There was a shower room with two stalls on each floor. There was also a big common area, where we could watch TV and socialize.

Most of the inhabitants of the long-term cottage had been convicted of violent offenses, like Lynette "Squeaky" Fromme. She was a devoted follower of Charles Manson, a notorious criminal and white supremacist cult leader whose followers, known as "the Family," carried out several high-profile murders in the late 1960s under Manson's orders. For her part, Squeaky had tried to assassinate President Gerald Ford in 1975. Squeaky was quiet and a bit strange. She kept to herself and often sang to herself. The only obvious remnant of her past was an X-shaped scar above her nose. Manson and most of his followers had carved Xs into their foreheads to protest his "persecution" while on trial for the murders of the actress Sharon Tate and others.

Squeaky and I were together a lot because we were both orderlies in our unit. Being an orderly meant we had to keep the place clean, mopping and buffing the floors and scrubbing the showers and bathrooms. I didn't clean the showers, because they were just too nasty. I let Squeaky do them. She didn't seem to mind. She'd get down on her knees and start singing as she wiped the disgusting mess of hairballs and menses away.

Squeaky wasn't too bad, but she was crazy enough that I didn't want to cross her. In her last prison, she'd beaten a woman with a hammer. She was also smart and attuned to whatever was going on.

Another prominent inmate was Jo Ann Harrelson, actor Woody Harrelson's stepmother. His father, Charles, a professional hitman, had assassinated a federal judge; Jo Ann was implicated and sentenced to twenty-five years for perjury and obstruction of justice. A drug kingpin, Jamiel "Jimmy" Chagra, had commissioned the hit; his wife, Liz, was also in our cottage, doing thirty years for conspiring with him.

Attempted assassination and murder were some scary crimes. Did I really belong in the same cottage as these women? I was different than most of these women. No matter what the Feds thought, I wasn't that kind of dangerous.

As it turned out, Jo Ann Harrelson and her girlfriend, Fay, became my friends. Fay was the first person I befriended at Alderson. A little ring of white supremacists, headed by Liz Chagra, began to taunt me about things like "talking white, like us," as if they thought I was putting on airs. Refusing to take the bait, I stayed pleasant and polite—until I couldn't.

There were two pay phones in the cottage. I was constantly on the phone trying to find a way out of prison. I'd found a way to call long distance for free. I'd call a hotel and ask to be connected to a certain room or department. Once connected, I'd say I had the wrong number and have them transfer me back to the operator. Then I'd ask the operator, who assumed I was an internal caller, like a guest calling from my room, to dial an outside number for me. The system was a version of my old call-in scheme with banks, and it saved me thousands of dollars in long-distance charges.

I was calling everyone I could think of who might help me. I was desperate for money to hire a lawyer for my appeal and even for little essentials from the commissary. Jim's family did nothing but make sympathetic noises, claiming they'd "try to get hold of him." Eventually, they stopped accepting my calls. I rang my parents daily to hear their voices and check in on Justin and Aiden; of course, I'd always ask if they'd heard from Jim. But Jim didn't even seem to want to know about his son, never mind about me. "Forget him," my parents kept saying. But how could I? He controlled the hard-earned assets that could win my freedom. I wasn't interested in romance or hearing how much he missed me. I wanted help getting out of prison.

Since there were only two phones, I was always careful to be courteous. I'd get right off if anyone else approached the booth. But it rankled Liz and her circle that I was on the phone. Since I'd told no one my scheme, they figured I was rich if I was always making long-distance calls.

Jo Ann and Fay warned me to be careful. "They're going to jump you," they said. "We're looking out for you, but watch your back."

One day when I was on the phone, Liz Chagra's girlfriend, a woman in her forties with fine black hair and black glasses, came up to me. "Get the fuck off the phone," she said. "You're always on there. Get the fuck out of the booth!"

If it had been anyone else—or if she'd asked instead of cursing—I would have. But I wasn't about to let her bully me. "No, I'm not getting off the phone. You wait until I'm finished."

I sounded calm, but my heart was pounding. I'd never even had a real fight. Liz and the others started to crowd the booth, boxing me in.

Just then, Jo Ann and Fay came and stood beside the booth, and some sistahs watching TV across the room got to their feet to come to my defense.

"You're a smart-mouthed Black bitch," Chagra's girlfriend snarled.

I said, "Fuck you!"

Then, seeing they were outnumbered, she and the others began to drift away, muttering.

Though I was proud of standing up to them, I knew that Jo Ann and Fay's presence had made all the difference, and I would need to be ready when the white supremacist posse came for me again.

The incident reminded me not to get too comfortable at Alderson.

During free periods when we were allowed to roam the grounds, I struck out in all directions, looking for unfenced stretches. On one edge of the campus, there was a river. I'm a great swimmer and considered trying to cross it. But there were snakes and God-knows-what-else on the banks—not to mention a strong current with a likely undertow. Besides, even if I made it across, where could I go? I was going to need help to get out.

The male guards at Alderson often hit on us, and lots of women screwed them, whether for favors or to break up the monotony. Cameron, one of the guards in my cottage, who took day and night shifts, was handsome, so he had lots of these trysts with "girlfriends." But he took a special interest in me.

After lights out each night, every three hours—at nine, midnight, three, and six—the night guards would shine a flashlight in each bed to count the prisoners. When Cameron was on duty, he'd take his time with me, letting his light play over my body and making remarks like, "Ummph, look at you," and, "You sure are fine."

I stayed covered up to prevent him from seeing much. I was one of the few who could resist his charms, which made him try even harder.

After a few more of these visits, I asked one of the inmates about him.

She said, "He's real cool. If you need something, he's the one."

Off that, once I started plotting my escape, I got more friendly—not exactly flirtatious, but chatty—with Cameron.

Sometimes when he finished the count, I'd get out of bed and go down to his office to talk. It's how I learned he was one of the guards who monitored and recorded inmates' phone calls from the administration building.

"We either listen in or record them. If something fishy is happening, we note it and write a report," he told me.

"So you could just ignore things if you want to?"

Reading me, he responded, "I could. Why do you need to make a private call?"

"I do, but every phone station in here has a big old sign on it stating that all calls are monitored and recorded."

"I'll let you know the next time I'm on duty monitoring the phones in the admin building," he offered. "That way, you can pick up any phone in here and make as many private calls as you want. I won't listen in at all."

"Thank you," I said.

Considering his generous offer, Cameron thought I should be more than grateful. His come-ons got more explicit. Grabbing his crotch, he'd say, "Tanya, don't you need to release some tension?" or "Girl, you know you want some of this." When I was out walking, he'd follow me in the white truck he drove around the grounds.

I stayed playful but chilly, telling him, "Cameron! Stop all that!"

"Don't you like sex?" he'd ask. "What's wrong with you, Tanya?"

Finally, his phone shift came through. By then, he had a full-blown crush on me. "You can have an open line as long as you want," he said when he came to tell me he'd be working in the administration building.

The first person I called was Jim's mother, who'd been ducking my calls since I always begged for money. This time, I got through.

"We all miss you," she said. "We're thinking of you. But Jim's not here." It was the same old song.

"Listen," I said. "Tell Jim I need to talk because I'm getting out of here."

I knew that would snap her to attention.

"Tanya! They're letting you out? I'm so happy." The woman actually sounded ecstatic. I supposed the whole family wanted me back so I could make them some more money.

"Yes. When can I talk to Jim?"

"I can have him here in thirty minutes."

Wow. A miracle. I frowned at how quickly she'd turned things around. I'd been in prison for almost a year. All that time, she'd claimed that she couldn't reach Jim. What a sorry bunch. I wanted to tell her off, but I held back. The idea of hearing his voice—after he'd lavished my money on his girlfriend, abandoned our son, and left me languishing in prison—made me sick to my stomach. But I had to get him on board—cash in hand—for my escape plan to work.

When I called back exactly thirty minutes later, Jim picked up on the first ring. He sounded overjoyed.

"Man, I'm going to get to see my girl again," he said. Not a word about his year of silence.

"Yes, Jim. But I'm going to need my money and some help."

"I'm here for you, baby."

"OK, good. I'll call again. Keep yourself reachable from now on."

With Jim on standby, I focused on the next step in my escape plan, which included Cameron. I told him how I was convicted on trumped-up conspiracy charges, how I would appeal if only I could get the right lawyer, and how badly I missed Justin and needed to help my parents, who were getting older and had health problems. He seemed sympathetic, but I knew he was just trying to find a way on top of me.

"Cameron, I want to offer you something, and I need you to say yes," I said one night in his office. "How would you like to make a hundred-thousand dollars?"

"I'd rather have some of you," he said, rubbing his hard dick, which I could see was actually big through his uniform.

I rolled my eyes, confused, and asked, "You mean you would rather have sex than a hundred thousand?"

Jolted out of his thirst, he looked at me seriously.

"All you'd have to do is get some clothes—a skirt, blouse, blazer, hose, shoes, and a briefcase. Oh, and some eyeglasses. And lipstick!—and leave them in a bag in the administration building bathroom."

"And then what?" he probed.

"And then I'm putting the clothes on and walking out of here. No one will ever know you were involved. I promise you I'll never tell on you, even if I get caught. Never."

"Oh, Tanya, I can't do that." He chuckled.

"I know you need money. And I can get it. Lots of it. Look me up. You'll see."

"OK," Cameron said. "I'll check you out."

A day or so later, he came to me with a serious look on his face.

"You are rich," he said. "They got you on bank fraud for taking a lot of money. I do need cash, but I'm scared, Tanya. I could lose my job and get arrested."

"I understand. In all things, there are risks," I said. "But this is easy money. You'll have a hundred thousand, and I'll have a chance for justice."

After a few more pep talks, Cameron agreed to help.

During his next phone shift, I called Jim to make a plan. After I told him about my idea to walk out of Alderson and that I needed him to be there to pick me up, he said, "I'm not getting near that prison. The Feds don't know about me. No way am I taking that chance."

With Jim playing weak, we decided that I'd get someone else to first drive me out of West Virginia—another state would be less focused on the escape—then Jim would fly out to meet me. I picked a tentative time, right after Christmas when the most-senior guards would be off and those on duty would be distracted.

"Be ready for my call," I told Jim.

As Christmas approached, I grew restless—a little excited, a little anxious. I had confidence in my plan that my disguise could get me to the parking lot. But after that, a lot could go wrong. I had to be ready for anything. The next time Cameron drew a shift to monitor the phones, I called some people from back home to help.

"I've been furloughed. Can you come pick me up in front of the prison on Christmas Eve?" I asked Wesley, my brother Mason's classmate who'd introduced me to J.D. and his sister Jackie. They were both good people who loved adventures, and I figured they'd bite. "I'll pay you," I added, sweetening the deal.

Knowing I was good for the money, Wesley and Jackie agreed to come get me.

The day before my planned escape, I was headed to the pay phone when I heard a strange, gurgling sound. There was

Squeaky, sitting in the phone booth with her head down. She was crying hard to the point of gasping for breath.

"Lynette!" I said. "What's wrong?"

She could hardly get the words out. "Charlie's sick. He has cancer," she wailed.

She looked up, and her bangs parted. I gasped as I could plainly see what she usually kept hidden: the deep X gouged into her forehead. The mark, which looked satanic, reminded me that "Charlie" was Charles Manson. Suppressing a shiver, I said, "Oh no!"

A short time later, the prison sirens blared. "Get off the grounds!" the loudspeaker boomed. "Go to your rooms! We're locking down!"

Everyone in our cottage was milling around, buzzing, "Escape! Who got out?" We gathered. Squeaky was missing.

That night, and for the next couple of days, national media camped outside the prison, with TV anchors doing stand-ups on Squeaky, the Manson Family, prison security, and the West Virginia terrain.

Meanwhile, locked down in my cottage, I thought miserably about how Squeaky foiled my escape plan. By breaking out right before Christmas Eve, she blew my chance to get away. I called Wesley and Jackie to let them know that the crisis meant that my "furlough" was postponed. I'd be in touch.

A day or two later, the media announced that Squeaky had been captured.

When I checked on her, she told me she hadn't actually been captured. She'd never planned to run. They'd found her walking along the railroad tracks, singing and talking to the birds, heading back to Alderson.

"I just wanted to feel free to think about Charlie out in nature and commune with his spirit."

I nodded along and told her I hoped she got what she wanted during her nature walk.

With Squeaky in custody, the prison recovered its normal rhythms. By New Year's, I was ready to escape. But Cameron was spooked by all the hubbub over Squeaky. It took a lot of coaxing, reasoning, pleading, and flattering, but I managed to convince him to try again.

"I'm going to pay you, right?" I said. "Just imagine how much easier your life will be when you get the money. I know you can do this."

Once he agreed, I gave him a warning. "Never trust anyone with what you're helping me with. No one. If you tell one other person, it's no longer a secret. It's the ones you trust, the ones closest to you, who can destroy you."

"OK," he said. "Just remind me of the plan. I leave the bag of clothes and stuff in the bathroom in the administration building and then you'll pick it up?"

"Right. Next, I'll need you to be in position to open the gate so I can walk out. Remember—I'll look like a lawyer who's just finished visiting a client. Just wave goodbye and open the gate. Got it?"

"I got it."

22

ESCAPE STATUS

Wesley, scared as hell being pulled over by a cop in West Virginia, rolled the window down and turned off the ignition as told.

"Did I do something wrong, officer," he asked, his voice shaking with fear.

The cop leaned down and stared into the car, slowly moving his eyes over each of us and scanning every inch of our bodies. After a few seconds that dragged on like years, he looked back at Wesley and asked, "Why were you speeding?"

"I'm sorry," Wesley said. "I didn't realize I was going too fast."

"And you back there"—the cop looked at me and Jackie—"you look nervous. What's going on?"

"No, sir, we're just anxious for a rest stop," I said calmly. The cop was alone, didn't have his gun drawn, and hadn't called for backup. All good signs this was a regular traffic stop.

Wesley handed over his license and registration, and the cop went back to his car to check the documents. Wesley kept peering at him in the rearview mirror.

We had only been in the car for forty-five minutes. I had a few hours before Alderson's 9:00 p.m. head count, when they would realize I was gone. It was more than enough time to get out of West Virginia.

"Keep calm," I urged him. "You've got to play the role. You're just on your way home, nothing more."

There was dead silence in the car as the guys and Jackie struggled to contain their nerves. As the cop started walking back to us, nobody dared to take a breath.

"OK," he said. "I'm not going to give you a ticket. But slow it down. I want you to get home safely." He smiled and handed over the documents before walking back to his cruiser.

After the cop left, Wesley pulled off, and Rob turned the music back on. I sat back and exhaled.

"You did great," I told them. "You earned yourself an extra ten thousand."

"Really?" Wesley asked. "I'll take it."

High Point, North Carolina, was about a four-hour drive from Alderson. When we got there, we checked into a cheap motor lodge. The four of us shared a room with two double beds, a couch, and a chair. I let them have the beds and stayed in the chair. I wasn't going to sleep.

When everyone had drifted off, I slipped out of the room to go to a pay phone to call Jim. I hadn't told him where to meet me. I figured it would be safer to wait until I was actually there. When he answered the phone, I didn't even say hello. I simply said, "I'm out."

"Oh, Tanya, you made it! You're free! I can't believe it! I'm the happiest man in the world!" he cheered. "I'll fly out this evening on a red-eye. I'm so glad I get to see my love again!"

Ignoring his usual over-the-top expressions of love, I said, "You need to bring some money. I have to pay the guys who helped me. I need seventy-five thousand for the drivers to split and a hundred thousand for a guy at the prison. Will you do that?"

"Sure," he agreed. "No problem. See you soon."

The next day, I told Jim to meet me at a mall in High Point. That way, if there was trouble, he wouldn't be able to identify Wesley, Jackie, or Rob—and vice versa.

When we got to the mall, I asked Wesley to drop me off at the entrance of JCPenney.

"Wait here. I'll be back to pay you guys," I said.

I walked through the mall and exited on the other side, where Jim was waiting in a different parking lot.

Jim jumped out of the rental and pulled me into his arms. "Baby, it's you. I can't believe it," he said. "My dreams have been answered."

Yeah, right, I thought. Jim was the absolute ghost I needed to protect me. The Feds didn't know him. While we were together, I was living under a veil, renting a house and driving cars under false names. There was no documented connection between us. I hadn't even named him as the father on Justin's birth certificate. My goal was to pay Cameron, Wesley, and the others for helping me and ride back to Los Angeles with Jim, where I'd reclaim my fortune, build my defense to beat the Feds, and, once cleared of their bogus charges, be reunited with my son and parents.

I got right down to business and asked Jim about my money.

Jim looked at me with big, sad eyes. "I don't have it," he said.

"What do you mean? You didn't bring it?"

"I mean there is no more money. It's all gone."

"What?" I was thunderstruck. "How is that possible, number one? And number two, how am I supposed to pay the people who helped me, who are waiting for the money right now?"

"You don't have to pay anyone, Tanya. Just get in the car."

"I can't do that! I promised them!"

"Forget about them. We've got to get out of here. They could be waiting for you with the cops," he said.

"No, they're not. I can't just take off."

"Who knows what they'll do if you can't pay them?"

Jim got into the car and started the engine. "Get in, Tanya. Or stay here if you want. But I'm leaving. I'm not waiting around to get arrested."

He started revving the engine, saying, "Are you coming or not?"

I had no money at all. Obviously, I couldn't just stay at the mall nor could I go back and beg Wesley, Jackie, and Rob to drive me someplace else. And surely my escape was known by now. I had no choice.

Jim and I stopped at a roadside Kmart, where I got a few toiletries and a change of clothes. We spent our first night in Atlanta and then took the southern route toward Los Angeles. At each stop, Jim tried to have sex with me, but I kept turning him down. I wasn't in the mood, and if I was, Jim wouldn't be my chosen suitor. My resistance was annoying him. Without any money, I was completely dependent on him. I definitely did not like that dynamic.

I asked about my things, but instead of answering my questions, Jim kept sweet-talking me. He went on telling me about how we were going to get our son, lead a wonderful life, and—he stressed this—"make lots and lots of money."

Of course, I knew he was lying. All the way to California, I alternated between fussing at him and silently fuming.

Finally, after four days on the road, we reached Los Angeles County. We stopped at a motel in Walnut, a city not far from Diamond Bar, where our saga began.

From a nearby pay phone, I called my mother. The US Marshals had already been in touch with her.

"Please turn yourself in. You're smart enough to find a way out of this mess legally. Your dad and I will do everything possible to help you, but you have to turn yourself in. I'm afraid for you," my mother pleaded. "And your sister too."

"Why? What's going on with Taryn?"

"As soon as you escaped, the marshals contacted Pleasanton and locked the entire facility down. They put Taryn in the hole.

They told her you were on your way to get her out too. They moved her to a state prison in Washington."

I wanted to lay my burdens down and pour my heart out to my mother, but I hung up the phone.

As I headed back to the motel room, I couldn't reconcile how my freedom—even my life—was in Jim's hands. I'd left literally millions of dollars with him, and he had the nerve to show up to get me without a dime. The first thing I did on opening the door was to light into him about all the shit he had taken from me.

Without a word, Jim popped up off the bed where he was sitting watching television and punched me right in the face.

His knuckles crashed into my right eye, and I saw blackness and stars. I'd never been hit like that. I was too stunned to cry. I took off running from the motel and kept going until my legs gave out. I collapsed on the steps of a restaurant to catch my breath. Then the tears fell.

One of the valets brought a napkin full of ice to put on my face. After sitting for several minutes, I had no choice but to return to the motel.

Jim was more stern than angry.

"Quit talking about your money," he said. "You need to start making more."

Bang! Bang! Loud knocking at the door stopped the conversation. Terrified, I started to run to the bathroom. Jim wasn't alarmed. He opened the door, and Randy was standing outside.

*　　*　　*

In those early days after my escape from Alderson, Jim and I stayed on the move to elude detection. We switched hotels several times while looking for an apartment. Finally, we found a furnished one-bedroom in Panorama City. I got myself some fake IDs, starting with a birth certificate to get my driver's license. I began talking to high-powered lawyers, including F. Lee Bailey and Robert Shapiro. But nothing could happen with my case until I had money. I did some transactions right away. My computer was long gone, and I resorted to my old method of transferring funds by phone into dummy bank accounts.

As before, Jim supplied the runners to withdraw money from the accounts. Knowing the kind of characters he employed, I tested the waters with small transfers. Even so, too often, their pickup efforts failed.

"Damn," Jim would say. "It didn't go through. Do another one."

After hearing this a few times, I was sure Jim was lying and pocketing the cash. I told him that I refused to do any more transfers until he handed over my take.

He grabbed me and pinned my hands behind my back. He pulled me to a chair in the kitchen and tied me to it with a scarf. He went to the stove and turned all the burners on without lighting them. Quickly, the room grew thick with the poisonous scent of gas. "I'm leaving," he said. "You're going to die."

I struggled to get free, but the scarf was too tight.

Snickering, Jim opened the door and crossed the threshold. He knew I was too scared to scream for help and attract the police.

"No!" I stopped him. "Don't go. I'll do what you want."

He shut off the gas and untied me. "You know I'd never hurt you. You're the mother of my son, the woman I love. You're my only girl."

It was a complete lie. The other women were still in the picture. He'd disappear for hours at a time and then come back demanding that I do a transaction. Then he'd be off missing again. I knew he was with them, enjoying the good life with my money.

"You're putting me at risk," I said one morning when he stumbled in. It was February 15, the day after Valentine's Day. "Those women know you're with me, and they don't like it. They could follow you here, make a big scene. Then what?"

"Ain't nobody doing nothing. Everyone knows who you are. The first lady," he said. "And I'm the president." He laughed.

I pulled away from him and said, "I don't like it when you leave me here. I'm a fugitive. It's dangerous."

"No, it ain't. Come on. No one knows we're here. Everything is fine."

"Randy knows where we are. He could tell Rita. She could tell someone else. And your women, they could show up at any time," I said. "I just have a bad feeling. We need to leave this place. Go somewhere else completely different."

A few days later, we drove to Denver, Colorado, and right away, I landed an apartment. It wasn't much, just a tiny, furnished studio. But it would do. Days after moving in, Jim left for Los Angeles, leaving me with no transportation—and, worse, with very little cash.

I was happy he was gone. I enjoyed my solitude and quiet. I didn't have to deal with his violent outbursts and constant demands for sex. A week or so passed, and I was running out of money. I needed to do a transaction. But who could collect the money?

I thought of Rhonda, an older woman who Jim called his "second mom." I didn't know her, but Jim used her as a runner to pick up some watches in Beverly Hills. I had sensed her empathy and could tell that she disapproved of the way Jim treated me. She knew I was the moneymaker and doing everything for Jim. I didn't want to bring trouble to her by asking for help, but she seemed like my only hope.

When I called and explained that I was stranded, Rhonda was sweet and kind. She told me she had been holding money for Jim. He'd taken most of it, but she still had $25,000. She warned me to get away from him.

I asked her to wrap the money in aluminum foil and then bundle it in clothes and put it into a suitcase. I told her to request counter-to-counter service at the airport. I had her address the package to Marcella Kendall, the name on my fake ID.

The money was there in a matter of hours. When I presented my ID at the counter, the attendant said, "Oh yes, Miss Kendall, just a minute."

She went into the back and then out came a white man with a leashed German shepherd. "Is this package yours?" he asked.

"Well, someone asked me to pick it up," I said, feeling uneasy.

"That's what I thought. Do you know what's in it?"

The German shepherd fixated on me with a fierce glare that made me feel self-conscious.

"No." I said, trying to ignore the dog. "I was just told to get it."

"Come with me," he said.

He led me to an interrogation room. I took a seat, and the dog, who sat down beside the man, resumed staring at me.

"This is a drug/money-sniffing dog," the man said. "He's detected money in your package. We think it's money from a drug operation."

"Drugs? Oh my God!" I surprised even myself by bursting into tears. My anxiety was running high enough that the reaction was real.

"Don't cry, Marcella," the man said. "We're not accusing you. Drug dealers use women like you all the time to move money and product. We need you to work with us."

"What can I do?"

The door opened and some men—presumably DEA agents— came in. The dog never even glanced at them. His eyes were trained on me.

"We just want you to answer some questions," the man said.

"Ask me anything," I told him. "I'm against drugs. I want to help you catch them."

Over the next few hours, I described an imaginary guy I met at a club, how he seemed nice, how he offered to pay me for doing him a favor, and so on. I painted a portrait of the trusting, even pathetically naive, young woman they had assumed I was from the beginning.

I played the role so well that the men bought it. They said they'd keep the package, but I was free to go. I was to alert them as soon as my guy got in touch.

I'd taken the bus to the airport but couldn't risk riding it home. When I saw a car driven by an older Black man, I asked for a ride.

As soon as I reached the apartment, I beeped Jim. When he called back, I said, "I just got busted. I need to clear out of here now. Send me a plane ticket."

In Los Angeles, Jim and I moved into a modest townhouse in Orange, which was about fifteen minutes from Anaheim in Orange County. We couldn't risk living any place fancy where we might stand out. I started doing transactions again, but Jim still wasn't giving me any money. He claimed he was using the cash to pay our rent and other bills. "I'm keeping us safe," he said. "You just keep the money coming."

I never recovered anything from the Cliff House—not a stitch of clothing, not a dollar from the safe—and Jim refused to say where it all had gone. Even asking sparked a violent outburst, as did any mention of my share of our current transactions. Clearly to protect my money, I'd have to keep it someplace where I could easily get at it.

By May, I'd been a fugitive for months. I thought I would have had the money for a lawyer by then, but between Jim's hoarding and the frequent failures of his low-rent runners to get small sums of cash (or so Jim said), I wasn't pulling in what I expected.

To make real money, I needed two things: a computer and Livilla, whom I'd been thinking about a lot. I missed her professional runners, who could credibly withdraw large sums, and her scrupulous fairness about our splits. My operation was stronger with her playing her part. Jim was weak. I still had to rely on him since it was tough to navigate alone as an escapee.

When he was off with one of his women, I went to a pay phone and called Livilla.

"I knew you'd get free," she said as soon as she heard my voice. "My people are so happy you're out." But then she gave me a stern lecture on how I'd let them all down. "Everything was going beautifully till you met that guy Jim. I told you he was no good."

I didn't respond.

"Oh no. He's still around?" she said. "We should have taken him out. We still can."

Even with all of Jim's transgressions, I wasn't about to condone his murder. "Please, Livilla, no! Don't talk like that," I said.

"Your call, but I'd hate to say, 'I told you so' three times. Now, let's get back down to business. Money is calling. Are you answering?"

"I am." I laughed, pleased to be reconnecting with my old partner in crime.

"Well, I have a few conditions," she said before explaining that for her to work with me, I'd have to make a commitment to not just do one or two transactions and then bail. Secondly, if her bosses had a specific wish or transaction—say, to buy gold or diamonds or cars—I'd have to fulfill it. Third, in case of trouble, we'd set up a code. If she and I didn't meet in person, no money would change hands unless both the delivery person and the recipient knew the code.

A safe-deposit box seemed too risky. I'd have to show ID and deal with bank officials. I'd once hidden some cash in a plastic bag in the ground, only to find that it quickly disintegrated. After doing some research, I decided to try burying the cash again, but I bought a few insulated, weatherproof aluminum safes for better storage. After driving a short distance, I crossed the county line into San Bernadino County and found a spot in Chino Hills with nothing around for miles. I planned to bury any money I made there.

Over the next few months, I kept doing transactions with Jim, but whenever he left the house, I got to work with Livilla. I collected my cut in public places, like malls and grocery stores, watching Livilla through binoculars to be sure she was alone. I began to amass a decent nest egg in the safes. I had enough freedom to leave Jim, but being a fugitive, I was afraid to be alone. I swore to myself that the minute I had enough money, I would escape Jim, hire a lawyer, turn myself in, and get my case reopened.

When I stopped nagging Jim about my cut or seeing his girlfriends, his harangues and beatings let up. He didn't even spy on me as much. He just let me make my transfers and then he'd go collect the cash. He was saving it, he always told me—the same song and dance—though he was likely blowing it in the casinos.

One day, Jim came home while I was talking to Livilla, organizing a pickup. I quickly hung up, but he'd caught enough to understand. He went nuts.

"You fucking bitch!" he screamed. "You're back with Livilla. How dare you cut me out?"

He jumped at me and dragged me to the standing beam between the kitchen and dining room. Slapping and punching, he shoved me against the beam and tied me there with a rope.

"No. Don't. You're going too far," I warned him, hoping he'd hear me through his rage and stop. As I sagged against my bonds, sobbing, he yanked a plastic bag over my head, clutching it tight at my throat, blocking my airway. With his other hand, he pummeled me, smashing his fist into my face, my breasts, and my stomach.

"You dirty, lying bitch!" he shouted as he beat me. Whenever I slid down the beam, he'd give me a breath and then yell, "Get up," and keep on slugging.

Blood blurring my vision, I was sure I was going to die.

Meanwhile, the phone kept ringing. I knew it was Livilla calling back because I'd hung up. The constant ringing finally broke through Jim's fury.

"That's her, isn't it?" he said. "She has money for you, doesn't she?"

"Yes," I admitted to get him off me.

Pulling the long cord along, he brought the phone to me.

Then there was a gun to my head.

"Call her back. Tell her I'm sending someone to get it."

When I reached Livilla, she could hear the strain in my voice.

"Are you OK?" she asked.

I told her I was fine and to give the money to Jim's runner.

"What's the code?" she asked.

I gave her the wrong one to alert her.

Jim stayed with me and sent his runner to meet Livilla at the designated spot at the South Coast Plaza. Since he had the wrong code, she wouldn't give him the cash. I'd vainly hoped that might discourage Jim. Instead, he proceeded to beat me until I gave up the correct code word: *Felix*. He left me tied to the beam when he went to meet the runner.

Tied to the beam, I lost consciousness a few times. I'd wake up and be surprised I was still alive.

When Jim returned, he gently let me loose, all the while calling me "baby."

"I'm sorry," he said, kissing my battered face. "But sometimes we got to do things this way. And you know I love my girl."

I said nothing. I was traumatized and could barely move.

"The money," I managed to get out of my swollen lips. "Where is it?"

"Don't worry about it," Jim said. "I got it."

From that moment on, I was Jim's prisoner. In the house, he kept me handcuffed to the furniture or to the bed at night. If we went out, he would handcuff me to the passenger-door grab handle, push the seat back, and make me sit on the floor of his Mercedes. My body crunched into a tight ball for long rides,

I could barely walk once I got out of the car. One day, I lifted my head and saw a police car had pulled up alongside us. For once in my life, I was thrilled to see them. I lifted my head as high as I could, trying to make eye contact with the cops. They didn't spare me a glance and pulled off. Once Jim caught on, he pushed my head back down.

I contemplated turning myself in. I'd get free and run to a police precinct. Then I could be done with Jim's torture.

The night I planned to escape, I was awakened by nausea that sent me running to the bathroom. I vomited in the toilet and sagged to the floor as I realized I was pregnant again. I couldn't have a baby with him and raise it in his hell house.

Without telling Jim about the baby, I started sweet-talking him, apologizing for dealing with Livilla.

"I just wanted money for the lawyer," I said. "I knew you'd saved our money, but I was scared there wasn't enough." I kissed him. "Oh Jim, I should have just trusted you. I know I messed up big time. Can you forgive me?"

Eventually, he took off my handcuffs in the house. He was probably tired of locking and unlocking me and having to fetch me things. Still, he rarely left me alone. I kept up the lovey-dovey flattery. "You know I'd be lost without you, Jim. My hero. Why would I run? Where could I go? Besides, we need to get our son."

There was a bounty on my head—a reward for information leading to my arrest. My mother, whom I called once a month to check in, had seen my picture on a wanted poster in the post office. I used that bit of information to convince Jim that I couldn't leave. "Anyone could see me and turn me in," I told him.

Soon enough, Jim became too restless to sit around the house and started venturing out. Certain that he was seeing his girlfriends, I again begged him not to jeopardize my freedom.

My fear of getting caught because of his sloppiness was real, but Jim dismissed it as jealousy. "Oh, baby," he said, grinning at me like I was crushing on him. "No one's going to come between us. Not ever again. You ain't going nowhere."

But each time Jim went out, I calculated my chances of getting away—whether I had time to reach the safe, retrieve the money, check into a hotel, call the lawyer, and so on. I ran a couple mental dress rehearsals, trying to judge how long he was usually gone.

One day Jim left without telling me, probably to avoid an argument. It was my chance. I started running around the townhouse, packing my things, planning my exit, but then I heard his key in the door. He was back.

I ran to the living room and hopped on the couch to pretend I was watching television—it wasn't on.

"Where were you?" I asked, hoping my interest would stop him from noticing I was out of breath from rushing to my seat.

He shrugged sullenly and headed toward the kitchen.

Bang! Bang! It was the loud, distinctive sound of law enforcement.

Jim and I both ran upstairs. There was a balcony off the bedroom. I thought I'd jump off and run away. But the backyard was swarming with plainclothesmen.

"FBI," called a voice at the front door. Jim went down to open it as I hovered on the stairs.

A group of US Marshals and FBI agents were on the porch. Jim tried to act innocent and charming as they explained that they were seeking a fugitive.

He said, "A fugitive? I had no idea . . ."

Seeing it was hopeless to try to run with the house surrounded, I went downstairs.

"Tanya Smith!" The agents and marshals were jostling, competing to try to cuff me.

Jim was handcuffed, too, for harboring a fugitive. He was flirting with a female marshal, telling her, "You sure are fine." She looked at him as if he were a virus. As shocked and upset as I was by the arrest, I felt a wash of relief at getting away from him.

One of the FBI agents said, "Tanya, I'm glad we got here in time. We were able to save your life." At the time I thought, *Save my life. What is he talking about?*

Jim kept chattering away, but I stayed silent as they escorted us out to the cars.

It was September 1988. I'd managed to elude capture for eight months.

23

HOLES

The Feds took me and Jim to the Orange County Jail. Local and state police hold prisoners on probable cause for a few days while they try to sweat them and come up with a charge, but the Feds tend to wait until they have a case before making an arrest, which permitted Jim to walk free right away.

I was held overnight and then transferred to Sybil Brand in Los Angeles. There, I learned how the Feds found me.

"They followed him right to you," one of the booking officers said, talking about Jim.

"How did they know to follow him?" I asked.

"A tip. LAPD got a call. A woman said she knew someone living with an escaped prisoner. She said what car he was driving and how they could find you if they followed him. She must've been pretty pissed to go through all that trouble. Guess she got her wish, huh?"

I'd been at Sybil Brand briefly before I was transferred to Chicago for my last trial. Sybil Brand was a jail, not a prison, which is for long sentences. Though inmates can spend many months in jail, they're designed for short stays, meaning without much attention to privacy and basic comfort. To make matters worse, people in jail are in limbo, feeling frantic and unsettled. They are the people least likely to cope well with poor conditions, overcrowding, intimidation by other inmates, and harassment by the guards.

It was built to house 910 inmates, but its typical population was 2,200. It had huge cockroaches, fearless rats, unrecognizable food, short meal times, little-to-no outdoor recreation breaks, unending noise, and vicious fighting among inmates and even with the guards.

After changing into my jailhouse attire—a shapeless brown dress with no belt, scratchy white-cotton underwear, plain white socks, and brandless sneakers—I was assigned to a dormitory of about two hundred women. It had a twelve-foot ceiling and only one row of windows that were too high up and only offered a glimpse of the sky. The room was harshly lit by dirty fluorescent tubes that hummed through the night. Luckily, I got the top bed in one of the metal bunks. Women in the lower bunks—and worse, in bedrolls on the floor—suffered most with nightly visits from cockroaches and rats.

The nights were the worst after surviving a day of witnessing constant chaos, fighting, and unimaginable human deficiency and neglect. All one wanted to do was rest in silence, but at lights out, everyone started talking, laughing, creeping into each other's beds to have loud sex, or sneaking into corners to smoke guard-procured weed. One night, two women got into it about sleeping arrangements, and the smaller one smashed the bigger one's head into the metal bunk. Blood seeped from her ear to the filthy mattress. As medics carried her away, the chatter was about the smaller woman beating the bigger woman's ass. No one mentioned the blood.

Most interesting about the setup at Sybil Brand was the wristband system. Inmates wore different colored bands on their left wrists to indicate their status. One color could mean the inmate had been arrested for a misdemeanor; others meant she had a mental health issue, protective custody, and so on through a rainbow of possibilities. The bands also revealed barcodes with personal information for the guards to know where to send different inmates and how to handle them.

While life at Sybil Brand was a complete reversal of the comfort and community I had experienced at the MCC in Chicago and the Federal Reformatory for Women in Alderson, the conditions barely fazed me. I was desperate to get out of there because I was three months pregnant, and I couldn't have another child behind bars. I wanted to be there for my children.

It wouldn't happen if I was transferred back to Alderson to complete the full thirteen years—and probably more after the escape charges. I would miss both of my kids' childhoods.

I started contemplating my departure from Sybil Brand during my recreation time. I scanned the perimeter through the window when I sat up on my bunk bed, high enough to see more than the sky. There were no woods to roam, no river to swim. The jail-yard fence was topped with razor wire, making it impossible to scale. I couldn't just slip away in the dead of night. I had to find a way to get out of Sybil Brand in plain sight like I had in West Virginia. Theoretically, that could be easier because of the crowding at Sybil Brand, which made inmates an anonymous blur to the overstretched staff.

I called Livilla. I waited until the guards were working the dining hall, which was always a chaotic scene. In such a short-staffed place, guards couldn't be spared to monitor the phones. Still, I knew I had to be cagey in case they were recording calls.

After trading hellos, I asked Livilla if she'd seen "Felix," hoping using our old password would clue her in on the fact that I was speaking code.

"I did. What's it to you?" Livilla caught on.

"I thought he needed help," I said. "He said he was going to reach out to his old friends. See if they were available."

"Oh, yeah. He did. I told him to let me know when he's ready. I'm available to him."

"That's good. Talk soon."

"Talk soon."

With Livilla onboard to help me out, I moved on to the next step. I started covertly questioning a couple of inmates.

"How much is your bail?" I asked one of the seasoned inmates who was in and out of Sybil Brand. "Can you pay it?"

"Leave me the fuck alone," she said. "I know you on some bullshit."

I moved to a dim-witted lackey who did whatever the longtime inmates told her. "How much is your bail? Can you pay it?"

"It's ten thousand. And no, I can't pay it. Why?"

"I could help with that."

"How you gonna come up with that kind of money? What do I have to do for it?" she asked.

When I told her my plan, she quickly backed off. "That ain't gonna work. I'd rather stay locked up in here than go down with you."

Next, I tried a new inmate, Gwen, who had been in and out of jail a lot. She was a street girl and small-time drug dealer. I wanted someone who was familiar with jails and police and wouldn't be nervous and easy to break if things went left. "What do I have to do?" she asked when I approached her after dinner.

"We are going to switch wristbands and sleep in each other's bed. I'm going to post your twenty-thousand-dollar bail and leave the jail as you. In the morning, when they discover they released the wrong inmate, they will come looking for you," I revealed.

"What am I supposed to do then?"

"Say they must have made a mistake when they put on your wristband because you are not Tanya Smith. Make sure to tell them it's *their mistake* and you didn't know you had on the wrong wristband. They can't charge you with conspiracy if you had no knowledge a crime had been committed. If you convince them, they'll have to release you because your bail will be posted," I said. "If there are any problems, once I'm out, I'll send one of the best attorneys to get you out."

"Whoa!" she stopped me. "Who are you? Are you with some cartel or something?"

"No, I'm not," I said. "I'm just using my brain to get out of here."

"It's risky."

"It is. And I'll pay you fifty thousand for taking that risk," I said.

"Fifty thousand?" Her eyes went wide. "You have money like that? I need proof."

"I do. I'll give you the money as soon as I'm released. But for now, I'll send five thousand to your people to prove this is serious. Deal?"

"Deal."

At mealtime the next morning, while the guards were preoccupied, I called Livilla to have her deliver the cash to Gwen's people and pay her bail. Wanting me to get back to work, Livilla's boss put up the money.

Hours later, Gwen reported that her people had gotten the $5,000. "So this is serious," she said with a tinge of excitement in her voice. "We're on."

At about 8:00 p.m., Gwen's bail was posted. She looked at me like I was some kind of genie granting wishes.

I told her, "It will take about six or seven hours to process the release. Now we wait."

Again, I called Livilla to launch the next phase. Not wanting her to get too close to law enforcement at the jail, I told her to pick me up at the McDonald's located at the bottom of the hill, a short distance from the Sybil Brand.

Before lights out, Gwen and I cut off our wristbands. It took some ingenuity to reattach them with string and home-made paste. She climbed into my top bunk, and, a few rows away, I crawled into hers, which was on the bottom. Lights out came at eleven. As usual, there was endless noise.

I was awakened at around 2:00 a.m. by a jostling guard. "Bail! Bail has been posted," she said. "Get up!"

I swung my feet out of the bunk. "Grab everything," she told me. "Pillow, sheets, blankets. Bring it all."

I shoved everything into the pillowcase and followed her. As I passed Gwen on my bunk, she was asleep.

We went downstairs to the storage room for inmates' personal belongings. The guard dumped the contents of Gwen's bin out onto the counter. "Give me your clothes and put these on."

I quickly removed and handed the guard the brown dress and took Gwen's clothes. She was several inches shorter than I was and petite. I couldn't even zip up her pants.

"Oh man," I told the guard. "These don't fit anymore. I gained weight. Do you have anything else?"

The guard rolled her eyes, exasperated, and rummaged around. She came up with some abandoned sweatpants and a T-shirt. The pants were long enough, at least.

"Thank you," I said, slipping them on.

The next step was fingerprinting, which I wasn't prepared for. Surely, they'd run my prints against Gwen's and see they weren't a match. My heart quickened as I let them take my prints and tried to remain calm.

As the sleepy night guard processed me, she hardly looked at the prints. She was just going through the motions. She didn't even compare them to Gwen's first set.

"All done." She yawned before handing me paperwork to sign.

Next, a guard took me to the exit. I entered a small steel vestibule that separated the inside from the outside. Facing away from the facility, I took a deep breath and waited to be released. It was taking forever. But then, all of a sudden, I heard the loud clanking noise of the sliding steel doors opening in front of me. I walked out the door.

I started walking to meet Livilla at McDonald's.

The road was pitch-black with no street lights. I walked for a few hundred yards and then started running. It was a long road. I was running fast. When I got to a curve, a car I couldn't see in advance came whipping around the corner. The driver flicked on the high beams, blinding me.

"Stop!" ordered a voice over a loudspeaker. Still blinded by the lights, I squinted to see it was a patrol car. The cop pulled up alongside me and said, "Hey, what are you doing out here?"

"My bail was just posted," I told him. "My ride is late, and I was going down the hill to meet them."

"Why are you running?"

"I'm afraid of the dark."

He didn't seem convinced. "Paperwork?" he asked.

I handed over Gwen's release paperwork. He looked it over and then said, "Get in the car. Let's go back inside and verify this."

*　　*　　*

Under the cold fluorescent lights, the guards, now on full alert, compared my fingerprints to Gwen's. Of course, they didn't match. It didn't take long before they recognized that I was Tanya Smith.

"Take her to the Bull Room," someone said.

I knew about the Bull Room and the beatings that went on there, where guards thrashed the will to fight out of prisoners. Abuse may have gone unchallenged in state facilities like Sybil Brand, but the federal jail contract, which I was classified under, forbade rough treatment.

"Hold it," I said. "I'm a federal prisoner. Nobody better lay a hand on me."

The guard confirmed my status and shrugged. "OK, take her to the hole."

It wasn't much better.

The hole meant solitary confinement. It was a block of tiny, dark, individual cells, each with a flap, known as a bean hole, near the floor, where they passed food—if you could call it food. Part of the punishment was that, most days a week, they served us "jute balls," which looked like solid blobs of vomit. It was the day's meal—sandwich or entrée, vegetable or salad, potato or rice, even dessert like Jell-O, whatever was on the menu—dumped into a blender, whizzed, and then molded into a lump that was served to inmates in the hole. This disgusting practice had to be illegal.

There were quite a few women in the hole. To check in on each other, we would talk by pressing our mouths against our cell door's "bean hole" or "bean slot."

"I refuse to eat that jute ball," I announced through my bean hole.

"It ain't that bad once you get used to it," someone replied. "Just get it down."

"I'm sorry, but I'd rather starve than eat that," I said.

The woman in the cell across from me heard me complaining. She always got a regular tray of real food. "Do you want my food?" she asked.

"Are you sure you don't want it?"

"I'm never hungry," she said. "It will just go to waste."

I gratefully accepted. She shoved her tray across the tile floor, and I grabbed it. It was a small mercy.

A day or two later, when the woman who'd been giving me food had to go to the infirmary, the inmate in the cell next door to me said, "Tanya, don't keep eating her food!"

"Why not?"

"She's in the hole because she's got tuberculosis."

"What? And you're telling me this after I took her food?" I asked, shocked.

I spent about three weeks in the hole until the Feds were ready to transfer me. This time, they didn't use regular ConAir for my transport. Instead, they put me on a private plane. When I was seated, a marshal installed ankle irons and a C & S Security "black box" handcuff cover, which was attached to a belly chain over my baby bump and sat between my wrists to keep them immobile. All I could do was wiggle my fingers. With all the gear, I wished I were Houdini.

Taking in my predicament, the marshal said with a smirk, "You're something else, Tanya."

The next day, we landed in West Virginia and reached Alderson around lunchtime. When we pulled up, the inmates were out in the yard and eagerly greeted me. All the women cheered. I'd become a legend as a prisoner who'd escaped and stayed free for nearly a year.

"Tanya, we love you!" a woman called out.

"Escape monster!"

"My hero!"

"Sign my titties!"

Depressing as it was to be back in custody, I had to smile.

The Alderson authorities, embarrassed by the escape, were more punishing than before. They made me submit to a humiliating strip search—squatting down and spreading my buttocks and labia, the works—and stuck me into Davis Hall, once notorious for abuses and Alderson's version of the hole.

The only other inmate in the hole was my old pal Squeaky Fromme. She was waiting to go to trial for her escape. We rarely had the chance to speak, but I could often hear her humming and singing. In the hole—the worst place to be in a prison, where most people fall into despair—she was happy.

24

A BIGGER THREAT

In November, I was taken by car to the Charleston, West Virginia, county jail to await trial on my escape. Once again, I was shackled like Hannibal Lecter in *Silence of the Lambs*, with leg irons and black box handcuffs attached to a belly chain. When we reached the jail, six US Marshals, three on each side, escorted me from the car to the lobby. It was deserted "for safety purposes," one of the marshals told me. He was implying that transporting me required lockdown protocols.

As I was processed, the guards stared and whispered among themselves.

"It's her."

"Be alert."

"She escaped twice."

I was fingerprinted, strip-searched, and then again encircled by six marshals for the elevator ride. Normally, jails are loud, with inmates milling around and talking, but the entire jail was dead silent. The guards took me upstairs to the women's floor and led me through the lounge, which was empty. No one was hanging out, talking on the phone, or watching TV.

"The inmates are locked down in their cells until you're secured behind bars."

I was dumbfounded. I wondered if other nonviolent, white-collar offenders got the same red-carpet treatment.

Beyond the lounge were the cellblocks. My cell was a six-by-eight concrete box fronted by a wall of bars with a rock-hard bunk, a stainless-steel toilet and sink, a cloudy metal mirror, and a blanket as gray and scratchy as a Brillo pad—stereotypical jailhouse decor. Even Sybil Brand had been more imaginative with their hellish design.

"You'll be in here twenty-three hours a day," a marshal said, leaving me in the cell as she stepped out to close the door.

"No. You can't be serious," I said. "Not twenty-three hours. There's no window. No light. I won't be able to read."

She pointed to a single light bulb in the hallway about thirty feet from my cell. "There's your light."

Once the marshals locked me in, the TV in the inmates' lounge quickly came back on. The other prisoners were released from their cells. As they started to circulate, I called out, "Hello! Hey!" but they all ignored me. It was as if I were a ghost.

The phones came back on, and everyone started making calls. From then on, whenever I was going to be out of my cell, the phones would be cut off. The reason? According to a letter from the probation office to my trial judge, government investigations revealed that, after my January 1988 escape, on sixty-seven occasions, I attempted the transfer of a total of $4,352,274.00 from banks throughout the country. They were planning to charge me and feared that if I had access to a phone, I might "arrange the disposition of this stolen money and continue my transactions."

Taking a shower became a huge production. I was allowed only three per week, supervised by four to six guards. Male guards recruited from other floors would stand outside while female guards would monitor me in the stall. My hands were uncuffed, but they kept my leg shackles on. Meanwhile, the entire floor would be locked down.

One day, another inmate slipped me some candy through the bars. Actually, she tossed it in and kept on walking. When she did it again, I asked her who she was. Looking around to be sure no one saw us, she said her name was Cathy. "Cathy, how come no one talks to me?" I asked.

She slid to the ground within earshot of my cell, pretending that she was chatting with someone else. "They said you're very dangerous," she told me. "If we talk to you, we could lose privileges and risk a new federal charge."

"Dangerous?" I had to laugh. "I'm a white-collar offender. I escaped. That's why they're so mad."

"I knew it!" she said excitedly. "All they do is lie. I knew you were someone important for these people to threaten us if we talked to you. Where are you from? I know you are not from here because you sound educated and proper."

I chuckled and asked if Cathy would make some phone calls for me.

NEVER SAW ME COMING

"OK, but I'll have to sneak. The women in here would snitch in a minute."

I discreetly gestured to the camera behind her in the hallway. "They have that camera pointed at my cell. I don't want you to get into trouble for standing here talking to me. Maybe you can stand on a chair behind the camera and turn it so it misses the corner and doesn't catch you by my cell."

"Easy." Cathy left and returned with a chair to turn the camera.

"You're amazing," I said. "Thank you."

After that first meeting, Cathy stopped by my cell every day to check on me and ask if I needed anything. If I was hungry, she'd bring me soup and potato chips from the commissary. She even slipped me her radio to listen to music. To communicate in secret, we'd exchange notes through the bars. I'd ask her to make calls each day—to my mother to tell her I was pregnant and to Livilla to say I needed a lawyer.

Cathy also kept me informed about gossip in the prison. The guards were asking other inmates what they knew about me. She said they all seemed scared of me.

"Fuck these people. You ain't no threat. They're just mad because you're Black and smart," she said one day. "Did you escape using a helicopter or something?"

I laughed, and we started playing cards between the bars.

Until Livilla came through with a lawyer, I was working with a court-appointed public defender named Oliver Caine. He advised me to plead guilty to the escape charge. He started asking questions about other aspects of my case not related to the escape, which was what he was solely assigned to handle. "How did you do transfers? How much money did you make? Where did you keep the money?" he asked in rapid succession, hardly giving me time to answer. Sometimes, it seemed like he was reading the questions from slips of paper.

I answered some of the questions, but his curiosity made me nervous. "Our conversations are confidential, right?" I asked.

"Yeah, sure," he responded and fired off more questions. "How did you escape?"

"I just walked out," I revealed.

"Wow, you just walked out." He leaned in like he was completely fascinated. "Did you get any help?"

"No." I lied.

"Hmm. Seems you'd need help to do something like that," he pushed.

"I didn't. Do you have any more questions?"

"No. Not right now. I just need you to speak to a marshal."

"For what? I'm not interested in talking to them."

"I think they have some things you need to see. Listen, Tanya, you're gonna have to trust me for this to work. Just sit tight and give it a try. OK?"

I nodded.

After flashing a smile, Oliver let a deputy marshal into the meeting room. I wanted to get up and walk out, but I followed the advice of my public defender. I stayed put.

The deputy marshal sat across from me and pulled a stack of photos from his bag.

"What's all this?" I asked.

"Something that may be of interest to you," he said. He started tossing the photos onto the table before me like a Vegas card dealer. There were surveillance photos of Jim going out with different women, driving my Porsche and Ferrari, and having a good time at a restaurant. Some of the women were wearing my clothes and jewelry. I even saw some of my furniture in the background.

"You really upgraded his life. It's a shame he's disloyal," the deputy marshal teased before slapping down more pictures of Jim at a home he purchased with Vicki. She was wearing my furs and driving my cars too. In some of the photos, Vicki was pregnant, and Jim looked on fondly. The deputy marshal also showed me pictures of Jim's mom and sister entering their new lavish homes, smiling and laughing as they brought in shopping bags. "It's time to stop all this. Help us shut him down. How was he involved? Were his mother and sister in on it too?"

I was sick, but I did not show emotion or answer any questions, knowing snitching on Jim would mean implicating myself in other crimes. I wanted to grab the pictures and turn them into confetti. I knew everything they had was purchased with money that vanished when I first went to prison. I felt used.

"You're going to rot in here if you don't wise up. Help us, and we will help you," the deputy marshal said. My public defender said nothing.

Disgusted, I got up and asked to go back to my cell.

"You can go, but just know I'll be back. You can't hide from the truth. No appreciation for us saving your life," the deputy marshal said as I walked out. *Save my life. What did he mean by that?*

Within days, Livilla came through. Six guards escorted me to the conference room to meet with Samuel Tolbert, a beautifully groomed and well-dressed Beverly Hills attorney. As we sat to talk in what was supposed to be a private attorney/client meeting, I was surprised that two of the guards stayed put right outside the open door. We weren't allowed to close it. We had to whisper, knowing they were eavesdropping and constantly looking in.

"Is this right?" I asked Samuel.

"No. It isn't," he said, glaring at the lurking guards. "But don't worry. I'll file a motion noting that you have a Sixth Amendment right to a private consultation with your attorney."

For the rest of the meeting, Samuel whispered.

Interestingly, his first question was not about the case.

"You have money hidden, right?" he asked.

"Yes," I confirmed. Before my escape from Sybil Brand, I'd told Livilla about my safe buried in Chino Hills and how desperately I needed its contents for my defense.

"Can you pinpoint the location? If not, I could have someone take aerial photos for you to circle the place where we should dig."

This line of questioning spooked me. He didn't seem interested in the case at all. Livilla had never cheated me, and I trusted her up to a point. Without the help of her people, I certainly had no way to get the money. I hadn't called her just to help me retrieve it. What I'd wanted was a lawyer to defend me, to be on my side.

I was faced with a ridiculous choice. To rely on a public defender who already seemed shady—as focused on my possible crimes as opposed to my possible freedom—or to rely on Livilla's bosses to dig up my safe and give me the cash.

Feeling defeated and scared, tears overwhelmed me.

"Oh no," Sam said, handing me his monogrammed silk handkerchief. "Are you OK?"

I told Sam all about myself—that I came from a good family, that my Chicago trial was a sham, that I'd escaped only to get a lawyer to fight the dirty conviction, that all I wanted was a reasonable sentence and to raise my children. I poured out my heart to a man I didn't even know, and he patiently listened.

I wound up by saying, "So, I'll have to take a chance. Go get those aerial photos. I'll figure out where the safe is. Even if I don't get all the money, I might have enough to—"

"No." He cut me off. "Stop talking about money. Don't ever mention it again to me or anyone else."

"What do you mean?"

"I mean that these are bad people. They're going to rip you off. That's their plan," he said.

"You mean Livilla?"

"Yes. She's in on it."

"I can't let that happen. If I lose my money, how can I fight back? I have to get out of here."

Rubbing my belly, which was just beginning to swell in my second trimester, I told Sam about my poor treatment in jail.

"They're treating you like a prisoner of war," he said. "I can tell that you're a nice woman. You just got in way over your head. Look—I can help you out. I'll take your case pro bono."

Once we agreed on the dynamics of our working relationship, Sam went to the public defender's office to retrieve my case file. As soon as he read it, he zoomed over to the jail to see me.

"Tanya, you need to review this with me," he said in our private conference. "Because some of what's in here shocks me. Did you know your assistant public defender, Oliver Caine, was sharing your private conversations with the AUSA? Looking through these documents, it seems Oliver was working with the AUSA to get you to tell them everything they wanted to know about your operation and plead guilty so they could lock you up for the rest of your young life. Some of the notes make it clear that other jurisdictions were working with them and would assist in making Oliver a federal public defender if he could pull this off."

"No. How could he do that? I thought everything I told him was privileged."

"That's what anyone would expect," Sam said. "That's why I can't believe what I'm reading. He probably never thought anyone else would see this. They didn't expect a new attorney to step in and retrieve the file. But when I requested it, the secretary had to hand it over after she saw I was the new attorney of record."

"I wondered why he was asking me all those questions. Could the AUSA use what I said to build a case against me?"

Sam showed me notes in the file suggesting that was exactly what the two of them had discussed.

"Is that even legal?" I asked Sam. "Can they do that?"

"Well, to me, this looks like the seeds of your defense," he said.

For the first time since my arrest, I felt a wave of relief.

Suddenly, the conference room doors banged open, startling us. There stood four US Marshals, demanding that Sam hand over the file.

"No way," he said.

They got aggressive, threatening Sam, surrounding him, insisting that the file belonged to Oliver Caine. Sam clutched the file to his chest, insisting, "You'll get it over my dead body." He was about to hop up on the table to get away from them.

"I'm calling this in," the lead marshal said, exiting the room.

When he was gone, Sam tried to leave with both arms folded over the file, but another marshal stopped him.

"No, you don't," the marshal said. "You're not leaving here with that file."

They blocked the door until the lead marshal returned.

"We're going to the magistrate to get an order for you to release the file or go to jail," he told Sam. "You might as well give it to us now."

Sam didn't budge. He said, "This file belongs to my client."

My head was spinning. As I watched them go back and forth, Sam turned to me and said, "I've never heard of a public defender and an AUSA fighting together to keep notes from a client and her attorney. This is unlawful."

Hours later, when I was back in my cell, one of the friendlier inmates who cleaned the jail office stopped by to let me know she'd heard gossip about what was happening with my lawyer.

"Chile, he got them marshals ugly mad. Word is they went to the home of the magistrate on duty and begged him to give them an order compelling your lawyer to give up the file or else there would be big trouble," she said. "They say people around here are fixing to lose their jobs and licenses and possibly go to jail if whatever is in that file gets out."

The story was confirmed ten hours later when guards came to take me back to the meeting room, where an exhausted Sam explained that he'd given the magistrate the file.

"They were going to arrest me. I demanded to speak to the magistrate over the phone. He assured me that he would personally take possession of the file, not reading it or sharing it with Caine or the prosecution, until there was a hearing," he revealed. "I'm sorry, but his word is the best we could get. I surrendered the file."

The hearing was held on January 12, 1989. There, in front of Judge Judith Murphy, Caine and AUSA J. Benjamin Connor, Sam called what he'd found in the file "disturbing." He noted that it rightfully belonged to me since it had been created to assist me in preparation for trial and described conversations between Mr. Caine and the AUSA, who then sought to prevent them from being discovered by me.

Sam added that some things that were done immediately after Mr. Caine talked to me stretched the bounds of propriety.

After pointing out that I had no knowledge that Caine and Connor were talking, he said that he didn't understand why Caine would object to sharing the benefit of all of his notes with respect to conversations both with Mr. Connor and me. Sam concluded that the only logical reason he would seek to prevent them from getting into my hands was either he had something to hide, felt he'd done something wrong, or thought Sam thought he'd done something wrong.

The AUSA stepped in to argue that Caine's notes were his personal work product, to which we weren't entitled, though Sam had pointed out that it was rather unique that we had such a confrontation. Generally, when you have two people on the same side, there is a free flow of information and cooperation.

Sam questioned why the AUSA was involved at all, saying he had taken the position of representing Mr. Caine who had previously been an adversary.

The judge ultimately bought the work product argument and said she would personally remove Caine's notes from the file. Presumably, without so much as examining them, she dismissed Sam's findings as "shadowy allegations." As a result, we lost the evidence of dubious dealings between the public defender and the AUSA, which might have helped me win my freedom.

One decent thing came out of the hearing, though. Sam objected to the unique restrictions I was enduring in jail. Judge Murphy seized on three of them—the lighting, the monitoring, and my inability to exercise—for immediate investigation. I wound up getting four hours a day outside my cell.

In February 1989, I was taken from jail in Charleston to court in Beckley, West Virginia. When I arrived, Squeaky Fromme was finally being led in for sentencing on her escape charge. I couldn't help noticing that her only restraint was ordinary handcuffs, not the wrist, leg shackles, and belly chain they used on me. Judge Murphy gave Squeaky thirty-six months to run consecutively with the sentences she was already serving.

Judge Murphy, who seemed to have disdain for Sam, dubbed him a "big shot Beverly Hills lawyer," as if that were an insult—which it may have been in Beckley, West Virginia.

She expressed the opinion that I was a menace and deserved to spend a long time in prison. Still, I was shocked when she delivered my sentence for my escape: forty-one months, consecutive.

It meant I now faced seventeen years in prison, minus the little time served.

I got to my feet, in my eight-months-pregnant state, and told the judge: "You're giving me more time than a Manson Family girl who tried to kill the President!"

"You are a bigger threat," she said. "You're a threat to the US banking system, to the United States of America."

I wondered who she was talking to, who she was talking about. I was Tanya Marie Smith. A twenty-eight-year-old young woman who'd grown up on tree-lined Washburn Avenue in suburban Minneapolis. I had started out wanting to help people in need. I got caught up in the thrill of transaction and all that money could provide. But a threat to the US? No. I didn't resort to violence. Squeaky was second in command to murderous Charles Manson and was treated with dignity in prison and perceived as less menacing than me. The disparities were glaring.

Sam tried to console me. "Don't lose hope," he said. "Because it will change you."

I was nearing the end of my pregnancy and was shipped to the Federal Medical Center (FMC) in Lexington, Kentucky. It was the facility designated for inmates, male and female, including the most violent, who had medical issues. It was my first experience in a coed federal prison. It was a party atmosphere. Prisoners were doing drugs and having sex right out in the open. The guards got in on the action too but more behind the scenes. Some days, with all of its debauchery and bacchanalia, FMC looked more like a scene from *Caligula* than a federal prison.

There was no maternity center there. So when I went into labor, I was transferred to the local hospital in shackles, including leg irons. The weight of the restraints on my swollen limbs made my labor pains more intense. My only escape was remembering Taryn being there for me in Chicago before I went to give birth to Justin. I closed my eyes and recalled her saying, "You got this. Take a deep breath. Relax."

At the hospital, the doctor demanded that they unshackle me, but the marshals refused, claiming, "She's an escape risk."

"That's insane," the doctor said. "There's no way she can run."

"We're not allowed to remove the restraints," they said.

"Well, I sure as hell will!" The doctor sent the nurse for bolt cutters and personally cut the shackles off my wrists and legs.

After hours of sweating, screaming, and crying, I pushed out the most beautiful baby girl I'd ever seen. My daughter Britney was born on March 9, 1989. I was amazed and humbled to hold such a tiny, perfect being. While I was exhausted from labor, I wouldn't shut my eyes for fear of missing a part of her. I couldn't bear the thought that they would tear her away from me. I said a silent prayer to God that he would give us a little more time together.

My blood pressure was elevated, and the hospital wanted to keep me. A nurse handed me medication and told me to take it every few hours. Holding little Britney in my recovery room, I secretly threw the medication away to stay with her. We were together a whole week before the staff caught on.

This time, my parents couldn't drive all the way to Lexington to pick up Britney. Sam, my lawyer in his fancy suits, flew out to get her and delivered her to them in Minneapolis.

On the phone, Mom and Dad were kind and uplifting.

"What a darling," Mom said. "It's great having another girl in the house. You and Taryn were my last girls."

Dad added, "These babies are keeping us young. We are up around the clock feeding little Britney and that's my grandbaby, so I don't mind one bit."

They could sense my depression over my sentence and the pain of giving up Britney. To comfort me, they reminisced about the old days in Minneapolis, the theater, and the fun we had with all six of us kids in the house. I missed those days. I just wanted to go back to my room and lay in bed with Black Power.

As usual, they put Justin and Aiden on the phone to say hello. I couldn't believe it when Justin said as clear as a bell, "Hi, Mommy!" and laughed. It brought me joy.

25

TRUST AND WILL

was transferred to the prison where I was to do my remaining time. The Federal Correctional Institution (FCI) in Marianna, Florida, housed some infamous inmates. I wasn't surprised to see Squeaky Fromme when I got there. It seemed we were tethered as we moved through the system.

Marianna was fairly comfortable, as prisons go. It was new and small, with only a hundred-plus inmates. The food was pretty good, and there was a small area in the yard with weights where I could exercise every day. There were single and double rooms. New inmates had to go to a double room with an empty bed.

My roommate Cielo was in for drugs and was a part of Pablo Escobar's cartel. I don't know how involved she was, but she was older and very kind, with a grandmotherly disposition. The moment I walked in, Cielo cooked me food and made me feel as comfortable as one can be in prison.

With no word about the exact length of my confinement, I went to receiving and discharge to get an accurate release date.

After some unnecessary eyeballing and confusion about why I was asking for the information, a desk guard handed me a document noting that I was set to serve fifteen years.

"That isn't correct," I pointed out. "My original sentence was thirteen years."

"Excuse me?" the desk guard asked before looking into my file for more information. She pulled out a document stating that I'd been sentenced to two additional years in Vegas, which were to run consecutively with my original sentence. "Do you know what 'consecutively' means? You have fifteen years, not thirteen."

I peered at the document. It definitely said consecutively.

"Yes, I do, but that's not what the sentence was. The judge in Vegas said in court that my two-year sentence was to be served concurrently with my original sentence."

"That sounds unlikely. Why would we have it wrong here in the system?"

"I don't know, but it is wrong. You need to change it."

"No one here can do that based on your word," she said. "Then everyone in here would be making up their own sentences."

Realizing I was talking to a brick wall, I went to the library to think. I knew I wasn't crazy. I was right in the courtroom when the judge had said, "Concurrently."

I started researching what happens when a judge's oral and written sentences are different. I discovered the oral sentencing rules. Armed with that information, I contacted the court reporter in Las Vegas and got a transcript of the hearing. Weeks later, I received the file. The judge had said, "Concurrently."

Using the legal precedent concerning mismatched sentences, I wrote the judge a letter stating the error. He quickly responded that the sentence was to be served consecutively, and he wasn't changing it. I filed a writ of coram nobis, representing myself, which is a challenge to the final judgment.

While I was waiting for a hearing date, in early October 1989, I got a phone call from a lawyer I didn't know.

"I'm representing Cameron Bates, a former employee of the Bureau of Prisons—Alderson," she said. "The Feds indicted him for helping you escape. Since you're a government witness, he has no choice but to plead guilty."

"What? This is the first I've heard of this. I never told anyone I'd testify." I didn't know Cameron was being charged and certainly wouldn't testify against him.

"You didn't?" His lawyer was shocked. I heard papers shuffling in the background. "Well, they have you down as their witness and said that you implicated him."

It wasn't true. I was not a witness for the Feds, which meant they probably had no case against Cameron. I never said anyone helped me escape from Alderson. Then I remembered that odd meeting with my court-appointed public defender, Oliver Caine. He was asking a lot of questions about the escape. When I'd told him I walked out the front gate, he said, "Did you get any help?" I said no, but as Sam discovered when he got my file, Oliver had been illegally sharing all of my responses with the AUSA. With that bit of information about my escape, it wouldn't take long for a smart person to land on Cameron as my accomplice.

A few days later, the Feds visited me to ask if I would give evidence against Cameron. Needing my help, they were extra nice and smiling at me like we were old friends. I wasn't going for it.

While I was uncooperative, a month later, they hauled me up to West Virginia, where I was confined in Beckley Jail until I was called into the courtroom. I shouldn't have been surprised to see Judge Judith Murphy and the assistant US attorney, J. Benjamin Connor. Seeing them all together again, I knew the information I shared during those early meetings with Assistant Public Defender Oliver Caine in West Virginia was the source behind Cameron's charges. I didn't let it throw me off. As I took the stand, I spotted Cameron to my right. Seated at the counsel's table with his lawyer, he looked terrified about what was ahead. Behind him was a woman who kept staring at me. I assumed she was his wife.

Since I was a hostile witness, the AUSA came on strong with his questions: "Tell us how you know the defendant and how he helped you escape Alderson," he pushed.

"I don't know the defendant," I said. "Nor have I ever spoken to him. This is my first time seeing him."

Already irritated, the AUSA frowned. He got louder and more leading in his questioning: "The defendant was a guard in your unit many times, and you don't recognize him?"

"No, sir, I do not," I said, unrattled.

"Do you understand that you are under oath, and if you lie, you are committing perjury, which is punishable by up to five additional years, which could be consecutive to the terms you are currently serving?" he pushed.

"Sir, I am under oath and I understand the penalty for perjury, so I would never lie to add more time to the sentences I am already serving," I said. "But it seems like you're trying to persuade me to lie so you can convict a man I have never talked to or seen in my life."

Observing my performance, Cameron looked shocked.

Annoyed, Judge Murphy rolled her eyes and said, "Please listen carefully to the question and then simply answer 'yes' or 'no.'"

I agreed to her request but then, rather abruptly, the AUSA seemingly thrown off by my ability to evade his questioning said, "No more questions, your honor."

Next, Cameron's attorney approached to conduct a cross-examination. "Tanya Smith, I have just one question for you. You testified that you never saw or talked to the defendant before, is that correct?"

"That is correct," I said.

"I have no further questions, your honor," the attorney said to the judge.

"At this time the government rests," the AUSA said.

After I was excused from the hot seat, I gave Cameron a tiny undetectable smile.

The next day, Cameron was acquitted.

After the trial, I was taken back to Marianna. Missing my children, I called home every day to check on them. Though they tried to hide it, my parents seemed to be stressed managing their three grandchildren while Taryn, who had been released from prison, was off using drugs. I confronted her about her behavior and why she wasn't helping Mom and Dad with the kids. She'd deny everything and say I had no right to judge her. On one of the calls, after speaking to Aiden and Justin, I asked to say hello to Denise.

"She isn't here," Taryn said.

"Where is she?" I asked. It had happened several times before, and Taryn always had some weak reason as to why I couldn't speak to my daughter. She was either asleep or unavailable. I felt something wasn't right. Finally, Taryn fessed up.

"She's living with someone," she said. "An associate of mine. She's fine."

"What do you mean fine? How come she's not at home with our family? Who is this person you gave my daughter to?" Denise was still a toddler, not even three years old. Suddenly, I couldn't breathe. Couldn't see. Couldn't even think. I dropped the phone and took a few deep breaths.

When I picked up the receiver, Taryn and I got into another argument, and she hung up. I called right back and asked her if I could speak to Mom and Dad, and she hung up again. We went back and forth like this a few times. When another inmate came to use the phone, I had to hand it over.

Shrouded in sorrow and shame, powerless to save my daughter, I went to my cell and cried in bed. A guard appeared at my cell door. "Tanya Smith, come with me," he said.

"Me? For what? I didn't do anything."

"We received a complaint that you've been making harassing calls. You're going to the hole. Take it up with the unit manager. Until he gets back from vacation, you'll be in the hole."

Locked up in segregation, I seethed with anger. I never liked feeling helpless or like I couldn't control a situation. I felt violated and disappointed. My connection with Taryn was weaker than it had ever been. I didn't think there was any way I could ever forgive her.

After two weeks in segregation, I was released back to the floor.

I went straight to the phone to call home. Luckily, I got my mother on the line.

She explained that when Taryn and I were locked up, she called an associate to ask if she would help our parents with the kids until she got out. The associate agreed, and Denise lived between two residences, which helped my parents a lot. When Taryn got out, she wasn't helping with the children as my parents had expected, and Denise went to live with the other family full-time. My mom's health was failing, and my dad was also sick and needed help caring for the kids.

Listening to Mom sound defeated, I was gutted. I realized that complaining would only make things worse. I backed off.

Meanwhile, the Feds were working hard to build a case against Jim and pin additional charges on me. Using our tumultuous relationship as fodder, they kept trying to get me to finger him as a major operative in my organization.

They popped up at Marianna and pulled me into endless interviews. During one encounter, the agents spread out more surveillance photos of Jim and Vicki in front of the big house he'd bought her. There were photos of Jim and Vicki posted in Vegas together as high rollers. One of the agents said, "You don't seem like the type to be with such a dangerous guy." *Dangerous*, I thought. *What did he mean by that?*

I didn't respond. Tormenting me with pictures of Jim's wonderful life was just one of the Feds' strategies to break me. It drove them wild that they hadn't yet managed to pin any large transactions on me. They still didn't fully understand how my operation worked.

They had many methods. In unexpected interviews, they tried to catch me by insinuating they already had information from someone else like, "Was a woman your contact at the such-and-such bank?" or, "Was your computer connected to the system?" I always kept cool, and my responses were brief, preferably one word: *no*.

One of their favorite gambits to try to wear me down was flying me all over the country. When a bank reported a mysterious loss, the Feds would deem me responsible and ship me to that location—Oklahoma or wherever—in hopes of uncovering some shred of connection or, better yet, manage to exhaust me and extract a confession.

Once or twice a month, I was hustled onto ConAir—often enough that the air marshals teased me about being a frequent flyer. They tossed me into whatever city's cold, smelly jail, and sometimes they put me in the hole. The Feds claimed they had all kinds of evidence to use against me if I didn't cooperate.

I didn't fall for their tricks, but my constant travels worried some inmates, who started asking if I was a snitch.

The state-hopping flights went on until 1991, when I got word that the Feds were ready. Marshals arrived at Marianna to take me to Los Angeles to face charges for wire and bank fraud. They drove me to a private airport where the van we were riding in pulled up alongside a small airplane. It wasn't ConAir.

There were about eight passenger seats on the plane. Two male prisoners were already on board. They were both good-looking Latino men who, even in their inmate threads, exuded wealth and charm. They also seemed to know each other.

I started chitchatting with one of the marshals, hoping I could get some information about the prisoners. I learned they were drug lords who tried to blow up a commercial airliner to kill a snitch who was traveling to testify against a cartel member.

I noticed that they were secured with ankle and wrist cuffs, but, unlike me, they didn't have the restrictive black box connecting their shackles. I was more restrained than two guys who tried to blow up a commercial airliner.

After landing in Los Angeles, the marshals drove me downtown to the Metropolitan Detention Center (MDC), a new coed federal facility for prisoners awaiting trial. I was taken to the women's floor, where the warden came to meet me.

"So you're Tanya Smith," he said, eyeballing me like I was already a big problem. "No one escapes from here."

His statement was my first indication that I had a bit of a rep. The rest came from the prison gossip. The rumors were about my wealth and the success of my escape: "She took a marshal hostage," "she was on the run for two years," "she stole diamonds from Tiffany," "she was heading to McDonald's when she got caught." It was amusing.

The charges the Feds pinned on me were extensive and included conspiracy to defraud the United States, bank fraud, multiple counts of interstate transportation of stolen money, and, surprisingly, money laundering—I suspected that was something Jim had done on his own. The evidence backing all the charges was related to pickups by Jim's people, none of whom I'd ever met. They stupidly used their government names and IDs. Though Jim was forcing me to initiate the transactions, I never made a dime from the charges I was facing.

The AUSA's office informed me by letter that I needed a lawyer to represent me in court, and if I couldn't afford it, one would be appointed to me. I found out from the AUSA that Sam had been disbarred on June 29, 1990. Though we spoke often, Sam had never told me about that.

Those court-appointed attorneys, like Oliver in West Virginia, were preferred by AUSAs looking for an easy win. I'd be defenseless.

I called Sam to ask why he hadn't told me he'd been disbarred. He said he'd wanted to keep helping me.

I was informed by the Feds that Jim had been arrested by the US Marshals and was in jail in San Bernardino waiting to be extradited to the MDC, where I was housed. I needed money really bad so Sam volunteered to go to the jail to ask Jim for money for me and the kids. I was skeptical.

As I suspected, Sam didn't get any money from Jim. What he got was an earful: "Tanya knew I had a woman, and I have a whole family with my woman. Tanya and I were never a couple, and she knew it. We made money together and that was it. She was never my woman and never meant anything to me. I want nothing to do with her or those kids she chose to have on her own. I don't have money to give her for anything. I have my own family to support."

It was a whole lot of chat from someone living off my dime. I was disgusted but not at all surprised by his stupidity. His miserable life was in my hands. I could clearly see that Jim's abuse was about him wanting to have power over me, to dominate me, to prove that though I was smarter and more savvy than him, he could beat me, both literally and figuratively. When a woman tries to build a man up, he actually comes to resent you for it.

Romance was far off my radar anyway. And I was having a whole different experience in prison. As a result of some facts and some fiction about my illegal activity and escape circulating around, I quickly reached celebrity status among women and men, which made some of the inmates not so fond of me.

"How come all the guys want to get with you? The women too?" a woman asked snidely.

I had no desire to respond to any of the constant come-ons being thrown at me.

My cellmate, Ginger Lynn Allen, was a porn star who'd been locked up for tax evasion. Famed for her popular triple-X films and romance with actor Charlie Sheen, Ginger Lynn was the typical LA dream girl. She was rail thin, petite, and blonde with blue eyes. Every night, the nasty guards would come to our cell and shine their flashlights on us to get a look at her.

It seemed everyone was hooking up at the MDC. In bathroom stalls, closets, and even the kitchen, inmates, guards, and sometimes visitors were heavy getting it on.

Aside from the sex, the atmosphere at this particular prison was cheerful. We all had our own radios and could sing and dance to music. We played spades and served snacks of commissary food or imaginative shoestring budget dishes cooked up in our little kitchen area. We also got to go outside on a little patio for fresh air or sometimes even up to the roof to play basketball and stare out at the diverse Los Angeles landscape dotted with buildings and mountains and glimpses of the ocean. We couldn't forget that we were imprisoned, but we could make the most of it.

The women were housed on the ninth floor, with the rest of the floors occupied by men. Communication between floors took place over the vents. The airshaft ran through each cell from the top to the bottom of the building. It was our in-house telephone system, with operators, customers, and long-distance calling capabilities. An inmate in a cell on an upper floor could stand on the toilet and holler down to cells on the floors below, and their occupants could respond. People not only talked through the vent but used it to pass notes, drugs, snacks, anything, by lowering the contraband tied in strips of bedsheets or even socks reimagined as baggies.

I had many suitors seeking my attention on the vent. While I wasn't looking for a lifelong connection, I enjoyed the conversations and got to meet some interesting and intelligent inmates. Though the guys loved staking claim to the women they chatted with, I considered myself a free agent. If I liked someone, I'd chat with them. If someone else caught my attention, I'd move on.

My best friend in the MDC was Lena. She was sweet and minded her business like me. Her boyfriend was Freddie Culver, who ran a huge PCP and cocaine ring in Compton. When she talked to him on the vent, I joined her on the chat and eventually developed my own friendship with him. Freddie, always generous with advice, became my big brother/protector in the MDC.

"Make sure you keep in touch with your family, Tanya, your kids and your parents. They keep you human," he often advised.

While I was talking to Freddie, a guy named Ricky happened to be listening. He began calling me on the vent, but I didn't respond until Freddie assured me that he was cool. Ricky, as it turned out, was Ricky Donnell Ross, known as "Freeway Rick," for the properties he bought along the Harbor Freeway, Los Angeles's Interstate 110.

Another one of Freddie's friends, Michael "Harry-O" Harris, also began calling me on the vent. A cocaine kingpin in his twenties, Michael produced the Broadway play *Checkmates*. He also bankrolled Death Row Records.

Though Michael and I chatted quite frequently, one of the women I sometimes ate dinner with said her prison boyfriend wanted to introduce me to his friend down on the fifth floor.

I was hesitant, but they kept talking him up, saying he was a secret admirer. After much coaxing, I went to the vent in her cell to speak to him.

"Baby, are you here?" he asked.

I immediately recognized the voice. "Jim?"

"Yes. I got arrested. How are you?"

"You can't be serious. What do you want from me?" I asked, ready to get up and leave the vent.

"Don't you like me no more?" Jim asked, trying to sound sweet.

"There's nothing about you to like," I snapped.

"I admit I'm not perfect. But I love you. I always have. I have my faults, but I thought you could see past them," Jim said. "I know I hurt you, but let's start again. We're all we got in here. We have to stick together and have each other's back, right? No need to talk to the Feds."

I started laughing. He must've thought I was a fool.

Sick of his nonsense, I said, "Don't try me. You're on your own."

Realizing I wasn't softening, the true Jim came out. His attitude changed, and he threatened me. "You know what's going to happen to you if you snitch," he said menacingly.

As I walked back to my room, I could hear Jim calling my name, "Tanya! Tanya! Tanya! Come back here."

Someone told Freddie, Lena's boyfriend, that they heard my conversation with Jim.

"Who's that punk threatening you?" Freddie asked me on the vent in Lena's cell.

"My ex," I said. "The one who took all my money and left me to rot in prison."

"I hate bum niggas like that. Can't get his own, so he fucked up your shit," Freddie said. "You're with us now. Don't worry about him. He'll never threaten you again. You are a queen, a legend, and a hero. I'll protect you."

It felt good knowing I had protection. I don't know what Freddie said to Jim, but he never got on the vent and called my name again.

Through his lawyer, Michael called me down to the attorney area of the visiting room so we could have some private time away from the general population. It was the only way we could visit and talk freely since attorney rooms weren't monitored. Freeway Rick had also asked me for a meetup in one of the visiting rooms. The two of them were so powerful at the MDC that they could get anything they wanted.

They were incredibly wealthy. Since I needed money for a lawyer, I wondered if Rick or Michael would be willing to help me. Though they knew each other and were cool, I was sure that dealing with two of the most powerful men in the correctional facility at the same time would cause trouble, and I chose to focus on Michael. I started seeing him in the visitors' room almost every day, just to flirt and talk. He told me all about Death Row Records and the artists he was developing. He would list all these rappers and groups and look at me like, "Where have you been?" when I confessed that I hadn't heard of any of them.

Michael was charming, as smooth as could be, and obviously very smart. Through our private meetings, which were often as many as three times a week, Michael and I developed a comfortable rapport. It was the only time I could laugh and joke and just enjoy someone's company.

I told him about my childhood and that I had a musical connection as well.

"I grew up a few blocks from Prince. I knew him as a kid," I said, knowing that would blow his mind as it had everyone I ever shared that bit of history with.

"Prince! You've got to be kidding," he said, amazed. "Man, I should have known you when I was out there. You not only would have had someone to treat you with respect, but I would have been so happy to be with a woman as smart and fearless as you. And no one would've mistreated you or put a hand on you, whether you were my woman or not," he said.

"Thank you, Michael. I really do appreciate the kind words. I never had a man who would protect me, watch out for me, and make sure I was good," I said with tears in my eyes.

"No problem. You need anything, just ask me."

"Actually, I do need something," I said. I told him about my legal situation and that I needed a lawyer.

"Oh, that's nothing for me, baby. I have lawyers."

"I don't have any money."

"Don't worry about that," Michael said. "Let me set you up with one of my lawyers."

On February 17, 1992, I got the worst news of my life during a call with my mother.

"I wanted to tell you myself," she said, and I knew what she was about to tell me, so I braced myself before she let out. "Your father died today." He was hospitalized in Minneapolis for cardiac disease and diabetes when his great, loving heart gave out.

While I half-expected the news, her words still cut through me, and my whole heart cried out in devastation. I got off the phone and walked straight to my cell. I just wanted to be alone. I felt so guilty that I wasn't present in his life and able to help him in his last days. Worse, I'd contributed to the stress that wore him down, and I couldn't even attend his funeral.

I stayed in my cell in solitude for a few days, only coming out to call my mom to help her get through her pain. Losing my dad, our patriarch, was the worst moment of my life.

26

THE LONGEST SENTENCE

In March of 1992, I got some really good news. The writ of coram nobis I had filed, challenging the judge's final written ruling adding two consecutive years to my thirteen-year sentence for the charges I pleaded guilty to in Vegas, finally produced a hearing. After waiting three years, I was transported by car to Vegas to dispute the judgment.

While I awaited my court date, I was sent to Clark County Detention Center, where I was given my own cell, but after a few days, a guard came to inform me that I'd have company.

"It's Dana Plato. Kimberly from *Diff'rent Strokes*," the guard revealed. When I asked what Dana Plato was doing in jail, he explained that her accountant disappeared with most of her money, and Dana robbed a video store with a pellet gun. All she got was $164. "We're placing her in here with you because you're friendly and nonthreatening and maybe you can calm her down," he added.

Moments later, Dana was brought to the cell. She was a weepy mess. Her eyes red and puffy from crying, she hardly said anything. She sat on her bed and sobbed for what seemed like hours until I sat beside her and asked, "Are you OK? Do you need a hug?" I had my own problems and was trying to prepare for my hearing, but I'd seen inmates like her, those unable to accept their imprisonment, and sometimes a kind word or gesture made a difference.

Dana fell into my arms, and I hugged her tight. "It will be all right. Don't cry," I said. "You got any people? Anyone coming to get you?"

Between sobs, she said some fans who watched *Diff'rent Strokes* wanted to bail her out, but her lawyer said she shouldn't take money from people she didn't know; there was no telling what their motives were. I understood, but later, when she got word that Wayne Newton also wanted to post bail and Dana was hesitant about it, I jumped in.

"Take it," I said.

When I finally made it to court, with the help of the public defender, I argued my case. The judge's first oral ruling for my two-year sentence to run concurrently with my thirteen-year sentence superseded his second written judgment for the two years to run consecutively, and as such, the original sentence should be reinstated. The AUSAs argued that the sentence should stay consecutive, but they had no legal argument to back it up, and the judge had no choice but to rule in my favor. My two-year sentence was made concurrent. Considering the block of time I still faced, it was a small victory, but it was a victory nonetheless. On the ride back to Los Angeles, I looked out at Sin City and remembered all the wild times I had had there. Back then, when I was a high roller with money to burn, I was up; I was winning. But right then I was down and had taken many losses.

When I got back to the MDC, Michael called me down for a visit. I told him all about the hearing I'd won, and he said, "Tanya, you're sharp. You should have been a lawyer."

My dad used to tell me that.

After the Vegas victory, I started coming back to myself, but the world around me was engulfed in chaos as the nation grappled with the senseless police beating of Black motorist Rodney King. Relations between the Los Angeles police and the Black community were already tense before the doomed traffic stop. Because he'd been drinking—in violation of his parole—King initially took off, but he surrendered after a chase. Rather than simply arrest him, four cops—two white and two Hispanic—beat him fifty-six times with their nightsticks and then threw him to the ground and stomped him.

The video of the event shocked the entire country. It was the first time such routine but vicious police brutality had been caught on tape and aired on network TV. The four officers were charged with assault and use of excessive force, but on April 29, 1992, all four were acquitted.

Los Angeles exploded. The city convulsed with outrage. Rioting over the next few days resulted in sixty-four deaths, at least ten caused by the police and the National Guard. More than three thousand fires were set, and more than a thousand buildings burned to the ground.

The government needed space at the MDC to house the National Guard. All the women and some of the men were cleared out. Riding on the prison bus on the way to San Diego, where I was being sent for temporary housing, I looked out the grated windows at the smoldering streets of LA. Looters darted in and out of shattered storefronts, buildings were in flames, and blackened ruins stood everywhere. The landscape was strewn with debris and half-demolished cars. It was a war zone.

As he'd been disbarred, Sam couldn't meet with me as an attorney any longer, but he remained a regular visitor. Entering the visiting room to see Sam one day, I saw Michael chatting up a woman who wasn't an inmate or his lawyer.

Knowing she would tell the truth, I went to my friend Lena to find out what was going on. She revealed that the woman was Michael's wife. Hearing that, I decided to step back from him. I wasn't angry. He never lied to me. He just didn't tell me he was married, and it wasn't something I thought to ask about. We'd talked about relationships we had, and marriage had never been mentioned.

Later, when I shared my feelings with Michael, he understood.

"I wouldn't expect anything less from someone like you," he said. "And don't think this changes anything about what I said. I'll get one of my lawyers to help you."

He contacted Lucas Peterson, a Los Angeles attorney specializing in major crimes, to represent me. The gallant gesture was humbling.

During one of our first meetings, Lucas presented the best and worst scenarios I could face in court. He also said he had been contacted by the AUSA, who asked if I would be willing to testify against Jim.

"They keep asking, 'How can she protect this guy? He's worthless. Without her testimony, he could walk. We need her testimony to clinch it. We saved her life. Seems like she would be grateful for that,'" he said. I thought, *Why do they keep saying they saved my life?*

"But I keep telling them you aren't interested. Won't even consider it. Is that still the case?"

I agreed but added, "This isn't about protecting Jim. Any fresh facts I give them could put me into a deeper hole. It's new ammunition for the Feds. They know that. It's a dead issue."

After the meeting, I returned to my cell and bumped into a male inmate who was on the women's floor collecting garbage, which he did twice per day. His name was Calvin. He was incredibly good-looking, not a pretty boy like Jim, but very manly and tall with a beard. He made his rounds quietly, keeping to himself, never stopping to engage with any of the women, who were all smitten with him, even the female guards. One day, I got on the vent in my friend's cell and called his name. After a while, he got on.

After that introduction, we communicated through the vent daily. Though he collected garbage from the women's floor every day, Calvin had no idea who I was because I played it mysterious and never told him my name. He kept asking how I looked and told me to come to the door where he picked up the trash for us to meet. I assumed he wanted to approve of my looks before continuing on.

The next day, I put on my best-fitting khakis, a tight T-shirt, tinted lip gloss, and mascara I had purchased from the commissary and stood by the door, awaiting Calvin. When he came by to get the trash, I smiled invitingly and flipped my hair. While we couldn't talk, because the guards were watching, the gestures made it clear I was his secret admirer. Our relationship blossomed after that.

Calvin was smitten. He always let me know when he was coming for the trash, and I waited nearby, all perked up, ready to put a smile on his face. After a while, the guards figured out we were becoming an item and let us talk for five or ten minutes through the door. In addition to chatting on the vent for hours about everything and nothing—from our dreams the previous night to goals after we got out—we'd trade letters, which we sent tied to socks through the vent. It was the sweetest prison romance.

After we'd been talking for a few weeks, I told Calvin about the things I had done that led to my confinement.

"Wow," he said. "I knew it was something white collar— you're so professional, but I didn't imagine you were involved in fraud. Would you do it again?"

"No. It wasn't like I was trying to be a criminal or anything like that. It started with curiosity and then a desire to do some good but then I was just acting out because I was mad that the police underestimated me. They were acting like all Black people only committed dumb crimes."

"I understand. People change. They grow. Is there anything you left out that maybe you'd do again?"

"No. Nothing else," I said.

"You sure?"

"You're beginning to sound like the Feds—so many questions."

Calvin said, "No way. I'm just saying that you're so smart. I figured you had more going on. Maybe stuff no one else knows about."

Put off by his line of questioning, I changed the subject.

Finally, in June of 1992, I was due in court to be arraigned for the Fed's charges. As I waited beneath the prison in a parking garage with the other women to be loaded into the van, the male prisoners were led out, and there was Jim. I hadn't seen him in a few years. Though he was in prison khakis, he looked neat. When he looked at me with puppy dog eyes and a sad smile, something inside me snapped. I pointed at him and shouted, "Why, you sorry motherfucker! Don't you smile at me! You beat me up, choked me, tied me up, and ripped me off, you punk-ass bitch!"

Hearing the commotion, the guards stepped closer in case I made a move. Everyone was silent. Their eyes darted from me to Jim, who appeared shocked and maybe a little afraid that I might indeed attack.

Just then, a man standing next to Jim pointed to his chest and said, "Miss, are you talking to me?" The interjection was so random and bold that it was kind of funny. It broke the tension and stopped me from doing something I may have regretted. Also, the man looked a little familiar, but I couldn't place him.

"No, I mean that piece of shit right there." I stabbed my finger at Jim, resisting a chuckle.

The guards began the van loading process.

The man who interjected got in beside me. We struck up a conversation. I learned that he was Charles Keating. I realized why I knew his face. Charles Keating's case was all over the news. I mentioned him in the letters I was still sending to judges to request a shorter sentence. In 1990, he was indicted by the State of California for duping his customers at Lincoln Savings and Loan into buying worthless junk bonds. He'd been jailed when he couldn't post a $5 million bond. Lots of other charges, state and federal, cropped up as people testified against him. On sentencing late in 1991, he received ten years.

From the moment we met, Charles and I became pals. We talked whenever we went to court together. In the holding tank in the courthouse, waiting to go before the judge, we were always in cells next to each other. We would spend the day talking, even through our bag lunches. Charles had a great sense of humor and was such an interesting man to talk to. In one of our conversations, I told him about my letters to judges about my sentence.

"Yes, the system is corrupt," he told me. "You got a raw deal."

He encouraged me to keep up my sentencing petitions.

At the MDC I also saw Michael Milken, the other white-collar criminal I often mentioned in my letters. I heard he was in booking and begged a friendly guard to take me down to the holding cell. Milken was being processed, doing his fingerprints and paperwork. When I tried to talk to him, he didn't offer conversation. He just looked as if he wondered how I knew his name.

After running into Jim, I couldn't get him out of my mind. His smug little smile. I called Lucas Peterson and said I was going to give them Jim.

"Tanya, no," he urged. "The Feds won't offer you a deal."

"I don't care. I'm not doing it for a deal. I'm doing it so Jim gets what he deserves. This is revenge."

In August of 1992, I pleaded guilty to the Fed's charges.

For Jim's trial, the AUSA planned to introduce the beatings I endured, his narcotics activity—which I never knew about—and the 9mm semiautomatic weapon they found at the house when we were arrested as evidence. The same gun that Jim put to my head. They were also going to bring in an FBI agent who would testify how dangerous Jim was. Sadly, Jim had been plotting to kill me. The mother of his two children. The agent's testimony would include how they learned of the plot to kill me and their rush to find me before Jim was able to carry it out. Jim made millions of dollar through my operation and no longer needed me to make money. Since I was the only person who could link him to my escape, harboring a fugitive, and his involvement with the wire frauds, Jim had planned to get rid of me. Now I understood why the FBI and US Marshals kept saying, "We saved your life."

Right before Jim's trial, his attorney filed a motion asking the court to exclude evidence of Jim's "bad acts." He argued that this particular trial was only about white-color offenses and that any narcotics or violence evidence would prejudice the jury. The AUSA told me that we could not bring up the bad acts at trial, because it could be overturned on an appeal as the bad acts were separate from the offenses he was currently being charged with. I felt differently.

At trial in December, I faced Jim and his family in the court-room. Once again, Jim kept looking at me with a "bitch, I'll get you" expression that made my blood boil. When I took the stand, I admitted to what the Feds already knew—that I was the one who transferred the money—but without explaining how I did it.

When the AUSA asked about Jim, I said, "He organized all the runners. They were just names to me. Jim found them, managed them, and collected funds from them. He then kept all the money."

"You didn't know any of the runners—none of them?" the AUSA pushed.

"Well, I knew two of them, Jim's sister and her husband, but I can't say exactly what they did," I replied.

Sitting behind Jim, his mother and sister looked shocked, like they thought I was still blinded by the fake family loyalty they had sold me. I ignored them and kept going. "I didn't know them very well. They weren't my kind of people," I said, twisting the knife.

The AUSA went on, asking about my relationship with Jim. Although I was told not to speak on it, I didn't hold back.

"Jim beat me. He tied me up. He kept me as a prisoner," I revealed, crying hard. His attorney stood up and said "objection," asking for my response to be stricken from the record. The judge said "sustained," which meant he agreed with the objection. Reliving those moments of terror with Jim made me angry and sad that I'd ever been with someone like him. Once I was done, I was exhausted.

Later, in the hallway, Jim's sister tried to attack me physically, yelling, "I'm going to kick your ass!"

Glaring at her like I had no idea who she was or why she'd threaten me, I cracked a little smile to let her know my loose lips and shade were intentional. Taking it in, she lunged at me, but the US Marshals who were guarding me pulled her away. Jim's mother didn't say a word. She stared at me but then looked away when I caught her gaze. I was surprised she could even look me in the face.

The trial lasted eight days. When the verdict came in after three days of deliberation, Jim was convicted on all counts and received ten years in prison. While I thought I would be happy, it was rather anticlimactic. This was the punishment handed down from the government for crimes against their system. No amount of time behind bars could make up for what Jim did to me or took from me.

Also, paradoxically, celebrating the government's sentence for Jim meant adding an ounce of legitimacy to their biased, racist sentences for me. By implicating myself in Jim's crimes, ninety-two months were added to my seventeen-plus-year sentence, which brought my grand total to more than twenty-four years. Even subtracting the time for my escape, it was one of the longest prison terms—if not the longest—imposed for a white-collar crime. Though I was expecting it, my heart ached with the realization that, by the time I got out, my children would be full-grown strangers.

As the US Marshals prepared to take me back to the MCC, the AUSA came to me and said I was the best witness he had ever put on the stand, but that couldn't help me get out of prison.

When I got back to the MCC, Lucas Peterson came to visit. I told him that I wanted to fight the sentence. I needed to find a way to get less time. He recommended that I get another attorney to fight that case.

Coming to terms with my newly extended sentence, my thoughts focused on my mom, who, having lost my dad, was suddenly raising Justin and Aiden on her own. I was also afraid for Denise, my baby girl, who was away from her family without anyone to ensure she was out of harm's way. I confided my fears to Calvin, my prison boyfriend, who was a good listener and helped me work through some of my fears about my children and nephew. His sentence was short enough that he was serving it entirely at the MDC, and before long, he would be released.

"When you get out, could you move to Minneapolis and help my mom," I asked during one of our late-night vent chats.

"Sure. I have nothing holding me in California. I want a clean break when I get out of here. A new life," Calvin said.

"You'd really do that for me? You know Minneapolis is like a whole different galaxy from Oakland?" I said, bringing up his beloved hometown, which he often spoke highly of, like most from Oakland do.

"Different could be good. And I'm not just moving there to help you out. I confess that the move would be mutually beneficial."

"How?"

"Because being there means when you get free, I'll get to be with you. And in the meantime, being with your mom and kids will be the next best thing," he said. "I could even bring them to see you—and your mom, if she's feeling well enough. I know she can't do it now, because she's so sick."

"You're amazing."

Hearing Calvin's promise to bring my kids and mother to see me, I went to bed that night thinking of how that could work when he got out. With him being a felon and not a relative, the visit likely wouldn't be approved. I realized there was one way around that.

On the vent the next day, I said, "If we get married, they can't stop you from visiting me."

Calvin quickly responded, "Sure, I can see myself married to you. But how can we do that?"

"I'll figure it out," I said.

Deciding to marry Calvin wasn't based on love or dedication. Though we'd been connecting for months and enjoyed each other's company, it wasn't a love thing. We were loyal companions, confidants, attracted allies. Maybe love would come later. Marriage, in a legal sense, ensured that he could be my advocate when he got out. There would be less legal tape to maneuver if he were my husband on paper. While we agreed to this arrangement, actually getting the paper to solidify our union would prove difficult. We had to do it after his release but before I was transferred out of the MDC to some faraway prison. Also, I had to get permission from the warden, which wouldn't be easy.

Other inmates at the MDC had gotten married. But the warden had disliked me from the moment we met. Perhaps he hated the reports of my wealth, which were greatly exaggerated, or the fact that I'd escaped and eluded capture.

Soon after, he flat-out denied my request to marry Calvin.

I concocted a plan.

When Calvin was released from the MDC, I called Lucas Peterson and asked if he could get a friendly judge to issue a writ so I would be called into court. The warden couldn't prevent that.

"Could we get that same judge to marry Calvin and me?" I asked Lucas.

"Sure," he said.

Calvin was released in October of 1992. We talked on the phone every day, and our plans were still in place.

Calvin met me in a courtroom on December 15, the day I appeared for the phony hearing, and the judge pronounced us husband and wife. As I was still a prisoner, we didn't have the customary rings, flowers lining the entry path, or rice thrown at us after we said, "I do," but that in no way detracted from the joy and excitement about what it all meant. In the eyes of the government, being an inmate meant I belonged to the penal system, but now, being married meant I, in some way, belonged to someone else. Someone who could fight for me and speak for me and promised in a court of law to be my partner. I was escorted out of the courtroom and driven back to the MDC.

I told everyone in sight, "I'm married!" The other women gathered around me and cheered with joy. I even got a few gifts at a makeshift bridal shower at dinner.

A few weeks later, in January of 1993, I was told that it was time for me to return to Marianna. Leaving the MDC was like walking out of the dance club at the end of the night.

On the ConAir flight back to Florida, I encountered two unlikely inmates. Seated a few rows from me was the Queen of Meth, Lori Arnold, whose $10 million methamphetamine production and distribution empire led to her being convicted of drug trafficking and money laundering in the early '90s. Lori was funny like her brother Tom Arnold and had a larger-than-life personality that kept everyone on the plane laughing as she joked about the terrible condition of the plane and the lack of adequate stewardess service. Even the marshals laughed when she suggested that we forget the flight itinerary altogether and go on vacation.

At the layover, before hitting the last leg of the journey to Florida, I was held in the same area as Jim Bakker, the televangelist scammer. Jim was a short, sweet-faced man who looked like he should be teaching choir at a Mississippi high school or raising chickens in Alabama. Bakker acted like he was in the wrong place. He cried so much his face was beet red.

I fell right back into my routine with my old associates at Marianna. By the time I hit the pillow at night, instead of feeling anguish and torment, I felt settled, like I could do what needed to be done until I devised a new exit strategy.

I was also feeling more relaxed because, as promised, Calvin moved in with my mother to help with Aiden, Denise, and Justin. On our calls, he said he was getting used to Minneapolis.

Soon, his good reports were outshined by Mom's bad ones. Contrasting what he was telling me, Mom said he wasn't paying rent or helping with any bills and stayed in his room when he was home, leaving her with the kids. She believed he had a girlfriend who was moving there from Oakland. My mother wasn't one to gossip or spread lies. Breaking her silence meant she was fed up.

When I asked Calvin if he was helping out, he got very defensive and elusive.

"I moved all the way to Minneapolis, left my family and friends to do something for you, and you question how I do it?" he said.

"I'm just looking out for my mom and my kids. You said you'd do it too. And what about bringing the kids to see me?

It's been years. I have to see their faces. I need to see my mom too. Make sure she's OK."

"Tanya, Florida is way too far for me to travel with kids and an elderly woman with diabetes. I just got a job. I can't take off. They're waiting for a reason to fire me. Florida is out of the question."

"You promised you would. Are you a man of your word or not, Calvin?" I pushed.

"I can't take this anymore. Not from you or your mother. I'm moving out. I'll leave my new number with your mom when I get settled," he said before hanging up.

A week later, Mom gave me Calvin's new number, and I reached out, but most times he didn't answer my calls. When he did, our exchanges were short, and as soon as I brought up my family and asked for help, he found a reason to get off the phone. Stonewalled, I felt foolish for ever thinking my plan with Calvin would work. Being stuck in Florida for the next seventeen years seemed impossible.

Years went by. I played a lot of racquetball, worked out, listened to my radio, and called home every day. I still knew how to maneuver the long-distance network operators and never had to pay for calls. I kept writing judges and begging for an early release based on my ongoing research of white-collar sentences. I told them I was a nonviolent criminal, and I had longer sentences than murderers and rapists. I told them my dad had died, my mom was ill, and I needed to help her and the kids. They kept denying me.

Exhausted by waiting for anyone to help me, I went to my unit manager, Michael Pettiford, who sprung me from the hole when I was put there after calling home about Denise. Pettiford was the best federal employee I had ever met. He was familiar with my story and believed in me. I explained that my mom was sick with high blood pressure, diabetes, and thyroid issues, and I told him about my kids.

I found out there's a state institution that houses federal inmates in Bismarck, North Dakota. It was closer to Minneapolis than Florida. The North Dakota State Penitentiary was a six-hour drive from Minneapolis—a long way but much closer. Visiting would be difficult but at least within the realm of possibility.

"If I could just get there, my husband or my mom could bring the kids to see me. I could see my mom again. Hug her," I told Pettiford. My voice petered out as I started crying at the idea of my mom passing away before I had a chance to say goodbye and bring her some peace.

Pettiford peered at me through discerning eyes and, without asking another question, said, "I'll tell the case manager to do the paperwork to get you to North Dakota."

I was relieved, but when we put in the transfer to be cleared by the Bureau of Prisons, it was denied by the review committee.

Pettiford was confused. "It's a simple request. No reason to deny you."

"They still have it in for me," I said. "Anything I want, they'll block it."

Unwilling to give up, I went to the parole board to plead my case. As I was still serving my first sentence of thirteen years, I requested that I be paroled for that sentence before starting the second one, cutting my time in half. It was a big ask, but I had nothing but time to put in these requests. Again, I was swiftly denied.

"Don't worry. I'm going to get you closer to home," Pettiford said when I went to him to commiserate my second loss. "Hold tight, and I'll figure this out."

When I returned to my cell, a serious-faced, short, full-figured woman approached me with four slightly menacing girls behind her. The woman smiled like we were good friends and pulled me into a hug before saying, "My name is Griselda. I hear many nice things about you."

She looked back at one of the girls who handed her a container of fresh soup. Griselda then gave me the soup and said, "Here is some food I had cooked for you. It's fresh and delicious. Enjoy."

"Thank you," I said before she left. The visit was strange but not totally unheard of for me. At all the prisons I'd been at, I'd racked up some admirers.

The visits became an everyday thing. While I was in my cell, she would come by and gesture to the girls to start cleaning. They would grab my dirty laundry and wash and iron everything to perfection.

My friendship with Griselda Blanco, Godmother of Cocaine, ended with news from Pettiford.

* * *

When I arrived at the North Dakota State Penitentiary, the warden, Timothy Schuetzle, proved to be a godsend. He presided over a coed facility housing about a thousand men and maybe 160 women. The women and men were strictly separated.

"We are here to keep you safe so you can do your time in peace. We will respect you if you respect us. Become a part of our community, and you will be treated well," Schuetzle said during our first meeting.

I became the unofficial librarian on the women's side, offering help to anyone who needed it. Divorces were a common issue. Sometimes a woman's husband would abandon her once she was locked up—start seeing other women, stop sending her money, and all too often, neglect his obligations to their kids. Sometimes, it was the husband who filed papers to divorce an incarcerated spouse. When women couldn't afford to hire lawyers—or if they could but had to personally file forms or whatever—they'd have me walk them through the process or even handle it on their behalf. I got to know all the ins and outs and pros and cons of prison divorce in North Dakota and, for federal inmates like me, beyond it.

Many women needed help petitioning to reduce their sentences, a process I had down to a science. Since many were state inmates serving shorter terms on lesser crimes, I was often able to get a year or two knocked off with a good petition. My own sentence, sadly, seemed set in stone.

I did so much of this administrative work that Warden Schuetzle honored me with the official title of Law Librarian. I got an office, my own private room with a desk, pens, paper, and a typewriter. I even got paid something like ten cents an hour, which wasn't much, but it did wonders for my morale. I had the whole prison library at my fingertips, and if I ever needed a resource such as a law book, Schuetzle's staff immediately ordered it. I even held office hours when inmates could make appointments or stand in line to consult with me.

My favorite part of the job was preparing my clients for internal hearings before the warden. Say there was a fight. It would be an internal matter for the institution to settle. The alleged perpetrator of the fight would be sent to the hole, where I'd be allowed to visit and interview her. We'd talk about what happened and why and then I'd work up a defense to get her time in the hole reduced from thirty or forty-five days to something reasonable. I discovered that I was good at crafting arguments to free my clients. I never lost a case.

After much begging, Calvin came to see me but didn't bring my mom and kids.

"You don't seem happy to see me," he said when I gave a cold, distant hug.

We were more like strangers than husband and wife. We hadn't seen each other in a few years, and any initial feelings of attraction I'd felt for him were gone. His disappearing acts and defensive attitude didn't make things any better. We were operating out of obligation.

"I was hoping you'd bring the kids and my mom," I said. "Isn't that what we discussed?"

"I ain't been over there. I work long hours just to get by," he explained. "I told you what it is. You can believe me or not."

As we regularly did on the phone, Calvin and I went back and forth like this until he left. When I called my mom to say I'd seen him, she told me to leave him alone.

"Just move on from him, honey," she said. "Don't worry about me. I'm getting by and keeping strong for my grandkids. You just stay strong in there and know I'm rooting for you."

"I know, Mom. I love you."

In March of 1998, a guard I hardly knew showed up at my cell to inform me that Bennie Smith had died. Without responding, I sat on my bed, overcome with grief. The shining light of my life was gone.

I was also in pieces with looming fears about the kids. My brother Mason was in the family home looking after Justin and Aiden, but he was on drugs and in no shape to rear two young boys. And what would become of Denise with absolutely no one to check on her? Taryn was back in prison, and Ryan remained disabled after his injury and still required care. With my mother gone, the center—the family's nucleus of love—was lost.

27

ALL THE SAME THING

The thing about doing hard time in federal custody is that at the outset, what appears to be the longest sentence, once it gets started—hour by hour, day by day, week by week and so forth—time smashes into a big ball of one second. It's like taking a cross-country road trip or reading a long book. At first, it seems impossible to complete but then you look up and you're somewhere farther than you ever knew you could be. That's the only way I can explain how I made it twelve years in prison. Well, eleven if you count my time off after my first escape. It's like I was Rip van Winkle. It was 1986 when I was sentenced. I closed my eyes. Waited one second. Opened them. And it was 1998. At thirty-eight, it was hard for me to fathom I'd spent over a decade of my prime adult years in prison, but the proof was in the undeniable markers of time all around me, such as my beloved parents being deceased and my children, Justin and Denise, being twelve and ten years old.

None of this made me complacent about my situation. Every single day, while I was mourning my losses, I continued to try to find a way out. In addition to helping the other women with their cases, I continued doing research to support my request for a shortened sentence, writing letter after letter to the court, praying someone would take me seriously. If the first twelve years in prison felt like one second, one second more was too many to bear. I wanted out, to experience real time with the luxuries of family and freedom.

My quest for release was interrupted by gossip circulating among inmates. The word was that the federal contract with the Bismarck prison had lapsed, which meant that all of us nonstate prisoners would be transferred out. Hearing the news between client appointments in the library, I rushed to get confirmation from Warden Schuetzle.

It was true. In a couple of days, I was to be transferred to a federal prison in Danbury, Connecticut. The good news was that the prison was medium security.

And what exactly was awaiting me in Danbury? For the past few years, in both Marianna and Bismarck, things had been running quite smoothly. I'd had sympathetic advocates on staff and, by helping others, had made a niche for myself. I'd achieved a position of respect among my peers—and, even more importantly, gained a new measure of self-actualization. At Danbury, I'd be starting from scratch—living in the dorm, working my way into a shared room—and in time, a single— trying to grasp the inmate pecking order, trying to eke out a few friendships, and so on. I'd be another anonymous inmate, little more than a case number.

A few days later when my flight was finally touching down in Connecticut, I promised myself I'd summon the energy to adjust. I could feel a deep sadness taking root. If I let it continue growing, it would consume me and then the Feds would have won in their final attempt to take me down and reduce me to a shell of a human being. I wouldn't be worn down by prison life. I'd stay the course and rely on what I always had to get through anything—my brain.

Once I was admitted to Federal Correction Institution Danbury (FCI: Danbury), I sought refuge in the law library, where I could keep my mind busy. By then, I'd exhausted every customary appeal for a sentence review. Since there was a time limit, I could no longer petition for a sentence reduction. My only hope of early release was to find some loophole, a compelling legal reason to reopen my case. To find it, I spent every free hour poring over the law books, searching for a needle in a haystack.

Whenever I came across a seemingly relevant decision, I Shepardized it, tracing its mentions year after year to see its ultimate interpretation. I went down a lot of rabbit holes and, more often than I want to remember, succumbed to tears of frustration.

And then, one day, I found it—the principle that could set me free.

Late at night, right before the librarian, Ms. Patricia, announced that she was closing down, I discovered the term "same course of conduct," meaning "offenses that through their similarity, regularity, and time between them are concluded to be part of a single episode, spree, or ongoing series of offenses." The cases where the term was defined weren't exactly like mine, but it certainly seemed to describe my actions. I'd made repeated transfers in short bursts of time. But what struck me was the way charges were lodged—and sentences given—in those cases. A charge was made for each "spree or ongoing series of offenses," not for each individual offense in the spree. Sentencing, too, was based on the spree, which added up to much less prison time.

For example, a person wrote ten bad checks in a week and the penalty for passing bad checks, according to the sentencing guidelines, was one to six months. If checks were considered as all part of one spree, the offender would probably get the top sentence of six months. But if each check was considered a separate charge, with a minimum sentence of one month for each, the total prison time would run much higher, from ten to sixty months.

That is, in effect, what had happened to me. Each of my offenses was charged and sentenced individually, with terms running consecutively, resulting in a huge cumulative prison term. But the case should have been framed differently, with the terms for the charges running concurrently.

I was stunned by the realization. Literally too shocked to breathe.

"Whatcha got there?" Ms. Patricia asked, leaning over me. I'm not sure why we all called her "Ms." She was an inmate, a lifer, who knew less about law than me, but she liked chatting and was a good listener.

"It's something called 'same course of conduct.' Ever hear of it?"

"No, I have not. You trying to use it in your defense?"

"Maybe."

"Well, I know we're not supposed to do this, but you go on and take those books with you tonight. Maybe if you can find a way out of here, you can help old Ms. Patricia too."

That night in my cell, I kept reading the cases over and over in the dark. By my reckoning, my sentence should have been no more than five years—less trauma, less loss, less estrangement, and less wasted time. If I'd drawn a five-year sentence, I never would have escaped and triggered the nightmare that followed.

The next morning when I returned to the library, Ms. Patricia asked, "So what you gonna do?"

"I don't know," I admitted. "I think I understand how this could help me, but I'm not sure it'll work, and I don't have money for a lawyer. I need a great one to argue my case. Someone a judge couldn't ignore."

After my chat with Ms. Patricia, I started cold-calling top white-collar defense lawyers all over the country looking for representation. The few I got on the phone weren't familiar with my case theory, and I wasn't surprised when I was rejected over and over, because I couldn't afford their retainers. Hitting another wall, I decided to file my own petition to the court for my release.

I'd filed a number of petitions in the past that had been denied; or when I'd reached the hearing stage, as in 1995, my claims had been dismissed. The time limit for a direct challenge of my sentence had passed. Any judge I asked to reduce it, for any reason, would decline. I needed to come up with a completely different angle, one without a time limit. I dug deep inside my inner strength, saying aloud, "Come on, Tanya. You can find a way. You're smart. You can do anything you put your mind to."

Then, bingo, it hit me. If I had been unjustly sentenced, the Danbury warden would be holding me illegally. I could petition for a writ of habeas corpus, one of our most basic legal principles, meaning that the warden would have to show cause for keeping me in custody. The only legal cause for holding me was a fair sentence. Then I could spring my "same course of conduct" argument to prove that my sentence, indeed, wasn't fair and I was eight years beyond what should have been my release date.

One night, after lights out, I wrote the first draft of the petition in a fit of anxiety, honing each point for clarity. The next day, I edited it and rewrote some parts. Days later, on September 3, 1998, when it was as airtight as I could make it, I filed the petition pro se (without legal counsel) with the US District Court. In it, I claimed Warden Margaret Harden of the FCI Danbury was keeping me imprisoned under an illegal federal sentence imposed by the district courts.

Over a month later, on October 16, I got word that my case had been assigned to Judge William Garfinkel. He ordered the warden to "show cause" for holding me, meaning that I'd scaled the first hurdle.

It took nearly three months before things really got moving. There was a lot of procedural back and forth, filing documents and responding to requests from the court. It all had to be done in a timely manner. While I was confident I could handle it on my own if I had more time and resources, I didn't want to miss anything and jeopardize my position and asked the court for a public defender who could assist me with the many steps. When she and I started working together, things ran smoothly, and I appreciated her input, but I always felt I was steps ahead of her. Maybe it was her workload, but she appeared less informed and often scattered. I couldn't let her lack of savvy mess up my defense. I knew our working relationship would be short-lived.

Though I was focused on ensuring not one stone was left unturned as we prepared to present my case, an equally important matter arose in February of 1999 when Taryn was released from prison. While we weren't on the best terms, I was excited she was free and hoped she'd get on the right track. I was happy when she got Justin and Aiden, who moved in with her, but Denise was still living with Taryn's associate. Hoping my girl, who was nearing her precious teen years, could be reunited with her biological family since Taryn was home, I contacted a lawyer to request assistance. Taryn went to see the lawyer, but since I didn't have money to pay, the case quickly fizzled out. My fight to get Denise home would have to wait.

On March 22, 1999, we filed a motion for oral arguments, meaning that we wanted to present our case. Judge Garfinkel granted the motion for a hearing the following month. Based on past experiences, I dismissed the public defender and planned to argue the case myself. Once again, relying on desperation and resolve, I'd go up against the US Attorney's Office.

As I prepared for oral arguments, I practiced in my cell with my cellmate, who would tell me how well I was doing.

The more I practiced and thought about what could go down in court, the more I kept thinking about how this was my only chance to get home. I was good, but I hadn't argued a case in court. Anything could happen, and I didn't want to be caught off guard. I realized that while I put the pieces of the case together using research and case-law knowledge, I needed a real powerhouse lawyer to bring it all home.

While reviewing recent rulings in the library, I stumbled upon Gary Lincenberg, a top white-collar defense attorney in LA. I called his office, hoping he'd give me a shot.

"Mr. Lincenberg isn't available right now. Give me your telephone number, and I'll have him call you back," his receptionist said.

"I'm in prison. He can't call me back. Please let me speak to him. I really need his help," I begged.

After a long pause, Gary hopped on the line. "What can I do for you?" he asked.

"Thank you so much for taking my call," I said before telling Gary I was being held under an illegal twenty-four-year federal sentence for crimes most convicts were given a maximum of five years. "I've been in here for thirteen years. I've already petitioned the court to be released."

"What's been the response?" he asked.

"I have an upcoming hearing in US District Judge William Garfinkel's courtroom. I just need someone to represent me, someone to argue the case. You wouldn't have to do any research. I've done everything. I can send you the paperwork and the motions I filed. All you have to do is read it and argue it in court."

"Do you have any money? I'm very expensive."

"Sadly, I don't, but the legwork is done—all I need is a speaker."

"I hear you. But that comes with a price tag too," he said.

"Please," I begged. "I lost both my parents. I've had two children while in prison. I've only held them once and that's when I gave birth to them." Feeling this was my big shot, I was nervous, talking fast, tears falling from my eyes. "This petition is my last chance to get to them."

"Send me all the research you have and give me a few days to review it. I'll think about it."

With that, he hung up. It wasn't a win, but it was something.

I sent Gary my petition and all the backup work I'd done. Not long after I'd sent the package off, one of the guards told me that my lawyer called the institution and asked me to call him. I ran to the phone and called Gary.

"I'm impressed. You did a great job, and you are right. The law is on your side," he said. "Look—if you'll pay for my airfare and lodging, you've got a lawyer."

After making a couple of calls to raise funds for Gary's travel, I managed to borrow the money from one of Dad's old friends, Senator Dave Durenberger, who wired Gary's airfare and wished me well. Once Gary received the money, he filed his appearance as my counsel.

Entering the courthouse in my prison khakis and shirt, I was nervous. But seeing Gary, I knew I made the right decision. When the bailiff removed my cuffs before I entered the courtroom, it felt like the beginning of me getting what I'd prayed for, what I'd worked for. If everything went my way, I wouldn't ever wear those cuffs again.

The judge seemed to listen intently as Gary meticulously laid out the "same course of conduct" argument, citing the precedents I'd researched, with a direct approach sprinkled with just enough Los Angeles suaveness. Gary closed saying, "Tanya Smith has been incarcerated for eight long years over and above the time to which she should have been sentenced. Justice demands her immediate release."

"What's your response?" the judge asked the AUSA.

The AUSA, who spoke like a windup toy the Feds had overnighted to Danbury, didn't even address our position but delivered a diatribe on how conniving I was, the money I stole, how I threatened the banking system, how I'd had the nerve to escape—on and on. Those were the claims that got me locked up to begin with—sins for which I'd already paid the price. Or way overpaid, as our case contended.

The judge, underwhelmed, shrugged off the AUSA's bluster. "I'll give you two weeks to counter Mr. Linceberg's argument," he said before banging his gavel.

Those were the longest two weeks of my life. Moments of anguish were punctuated by hope, no sleep, pacing, and then anguish returned exponentiated.

Before I could figure out how to regulate my emotions, we were back in court.

Once again, on May 25, 1999, the wind-up toy AUSA rose and launched into a recitation of my crimes, assailed my

NEVER SAW ME COMING

character, and warned the court of the dire threat I posed. When he was done, he took his seat and crossed his arms like he'd really done something.

My eyes darted to the judge, who suddenly had the most unreadable poker face I'd ever laid eyes on. He wasn't impressed or let down. Angry or happy. Entertained or bored. As everyone in the room awaited his response, he sat back in thought. I dug my nails into my thighs to stop myself from hollering.

"Tanya Smith, you're free to go."

"What?" I said. Years of my life had been restored with just a few words, like a magic incantation. I nearly collapsed. My tears flowed freely. They could have filled Lake of the Isles in no time.

I looked down at my wrists. No more cuffs. I was free. US District Court Judge William Garfinkel was a fair judge who followed the law and did what he was appointed to do.

While I'd won, the US Marshal had to return me to Danbury for processing. When I told the other women about the ruling, they went wild, clapping and cheering. "Whoo! Tanya's free!" It was like a party. Even the guards seemed excited.

Gary had thought I'd be released in a matter of hours, but it didn't happen that night. Or the next day. Finally, on May 27, 1999, I went to the administration office to ask if they'd finished my paperwork.

"No," the case record administrator said without looking me in the eye. "We've been instructed to hold you."

"Hold me? Why? I'm free."

"We were contacted by the Los Angeles US Attorney's Office, who halted the release," she revealed. "You won't be released until it is confirmed through that office."

"The US District judge released me. A US attorney's office can't override a judge's court decision."

She turned away from me and went on about her business.

Alarmed, I immediately called the judge's clerk to ask if there was some kind of change in the order. When she said no, I called Gary to complain. He said he'd reach out to the judge to tell him that I wasn't being released and let him know what the case-record administrator had told me about the Los Angeles US Attorney's Office halting my release.

Once the judge got all the information from Gary, I was told he called the warden to say, "If Tanya Smith is not released in one hour, I am going to have you arrested."

With the judge's orders, a guard came to my unit in a hurry and told me, "Let's go. We've got to get you out of here now!"

"One second," I said. I didn't have much to pack. I'd been preparing to leave for days. I'd already given away all my commissary, clothes, and practically everything else. All I had was my legal papers, which I put in a black garbage bag and rushed out.

When I got into the transport van, the marshals informed me that, courtesy of the Bureau of Prisons, I had a plane ticket to Minneapolis. En route to the airport, I was a mess of emotions thinking about what it would be like to return to my hometown.

Thanks to traffic, I missed my flight—the last of the day as it turned out. The marshals didn't give that a thought. They just pulled up to the terminal and dropped me off, leaving me on the curb with my garbage bag. I was no longer the Feds' responsibility.

At least I was free. I walked into the terminal, overwhelmed by the bright, cavernous space. Stores and restaurants—elements of a world that I hadn't seen in years—beckoned. I poked around, looking at souvenirs, like T-shirts and mugs and shot glasses, trying to imagine how they'd fit into my life. I didn't know my kids well enough to buy them gifts with my small parting stipend from the Feds.

I thought about sitting in a restaurant to eat but got a Styrofoam takeout box with a Coke and chips. Dragging my bag, I found a quiet corner where I could eat and camp out until my early-morning flight.

EPILOGUE

Being released from prison wasn't a ticket to some big, loving reunification with my children and siblings. After landing in Minneapolis, I hopped in a cab with my black trash bag and headed to Taryn's place. Had my parents been alive, when I arrived, there would've been some jubilation, some celebration, a welcome-home party followed by a big family dinner. But there was none of that. When I walked in, Taryn and Mason greeted me with a big, long hug. Tears flooded my eyes. I was happy to see them. They were living together in a duplex; we'd lost the family home while I was in prison. Mason stopped using drugs and looked much like our father. Peering at him was a treat, like I was getting to spend time with my dad once again.

When my parents passed, Mason looked after Justin and Aiden, so they were there on the couch playing video games. Neither stood to embrace me. The lack of reception stung. Ex-convicts, whether having served five years or fifty, want to be embraced and loved by those we fought hard to get back to. But I understood that I was a stranger to them. Taryn told them to get up and give me a hug. When they did, I didn't want to let go, and I couldn't stop crying. The last time I'd held them, they were literally babies. And now they were almost grown men.

I wasn't prepared for how high the walls between us would be, but it wouldn't stop me from trying to connect. I was Justin's biological mother, and I was going to be present in his life from that day forward.

Immediately, I started asking if he wanted to go to the circus, movies, the mall, dinner, and on and on. The response was always no.

Seeing my soft asks went unrequited, I tried a grand overture, hoping it would lead to a more positive reception. I told Taryn I was going to buy a house, and Justin and Denise, who was staying in Florida with the woman who'd taken her in, would be with me. But Taryn said Justin called one of her associates "mom," and he didn't want to live with me; neither did Denise, who also called her caretaker "mom." Taryn had a smirk on her face as she spoke those words. It was as if she was enjoying seeing me hurt.

I was getting nowhere fast. My fractured relationship with Taryn was a part of the disconnect with my children, who were loyal to her and all the often-questionable people she had in her circle. It hurt me to the depths of my soul. I fought for my kids for years, but nothing worked out.

*　　*　　*

I also reached out to Calvin. Due to everything that transpired when I was incarcerated, I wasn't happy to see him, but we talked at length about the past, and he apologized. We caught up and discussed how we could make things work. He was working and making decent money. He said he was ready to start his life with me.

Using money lent to me by one of my dad's friends, Calvin and I moved into a three-level, newly built 2,500-square-foot home with a three-car garage. It felt good to turn the key to my new home. I hoped and prayed to someday fill it with my children. I made room for my brother Ryan, who had been staying in a nursing home.

As much as I wanted things to work with Calvin, things quickly dissipated between us. We just weren't compatible. All he did was go to work, come home, expect dinner, and play video games. He never smiled and barely talked to me. When he did, he was mean. It bothered him when I seemed happy or had a smile on my face.

Though the disconnect between Calvin and me was predictable, seeing my marriage crumble felt like yet another blow. I worked hard not to let it get me down and to find joy and happiness in little things. And then I got pregnant. I was overcome with joy.

"The last thing I want is another child," Calvin complained when I told him. But I didn't care. I was blossoming, growing radiant and full, while he looked at me with disgust. I was having my baby and cherishing every second of my pregnancy.

In March of 2002, Makala was born. When I got home with my Makala, every one of her milestones was a miracle: her first gurgles and smiles, her tight baby-fist grip, the way she rocked on her hands and knees trying to crawl.

I threw myself into motherhood. Being deprived of the chance to raise Justin and Denise had been the greatest sorrow of my life. I was determined to change that with my third child. No matter what, she'd grow up in a stable, loving environment. That motherly instinct led to us parting from Calvin.

After many joyful years of making a life for us as a single mother, I decided we needed a fresh start outside Minneapolis. We landed in Chevy Chase, Maryland, where Makala would get a world-class education and surround herself with inspiring people. Dedicated to our new existence, I didn't tell anyone, including Makala, about my past. Life was simple and easy. Filled with school drop-offs and weekend slumber parties. But then, the past came creeping in.

One night, when she was twelve, Makala was playing dress-up. Leaving me on the couch downstairs, she'd go up to my bedroom, put together a fabulous ensemble, and come down to model it for me. After one of her catwalk appearances, I sat waiting for nearly thirty minutes before it occurred to me that things were too quiet. I went to check on her.

When I got upstairs, I found Makala sitting on my bedroom floor. She looked up at me, dazed and in shock. Spread out on her lap were news clips from the box I kept hidden deep in the closet. I glimpsed at a familiar photo of myself in handcuffs being led into court by FBI agents.

Makala didn't speak. She didn't have to. Her face said it all. She'd been blindsided with unfathomable historical information about the one person she thought she knew more than anyone in the world. She was confused. How could the lawless criminal and felon described in the papers at her feet be the dedicated and loving mom standing before her? And if those two realities could exist in the same person, why hadn't I told her about my past? The lack of transparency was the worst. Makala was hurt that I'd kept my past from her and sad that I felt I had to.

At that moment, I realized I had to make a change. I had tremendous guilt and some regret over losing nearly a quarter of my life to prison, over my fractured family relationships, over my failure to achieve the potential my parents had selflessly nurtured. I had a mixture of confusion and shame over my mis-judgments of men. But I wasn't about to let the guilt, regret, confusion, or shame from my past ruin my relationship with Makala. I couldn't lose her.

I decided that all I could do was tell it straight. Whatever Makala was going to think, I'd have to accept the consequences.

It took a long time to unspool the whole tangled tale. I covered the broad strokes in one marathon session and then we kept talking over the days and weeks ahead. To my relief, Makala's love and empathy proved expansive enough to accommodate the sins of an all-too-fallible mother. As she put it in her college admissions essay:

When I recovered from the initial shock of my mother's past, learning about it actually inspired me in a number of ways. It let me know that people have a great capacity to change and that mistakes made yesterday do not have to set the arc of your future. Her story also inspired me to work hard and achieve in school and present myself respectfully at all times. I am the best example of the goodness in my mother—I am a person of self-worth and integrity. I embrace who I am, and I am comfortable with myself because I know the darkest and brightest of the woman who birthed and raised me. I have no illusions about her and being able to identify with who she is helps me identify with myself.

How generous and loving she was. It was hard to feel worthy.

Makala's encouragement inspired me to think that I could finally come clean, once and for all—to stop lying about my past, papering over my slipups—and trust others to accept me as she had. She kept saying, "Mom, you have to be honest," and, "Maybe your story could help someone else."

It took a while, but eventually, I did share my true identity with a few friends. At first, many didn't believe me. But I was happily surprised to find understanding—even a degree of fascination—where I'd feared rejection and contempt.

In time, opening up got easier, and soon, I realized Makala was right: my story could help someone else. Maybe that someone was a person I didn't know. That led me to begin recording my story, the good and bad, every part, in a memoir. My hope is that the journey I went on inspires everyone to uplift those in need and see the good in people.

*   *   *

In 2020, I decided to return to California, a state I've always loved. I settled in the Greater Los Angeles area with Makala and my brother Ryan. Makala started college at the University of Southern California, where I had once enrolled.

Though I was committed to living a simple life, I had a mystery to solve—the fate of those insulated, weatherproof safes I'd buried in Chino Hills. They contained a few million dollars in cash, along with bars of gold and uncut diamonds. What were the chances that I could find them?

What I found were subdivisions sprouting from the once-bare hills, like quills on the back of a porcupine. I combed the sterile suburban landscape, looking for my buried treasure, but it was hopeless. The safes were lost—maybe caught in the mouths of backhoes by workers who opened them and kept the spoils, or maybe buried in a slab of cement that formed a basement floor. I would never know.

If I needed a sign that my life of crime was over—as daring, exciting, and ultimately destructive as it had been—that was it. It's enough of a thrill to try to reinvent myself, yet again, at midlife.

ACKNOWLEDGMENTS

Turning my personal story into a memoir to share with the world was no easy task. While I never shy away from hard work, I didn't cross the finish line alone. Without support and faithfulness from my team, family, and friends, this book would not exist. I'd like to acknowledge those who've stood by my side while on this journey and dear friends and family who were there for me as I lived through the trials, tribulations, and triumphant victories documented in these pages.

Mom and Dad, you taught me that we are all human beings—regardless of race, religion, class, or creed—and we should support each other. You taught me to be kind and caring and to always help others. You gave me the strength and confidence to believe in my abilities as a woman, a Black woman, and to always persevere—if I can dream it, I can be it. Your love, teachings, and memories remain with me always. Thank you, Mom and Dad, for your continued eternal guidance and love in spirit, each moment of the day.

Makala—my sweet daughter, my great teacher, who came into my life right on time—you gave me the courage to write about my life. Hearing you tell me that I could help others and also free myself spoke volumes to the young woman you are—always thinking of others, always looking out for your mother, honest, trustworthy, and kind. Your morals and values are like no other. Seeing you grow and fight for change in the world makes me proud to have raised you. You are my confidante and best friend, my reason for pushing forward through all obstacles. Being a mother to you has been my greatest joy.

Black Power—the most magnificent Doberman pinscher a girl could have by her side. For so much of my life, you were my partner, companion, and best friend, always along for the ride. You brought me joy, made me laugh, and no matter what I was going through, you were there to show me love. The bond we shared was like no other.

My big brothers—Mason, it doesn't matter who you're talking to, your final words about me are always, "No one is badder than my sister Tanya." Thanks for showing me so much love and always being a great brother. Ryan, thank you for allowing me to look after you. Caring for you is what Mom and Dad always knew I would do if they were ever gone. It feels good knowing they are smiling down on us and seeing you content and thriving. I will always be here for you.

Justin, Denise, and Aiden, I hope this book helps you understand who I am. I really want you to know that I made it through all those difficult times with thoughts of getting home to you. I am so sorry that I couldn't be there for you when I should've been. I pray you are covered and finding your way on your journeys.

Grandmother Grace, thank you for visiting us every summer and bringing us turtles. Your warm hugs were so loving. I remember asking you why you always wear dresses. Your response was "It shows femininity and elegance." You've always been a class act and made the best banana pudding.

Babs, you were the big sister with big dreams. I won't forget your dancing, laughing, and wonderful stories. You were so much fun. I will never forget the talent shows at the house you would put on. Taryn and I were in a trance when we would watch you entertain us while you would pretend to be a movie or Broadway star. I miss you dearly. Heaven has an angel.

Iris, when you won the title of Queen at North High school, it certainly fit your attitude. I still haven't seen a woman who has a basketball shot as pretty as yours or who could choregraph a dance as well as you could.

Samuel Tolbert, my friend forever, thank you for fighting for me and helping me when no one else would. You were my advocate and a true friend.

Tracy Sherrod, no one can tell me that I don't have the best editor in the business. You know what it takes to have a great book. You believed in me. We talked for hours about our vision for the memoir, and we were always on the same page. You have helped many authors to reach their dreams, and I appreciate the opportunity to work with you.

Little Brown and Company, I appreciate all the great work you have done for me. Everyone has been so wonderful and helpful in every direction. Kathryn Myers, Danielle Finnegan, Peyton Young, and Marieska Luzado. Wow, my media team is the absolute best. Your reach and love for my story has been heartwarming. Thank you for publishing my story and helping me share it with the world. I only choose the best, and that's why I chose you.

Janelle Monae, the passion you share for my story is mind-blowing. I feel it in my heart, and I knew that there was no one else to play my role but you. I appreciate you and what you do to uplift people and make all of us feel good about who we are. We are here together for a reason. Fate. Thank you for giving my journey a voice. Prince, my childhood friend and your mentor, is proud.

Wondaland, you believed in me wholeheartedly and what we could do together. When I heard each of you speak about my journey, it touched my heart. I am tremendously grateful to be working with such a diverse, brilliant team.

Universal Pictures, I couldn't believe it when I was told the top studio in the world was interested in my life story. You have done a terrific job bringing diverse entertainment to the world. I am very proud to be a part of the Universal team who has made us all cry, laugh, scream, and love. Your hard work and gift for choosing talent, filmmakers, cast and crew speaks for itself. Thank you for believing in me and allowing me to use your platform to bring my story to the big screen.

Katrina Escudero, when you were my agent, I never forgot how kind, helpful, and smart you are. That's why when I was searching for a manager, I came looking for you. You have exceeded my expectations in representation. I appreciate your honesty, hard work, and always being there whenever I needed you. You supported my goals and aspirations and made them a reality. I'm proud to say, I have a manager who really cares about her clients. Your support and advice made everything so much easier and I appreciate all that you do.

Alex Kohner and Mitchell Ostrove, I want to express my deepest gratitude for your outstanding and professional representation. Your demeanor, dedication, and expertise ensured the best outcome on my behalf. I am immensely thankful for your commitment to making sure that I was getting the best deal possible. I am happy to say that I have the best lawyers.

Christy Fletcher, you are an outstanding literary agent. You have always acted in my best interest and have been in my corner when needed. I chose you because you are smart, positive, and a great communicator who gets things done. I truly appreciate all that you have done for me. Thank you for your guidance and support.

Calaya Stallworth, you were such a joy to work with. No one does it better than you.

Elisa Petrini, thanks for your contribution to this project.

Thank you, Gary Lincenberg, for representing me when I needed help.

Lita Rosario Richardson, you are a brilliant and true fighter for me. With you on board, I could relax because I knew I could trust you to protect me and my interests. You make sure I understand everything and are always available any time, day or night, for me. You are the type of entertainment lawyer everyone should have. You really care about your clients. Thank you for being my most trusted advisor and my friend.

Judge William Garfinkel, thank you for being a fair judge and following the laws of the court.

Michael Pettiford, thank you for being a fair and caring unit manager to all the women in Shawnee Unit at Marianna, Florida. You treated us like human beings.

Maya Angelou, James Baldwin, and Toni Morrison, thank you for helping me survive moments of draconian treatment in solitary confinement.

President Barack Obama and (my forever first lady) Michelle Obama, thank you for being the best examples to the world.

Federal Bureau of Investigation, when I discuss the unfair treatment I received from the FBI, it does not reflect on the entire bureau. While there were instances of misconduct by individual agents, most of those I encountered showed curiosity, respect, and appreciation for my abilities. They conducted themselves with humility and honor. My grievances were not with the FBI but with those agents who failed to uphold their oath to fairness, to protect all citizens, and to uphold constitutional laws. Therefore, I harbor no ill will or resentment toward anyone within the FBI. I thank you for your service and encourage your continued growth and evolution.

To the children, women, and men who are being abused in any way, let your voices be heard. To all the members of the LGBT community, I got your back.

To the women and men who have been unjustly incarcerated, don't ever stop fighting for yourself and your family.

To everyone, treat people as equals, no matter how you interpret their social standing.

May God bless you all.